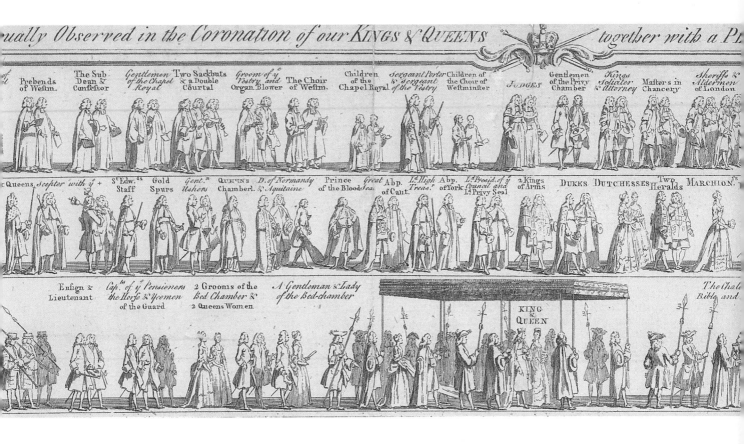

ually Observed in the Coronation of our KINGS & QUEENS *together with a Pl...*

Prebends of Westm. | The Sub Dean & Confessor | Gentlemen of the Chapel Royal | Two Sackbuts & a Double Courtal | Groom of y.e Vestry and Organ Blower | The Choir of Westm. | Children of the Chapel Royal | Sergeant Porter & Sergeant of the Vestry | Children of the Choir of Westminster | JUDGES | Gentlemen of the Privy Chamber | Kings Solicitor & Attorney | Masters in Chancery | Sheriffs & Aldermen of London

Queens Scepter with y.e + | S.t Edw.ds Staff | Gold Spurs | Gent.n Ushers | QUEENS Chamberl. | D. of Normandy & S.t Aquitaine | Prince of the Blood | Great Sea. | Abp. of Cant. | L.d High Treas.r | Abp. of York | L.d Presid. of y.e Council and L.t Privy Seal | 2 Kings of Arms | DUKES | DUTCHESSES | Two Heralds | MARCHION.ss

Ensign & Lieutenant | Cap.t of y.e Pensioners the Horse & Yeomen of the Guard | 2 Grooms of the Bed Chamber & 2 Queens Women. | A Gentleman & Lady of the Bed-chamber | KING & QUEEN | The Chal... Bible and

LONDON   A Life in Maps

Peter Whitfield

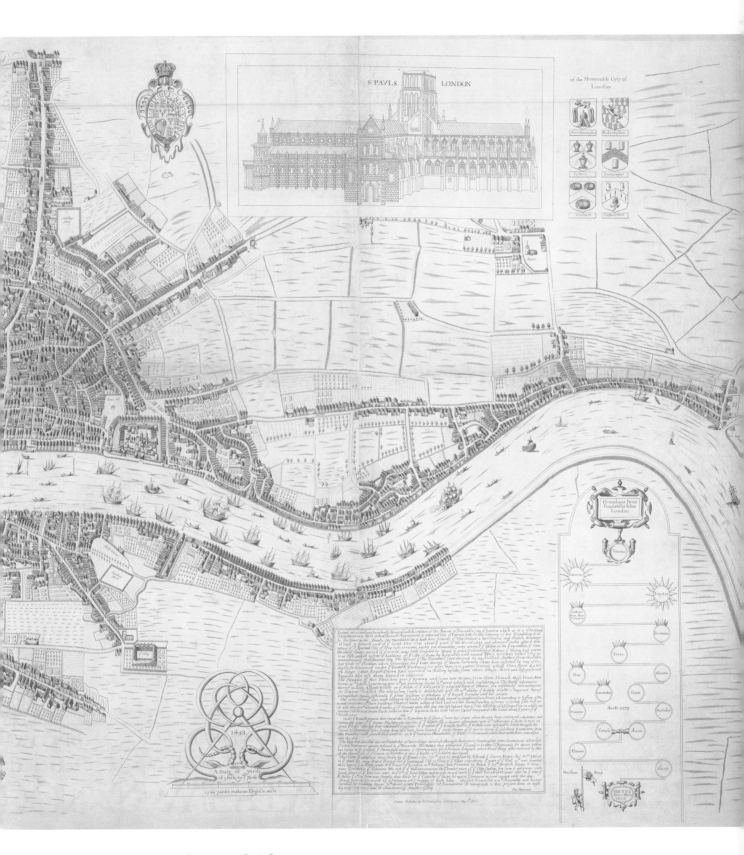

The British Library

First published in 2006 by
The British Library
96 Euston Road
London NW1 2DB

Text © 2006 Peter Whitfield
Illustrations © 2006 The British Library and other named copyright holders

British Library Cataloguing in Publication Data
A catalogue record for this book is available from The British Library

ISBN 978 0 7123 4918 5 (HB)
ISBN 978 0 7123 4919 2 (PB)

Designed and typeset in Mentor by Alison and Peter Guy
Printed in Italy by Printer Trento S.r.l.

Illustrations

Jacket
Plan of London, Westminster and Southwark, 1745, by John Rocque.
B.L. Maps Crace III/107.

Half-title page
Plan of Buckingham Palace (detail) showing order of precedence at coronations, 1761.
B.L. Maps Crace XI/39a.

Title page
Plan of London, 1658, by Newcourt and Faithorne.
B.L. Maps Crace I/35.

Page 7
Plan of London and its environs (detail), 1746, by John Rocque.
B.L. Maps Crace XIX/18.

Contents

London Before the Fire

The first comprehensive images of London, in the shape of maps and views, began to be drawn and published around the year 1550. Before that, surveys and plans of particular areas and estates were occasionally made for their owners, but the idea of a map or view portraying the whole city was a new concept. The making of urban maps had been developing in continental Europe for perhaps a century before this date. Just as Renaissance artists rediscovered the world of nature, so they began to look with fresh eyes at the human environment, and the city became a subject of study for scholars and artists, and, of course, for the rulers of cities. Before 1550 small images of London had occasionally been produced, but these were stylised in form, and they were always secondary to a text, most commonly illustrations in a manuscript. What was new after 1550 was the idea that the city was now, in its own right, a subject of interest for artists to focus on, and to embody in both manuscript and printed images, drawn on a large scale, so that they became both functional and aesthetic. These early maps of London had a strongly pictorial element: buildings are seen in elevation, human figures are placed here and there, flags are to be seen, and ships sail on the river. They are, in fact, halfway to being views, or

pictures of the living city, rather than impersonal plans of it. Despite not being strict plans, they did, nevertheless, embody an instinctive grasp of scale - the idea that each part of the map must relate proportionately to all other parts. However, the prospects and panoramas of the city were not naturalistic views: the artists who created them had to manipulate space to display the principal features in an attractive way.

When these earliest maps and views of London were being made, the city was one single community, covering just one square mile, almost all of it still squeezed tightly within its encircling walls. Its only satellites lay a mile away in Westminster, seat of the national government, and across the river in Southwark, home to taverns, theatres and brothels. Physically this was still, in essence, the medieval city, reaching from the Tower in the east to Temple Bar in the west. London Bridge was the only crossing of the Thames (and would remain so until 1750) while the northern boundary was plainly marked by the ancient walls, whose gates were still locked shut each night. Virtually all the houses were of timber, with the characteristic Tudor overhang, while St Paul's was a spired Gothic cathedral resembling those we now see in Salisbury or Norwich. The city's life was

governed by the mayor, his aldermen and the craft guilds, according to the terms of the royal charter granted by King John in 1215. Together these bodies regulated work and trade, law and order, water supply, hygiene, building, river traffic, and a hundred other

Above: Visscher's classic view of pre-Fire London, 1616, seen from Southwark, looking across old London Bridge to the Tower, the spires of the City, and St Paul's.
B.L. Maps 162.o.1.

Right: King Edward I at the gates of London, from a 14th-century manuscript.
B.L. Egerton MS 3028, f.62.

matters. This was a self-governing community, but in the last resort it could not defend itself against an outside force (witness the violent events of the Peasants' Revolt in 1381), or against a determined king, just one mile away in Westminster or even closer in the Tower. But the City's great defence was its wealth: its money-raising powers on behalf of the Crown reached back to the crusade of Richard the Lionheart, and all monarchs until the end of the seventeenth century would continue to need and deal directly with the

City; so the two powers co-existed for centuries, often in an uneasy truce. The population of this community may have been perhaps 60,000 - the size of a modern town like Hereford - but its citizens were far more tightly packed, squeezed in, and almost literally crawling over one another amid an extraordinary array of medieval dirt and smells.

Nevertheless, after centuries of stability in terms of physical size, London in 1550 now entered a new phase of growth and change, a phase which would never really stop, but which would go on accelerating for the next four centuries and beyond. Some of these changes are evident in the maps of the Tudor period, while others lie hidden, their effects waiting to make themselves felt over the next hundred years. The most obvious sign of growth is the ribbon development that began to appear on maps, both to the east and west, outside the gates. Outside Aldgate and Bishopsgate, rows of houses reach out between the open fields, while beyond Aldersgate the hamlet of Clerkenwell is evidently a community in its own right. The buildings west of Newgate, towards Holborn, suggest that the Fleet River rather than the wall was now the natural boundary of the City. Most striking of all is the roadway, almost a mile long, from Fleet Street through the Strand to Charing Cross: it is lined by buildings on both sides, those on the south side being substantial houses with gardens running down to the river. It is clear that by the 1550s the two centres of London and Westminster were now linked by this broad highway, and it would be easy to conjecture that its inhabitants were

[9]

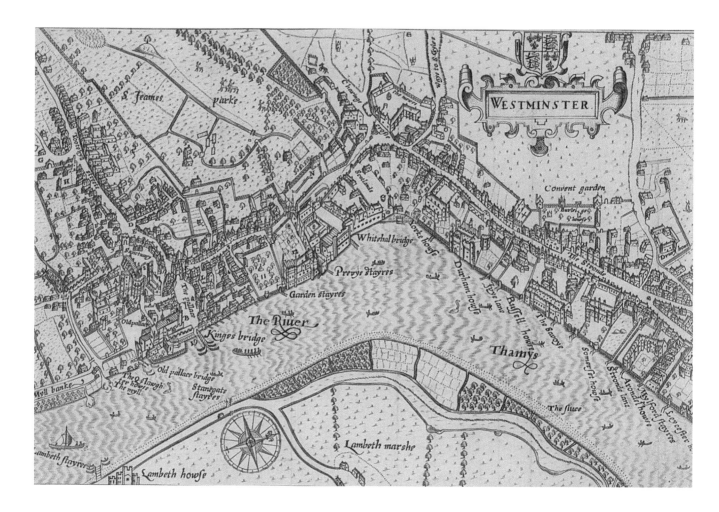

Above: John Norden's map of Westminster, 1593, showing the aristocratic riverside houses which lined the Strand. B.L. Maps Crace 1/22.

Below: the seven gates of the City, 1720, plus Temple Bar. These gates, traditionally locked at night, defined the City's geographical identity until they were demolished in the late 18th century, because they were a hindrance to traffic. B.L. 171.d.5(1).

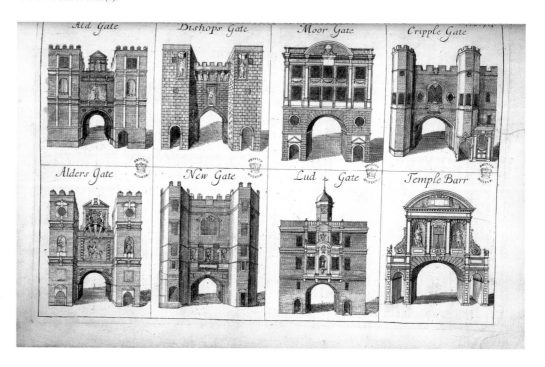

Above: John Norden's map
of the City, 1593, half map,
half view.
B.L. Maps Crace 1/21.

wealthy, and were more likely to be connected with the court to the west than with the City to the east. In fact, many of these riverside houses were virtual palaces, belonging to the noblemen whose names are still attached to the Strand area: Somerset, Savoy, Exeter, Arundel and Suffolk.

This westward movement was to be one of the great factors of London history throughout the seventeenth and eighteenth centuries. It had originated with Edward the Confessor's decision to build a royal palace in Westminster, close to the great Abbey of St Peter. Here the embryonic offices of state and the Parliament were established, creating a social and economic focus second only to the trading community in the City itself. This westward pull was complicated and intensified when King Henry VIII, restless seizer of property and builder of palaces, adopted St James's as the site for another new court and royal dwelling-place, so that London now had a third centre of gravity, which would in time inevitably develop and become linked to the others, as Westminster had to London.

In the foreground of most of the early maps

and views stands Southwark, the access point to London from Kent and Surrey and all points south. Even more extensive than Clerkenwell, Southwark was noted for four ill-matched types of building: the houses of prelates, many of them effectively palaces; large inns; prisons; and pleasure resorts, including theatres, brothels and the Paris Garden, a disreputable meeting place for rogues and criminals. Until 1556 Southwark lay outside the jurisdiction of the City, and it developed a freewheeling character of its own, which was not much changed when the area became a City ward, called Bridge Ward Without. This was a place where noisy public entertainments, such as the bear-baiting pit and the theatre, could flourish without disturbing the peace of the City.

All this change was highly visible on the map, but behind much of it lay one of the most significant events in London's history, which had occurred a couple of decades before the first maps of the city were drawn, namely the Dissolution of the religious houses. Henry VIII's manufactured quarrel with Rome, and his natural avarice, led him between 1535 and 1540 to abolish the twenty

or more major religious foundations in London, and to take possession of their lands and goods. Dozens of very large buildings, and hundreds of acres of land, much of it lying in a great arc roughly following the line of the City walls, were seized, demolished, sold, given away to royal servants, built over or transformed into secular use. The former religious inhabitants were turned adrift with pensions, large or small depending on their status, except for the few who refused to cooperate spiritually or practically in this process, who were summarily butchered. It was the greatest single transfer of land in London's history, and it had enormous implications, for the new secular owners became free to develop this property for their own use or for commercial ends.

It is true that this did not happen overnight, for other conditions had to fall into place to make this strategy attractive, but it was the beginning of a property market in London, which has grown steadily ever since, and which was the basis of hundreds of great personal fortunes, and of the far-reaching physical changes which overtook the capital over the next two hundred years. It also marked a huge intellectual change in urban life, an end to the consensual vision of the world and the religious life which had ruled England, as it had the rest of Christendom, for a thousand years. As the very fabric of the City became secularised and commercialised, so inevitably did its customs and its values. How London would have developed without the Reformation and the Dissolution of the religious houses no one knows, but it is extremely hard to imagine the London of Inigo Jones, Wren, Hogarth, Fielding, Nash and Dickens emerging exactly as it did, in an unreformed, post-medieval, Catholic community. The English Reformation may have originated in a royal whim, but its reception by the people of London must equally have sprung from a recognition that this was what they wanted, that this could be in their interests. The confusion sown by the restoration of the old faith under Queen Mary showed that it was too late to turn back the clock, a feeling hardened by the martyrdom of London Protestants at Smithfield and elsewhere.

Criticism of change and development in London has a fairly long history. John Stow, the contemporary of Shakespeare and great chronicler of Elizabethan London, published his *Survey of London* in 1598. Stow seems to have had Catholic sympathies, for one of his constant themes is regret for the demolished churches, for the alienated religious lands, and the incessant, disorderly growth of the city, both inside the walls and outside. This growth was, of course, driven by the basic fact of a swelling population. Mortality rates in Tudor and Jacobean London were terrifying,

Above: Hollar's engraving of the old St Paul's which was destroyed in the Fire; its spire had collapsed in 1561.
B.L. Maps 3545(4).

Right: a vivid reminder of the shadow which the plague cast over London, 1625.
B.L. Ashley 617.

the deaths always exceeding the births because of the insanitary and overcrowded state of the city. This deficit was, however, counterbalanced by the ever-growing tide of immigration into London. From the time when reasonably reliable figures become available, around 1650, we can calculate that the known growth of London, which took place despite the appalling death rate, must have required a constant inflow of around 10,000 people per year. This influx was always one of the basic conditions of London's life and continued growth: London was a perennial magnet to people from outside - some rich, but many more poor, some foreign but many more British, some industrious but many idle and villainous. It was always a place to work and make money, to find a better life than that available to the rural poor. Much of this incoming population settled outside the City walls, often in squalid, makeshift housing. In some ways perhaps they preferred to live outside the City limits, because they would not then be subject to the strict regulations, especially labour regulations, which held sway within the walls. The powerful craft guilds could not prevent a man pursuing his trade if he lived in Whitechapel or Wapping or Spitalfields. In fact, the City realised in time that it suited them to banish to these districts certain noxious but necessary trades that were not welcome in the City itself, trades such as leather-tanning, brick-firing, carcase-rendering, tin-smithing, soap-boiling and so on.

This extramural growth greatly alarmed the City and the Crown throughout the Tudor and Jacobean periods. They feared that the hordes of this new uncontrolled population boom would be ungovernable, that they would bring disease, famine and disorder to the capital, and undermine the power of the guilds to control labour and commerce. Years of royal and municipal proclamations attempted to prevent this growth by forbidding all unlicensed building within three miles of the City gates. This policy proved unworkable, first because the authorities were all too often persuaded to accept a fine from an offender rather than removing the building, and second because if enforced it would only serve to increase the overcrowding it was meant to prevent. London's mayors and the nation's monarchs, from Elizabeth to Charles II, slowly learned that social history cannot be shaped by official decrees. By the 1680s the policy was abandoned altogether, and a completely different and more orderly approach to city planning was adopted.

It is intriguing to speculate whether this approach might have emerged sooner had not the Civil War in the 1640s intervened. It seems that both James I and Charles I were meditating some imaginative schemes for the modernisation of parts of London. These were the years when Inigo Jones was Surveyor of the King's Works, when grandiose designs for a new Whitehall Palace were made, when the Queen's House in Greenwich was built, when the renovation of St Paul's was planned, and when Jones was seconded by King Charles to design the great innovative residential district being planned by the Earl of Bedford on his land at Covent Garden. This, the first of London's new squares, was immensely important as an architectural and commercial model of the way London's western suburbs would develop, with an aristocratic patron developing and leasing elegant houses as a handsome long-term investment. Completed

Opposite: part of the Agas Map of 1633 showing the beginnings of suburban building outside Aldgate and Bishopsgate.
B.L. Maps Crace 1/8.

[14]

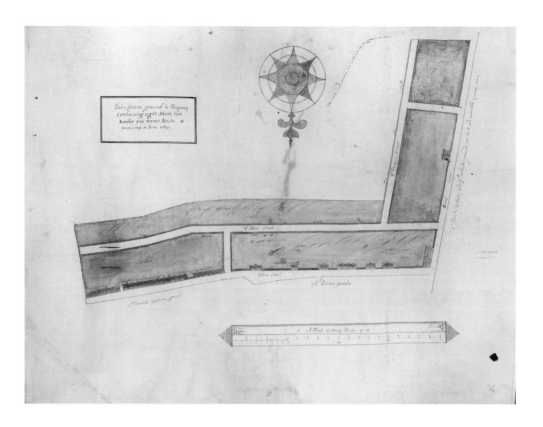

Above: a request for a royal licence to build houses in Brick Lane, Whitechapel, 1671. B.L. Harley MS 7344, f. 72.

Below: a rare pre-Fire house still surviving in Fleet Street in the early 19th century. B.L. Add. MS 42506, f. 81.

by 1640, the piazza was an aesthetic and commercial triumph, but the disruption of the Civil War meant that the experiment would not be repeated for another thirty years.

One district in which urban expansion was not opposed was along the east riverside, where the great increase in English maritime trade fostered the growth of the hamlets of Wapping, Shadwell and Ratcliffe, where ships were built and serviced. International events played their part here: the long conflict in the Spanish-ruled Netherlands greatly damaged the Dutch carrying trade and benefited the English, who were in any case now opening their own exciting new trade routes around the world. From these little East End wharfs, explorers set sail for America, for Russia, and the East Indies, and to them came successive waves of Protestant refugees from a Europe torn by religious wars. The fate of Antwerp at the hands of its Spanish rulers also gave the City of London its great opportunity to expand its financial role, and Sir Thomas Gresham opened his Royal Exchange in 1570 in direct imitation of the bourse which he had seen in Antwerp; it was the first of the great institutions which were to build the City's power and prosperity. A Tudor commentator boasted that 'the beauty of London has become a terror to other countries, by reason of its great wealth and frequency of trade; it spreadeth

Above: Hollar's engraving of the Covent Garden piazza soon after its completion in 1639; the first planned residential square built in London. British Museum, Dept of Prints and Drawings.

the honour of our country abroad by her navigations, and maketh our power feared even of barbarous princes,' while another wrote that 'the wealth of the world is wafted to it by the Thames'. Rather strangely, in view of these sentiments, the very existence of the East End seems to have been ignored by map-makers, and all maps of London before about 1650, and many afterwards, stop at the Tower.

The growth of Tudor and Stuart London is illustrated by one striking event from the beginning of the Civil War. After the Royalist army had briefly threatened London but withdrawn without fighting, Londoners in their thousands spent months throwing up a line of earthen ramparts and a series of forts around the capital, in preparation for a second attack. These fortifications followed a line far outside the ancient walls, which were themselves clearly seen to be ineffectual. They took in the whole of St James's, Westminster, St Giles, Clerkenwell, Shoreditch, Whitechapel, Wapping, Southwark and Lambeth:

in other words those who built them recognised the fact that the London of 1642 was at least double the size of the original City. And when King Charles's head was struck off in front of thousands of Londoners, it seems symbolic that this act was carried out not on Tower Hill or some other ancient place of execution, but before the Banqueting House of the new Whitehall Palace, which the king's father had planned with Inigo Jones just twenty years earlier: the weight of power and history in London had shifted decisively westwards.

It was because of these changes that when the Great Fire ravaged the City, it did not destroy London, for London had now outgrown its historic core. But the Fire was undoubtedly a great watershed in London's history, wiping out the medieval city of timbered houses and Gothic churches, and opening the way for a more elegant new city built of brick and stone, closer in character to the new London that was beginning to emerge to the west.

Medieval London: The Earliest Images of the City

City maps in any formal sense did not exist in Europe in the Middle Ages, but from time to time scholars and artists did attempt to illustrate their works with images of cities. These pictures were usually very small, and the features of the city were simplified into an anonymous cluster of walls and towers; however, the oldest surviving image of London is rather more than that. It occurs as a detail on an illustrated road map showing the pilgrims' route from London to the Holy Land via Italy, and it was drawn around the year 1252 by Matthew Paris, a monk of St Albans and a prolific writer and chronicler. The image is a mere thumb-nail sketch, but it nevertheless contains the essential features of medieval London.

Opposite: the Tower and the City from the Charles D'Orleans manuscript. B.L. Royal MS 16.F.2, f. 73.

Below: the image of London from the Matthew Paris manuscript. B.L. Royal MS 14.C.7, f. 2.

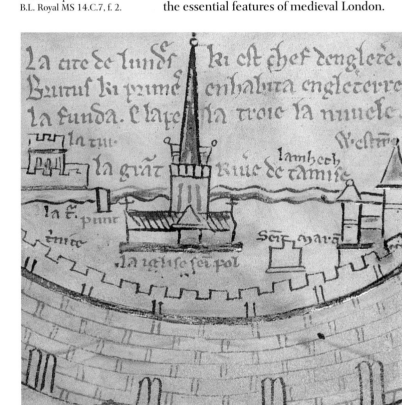

grasp of geographical layout was very hazy: the Tower is on the wrong side of the river, and it is not clear that Westminster lies outside the city walls. Nevertheless this little icon does display some fundamental historical features now vanished: the centrality of St Paul's with its medieval spire, which collapsed in the fire of 1561, and the survival of the Roman walls, which defined the city limits for 1,500 years. The names of the city gates are rather mixed up, but they show one intriguing detail: along with Aldgate, Bishopsgate and so on, Billingsgate is named. Yet we know that Billingsgate was not a gate at all as the others were, but was for centuries the famous fish market on the riverside. But, in fact, there was a riverside wall, built towards the very end of the Roman occupation, parts of which still survived in the twelfth century according to medieval descriptions, and traces of it have been excavated. Behind the quayside east of the Tower there must have been a gate in that wall which became Billingsgate. Matthew Paris's little sketch does, therefore, contain authentic geographical elements, and, elementary as it appears, no larger or better image of London survives from the entire Middle Ages.

More than two centuries separate this sketch from a second medieval miniature of London. Drawn by an unknown French artist around 1485, this shows Charles, Duke of Orleans, in the Tower, where he and several others were taken after their capture at the Battle of Agincourt. The timescale is compressed into three simultaneous scenes, which show his confinement as a noble hostage, his face at a window during his imprisonment, and his eventual release after twenty-five years. The walls of the White Tower are opened to reveal the theatrical scene within. Stylistically far advanced from Matthew Paris, the layout here is just as confused, for we are facing the Tower from the south, yet it appears to stand on a peninsula, with the river curving around it, and London Bridge with its houses and shops lying to the north. The artist must have been well informed about the bridge, the White Tower and the Traitor's Gate, but he could surely never have painted this view on the spot. Nevertheless this is still an invaluable vignette of medieval London, and it is a strangely attractive, almost idyllic, image of a long, weary captivity, during which Charles d'Orleans pursued the art of poetry, writing courtly verse in both French and English. He lived to enjoy twenty-five more years of life after his return to France.

The city seems to be portrayed from an imaginary hill to the north, so that we see the city walls, pierced by several gates, and beyond that the Tower, the river, St Paul's and Westminster. Lambeth is named, along with 'the great River Thames', while London Bridge is briefly labelled 'pont'. Matthew Paris has written a little text endorsing the legend that London was 'founded by Brutus, the first inhabitant of England'. But although the artist has highlighted the city's main features, his

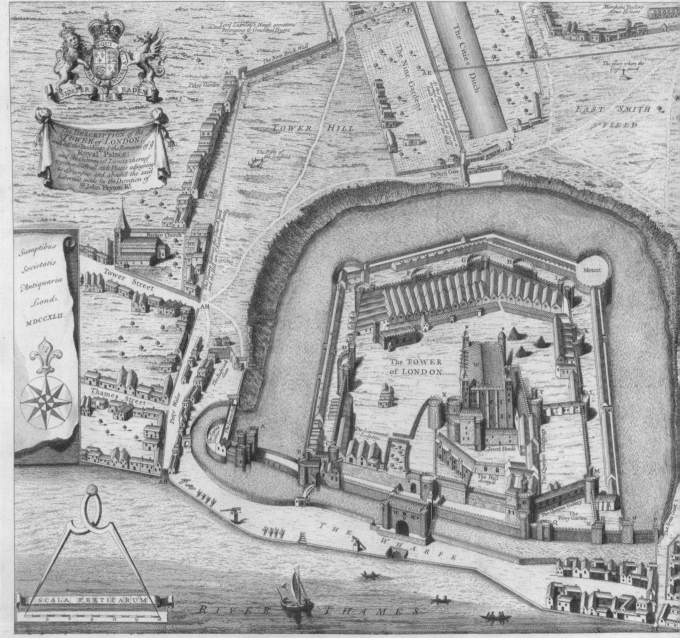

Above: Gascoyne's 1597 view of the Tower of London, which conveys a sense of the fortress as a private realm, separated from London by its walls, broad moat and the open space of Tower Hill, where the place of the scaffold is plainly marked. B.L. K.Top. 24.23.b.

Opposite: an 18th-century plan of the Tower of London. B.L. K.Top. 24.23.a.

The Tower and Westminster Abbey

The Tower of London and Westminster Abbey are our great surviving links with medieval London. Destruction by fire or deliberate rebuilding has erased every other trace of those distant times, and, historic city though it is, the 'historic' London that we see today is primarily a creation of the eighteenth and nineteenth centuries. The White Tower is the most perfect example of Norman military architecture in England, although the windows and the four turrets on the towers were added by Christopher Wren in the 1690s. The abbey, too, has been modified over many centuries – it comes as a surprise to learn that the famous twin western towers were added only in the eighteenth century, designed by Wren and Hawksmoor.

The immense continuity of the Tower gives it the appeal of a great theatre, on whose stage a centuries-long pageant was played out, whose themes were power, conflict, conspiracy and above all blood. The Tower has been a fortress, a palace, and a prison, and in our more democratic age it is now a magnet for tourists. It was never the seat of government, either of England or of London, but instead it was a citadel of absolute royal power, where monarchs pursued their pleasures and their enemies, immune from the outside world. The area of almost twenty acres, which was enclosed by the moat and the great perimeter wall, was a complete miniature kingdom, with banqueting hall, chapel, armoury, jewel-house, dungeons, state rooms, private chambers, gardens and private zoo.

Although it was Henry VIII who ceased to use the Tower as a royal residence, moving instead to the palaces of Whitehall and St James's, it is perhaps with his reign more than any other that the Tower is identified. So much intrigue, ambition, betrayal and revenge have been enacted there that it seems to symbolise the personal dimension in history, when the royal will was supreme, and everyone else had to bend to it or escape it. Its list of prisoners must be the most elite of any prison in the world: the kings Richard II, Henry VI and Edward V; the poets Charles d'Orleans and Sir Thomas Wyatt; political and religious martyrs, Thomas More and Edmund Campion; disgraced royal wives like Anne Boleyn or Catherine Howard; dangerous heirs like Princess Elizabeth or Jane Grey; fallen ministers or archbishops such as Thomas Cromwell or William Laud; conspirators and rebels like Guy Fawkes, the Duke of Monmouth, Lord George Gordon or Roger Casement; and innumerable unfortunate chance victims including Sir Walter Raleigh, Samuel Pepys and John Wilkes.

For most of these people their place of imprisonment became their place of death, and there is no doubt that the roll-call of executions is at the heart of the Tower's macabre appeal. The scene of execution was the relative privacy of Tower Green for the king's more personal victims, or the public

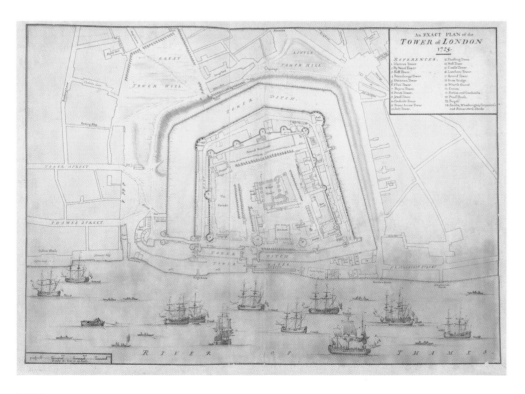

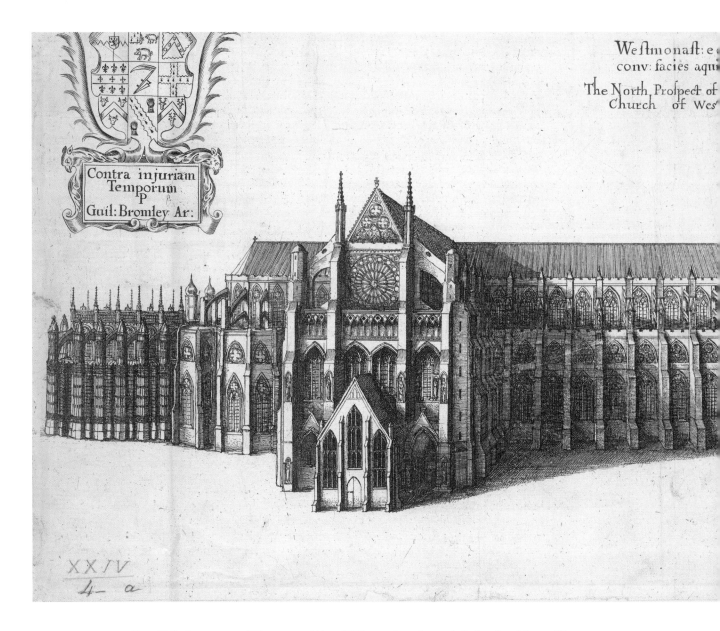

Westmonaſt: e
conv: facies aqui

The North Proſpect of
Church of Weſ

Contra injuriam
Temporum
P
Guil: Bromley Ar:

XXIV
4 — a

Above: Hollar's engraving of Westminster Abbey, 1554, seen from the north, before the addition of the two west towers, which were designed by Wren and completed by Hawksmoor. B.L. K.Top. 24.4a.

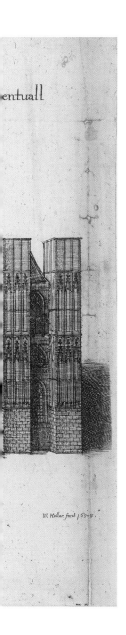

entuall

W. Hollar fecit / 1647.

arena of Tower Hill for those reckoned to be enemies of the state. The last public beheading in England was that of the eighty-year-old Jacobite Lord Lovat, in 1747, on Tower Hill; on that occasion the spectators' stand collapsed, killing half a dozen people, much to Lovat's delight. It was very soon after this that the Tower's unique role as a repository of English history was recognised, and by the 1750s the public was being admitted to gaze at the weapons, the ravens and the other animals in the royal menagerie, including lions and bears, and to absorb the atmosphere of the dungeons and torture chambers, which now seemed to belong to another age.

If the Tower was the private citadel of royal power, Westminster Abbey marks the public ceremonial face of monarchy, the place of coronation and burial. We now see it as only a building, and it is easy to forget that it was the church of a large community of monks, with extensive living quarters attached, and the centre of a very wealthy estate. Architecturally full of beauty, where the Tower suggests mere strength, the abbey, too, reminds us that the two most potent forces in medieval life, besides the Church itself, were royal power and death. The magnificent nave was constructed in stages in the thirteenth and fourteenth centuries, but the Henry VII chapel, with its miraculous lace-like stonework, dates from the early sixteenth century. The succession of tombs and monuments from Edward the Confessor onwards has made the abbey a national shrine, perhaps inspiring meditations on the passing of worldly power, as Beaumont wrote:

Think how many royal bones
Sleep within these heaps of stones;
Here they lie, had realms and lands
Who now want strength to stir their hands...

The royal tombs also catered for more unusual tastes: the embalmed body of Henry V's queen, Catherine of Valois, lay in an open coffin for three centuries, enabling Samuel Pepys to 'take the upper part of her body in my arms, and I did kiss her mouth, reflecting upon it that I did kiss a queen'. These royal burials inspired imitative traditions for statesmen, military figures, writers, scientists, architects, actors and even a few churchmen, although many of those commemorated here are actually buried elsewhere. One of the abbey's most famous features – Poets' Corner – seems to have grown up around Chaucer's tomb, out of the mistaken belief that he was buried there in recognition of his poetic skills; in fact, it was because he was a royal servant, but the growth of the tradition became unstoppable. Not a few writers have presented ticklish problems for the dean and chapter of Westminster Abbey, and we can easily wonder what exactly Burns, Byron, Keats or Hardy contributed to Christian life or thought to justify their place in the abbey. Blake had to wait two hundred years for his memorial, unveiled in 1957. Many of the monuments, especially those carved by Roubilliac, are spectacular fantasies in stone, as one critic remarked, 'more theatrical than sepulchral'. All these tombs of the famous are counterbalanced, perhaps even overshadowed, by the symbolic tomb of Everyman – the unknown soldier – probably the most visited and the most moving of all.

In addition to the formal monuments, the abbey also possesses a unique collection of wax effigies of monarchs and statesmen which were exposed during state funerals, their features modelled from death-masks. The twin themes of worldly glory and mortality appear to pervade the abbey, and for this reason perhaps all the secular history to be found there does have a religious dimension after all.

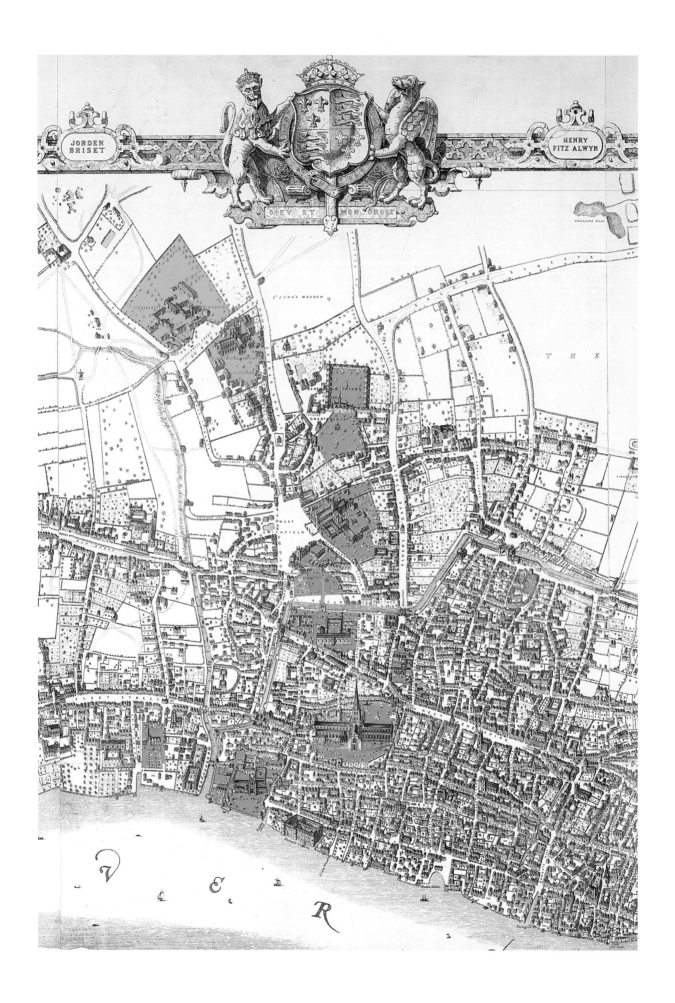

JORDEN
BRISET

HENRY
FITZ ALWYN

DIEV ET MON DROIT

The End of the Middle Ages in London

One of the greatest turning points in London's entire history occurred just a few years before the era of maps and urban views dawned in the capital, and it is therefore impossible to trace in the plans or images of the city. Henry VIII's quarrel with Rome - allied to his personal avarice - provoked him in 1535 to dissolve all England's religious communities, and to seize all their buildings and property. In London, more than twenty substantial priories, hospitals and colleges, which had been landmarks in the city for centuries, were emptied of their members and taken into secular hands. Over the next twenty years their lands and buildings were sold or given to the king's friends, converted into houses or demolished. The moral justification of what happened is arguable: no doubt many monks and friars were idle and some were corrupt, but others fulfilled a valuable role in the city, and the hospitals in particular were soon re-established by the city governors.

It was not only the land lying directly inside the City which changed hands as all these institutions owned extensive property throughout what we would now call Greater London - in Middlesex, Essex, Kent and Surrey - and all this now passed into new ownership, creating the conditions for the development of London that was to follow from the seventeenth through to the nineteenth century. For the new landowners, the foundations of great private fortunes were laid, and for London at large a market in property was created which saw these private estates steadily subdivided and broken up into smaller and smaller blocks. Would this have happened anyway, whether the owners were monasteries, dukes or land speculators? In some cases possibly it would, but it is hard to believe that it would have happened at the time that it did or in the way that it did. The map of London and the face of London which we know from the years 1700 and 1800 and 1900 might have looked very different without the widespread development of secularised property, all made possible by the Dissolution of the religious houses in the few years after 1535.

To give just one example, the Saxon manor of Eia consisted of over a thousand acres, much of it marshy or scrubby pasture, and it was one of the many properties owned by Westminster Abbey. Seized by Henry VIII in 1540, it remained Crown land, although leased to various court servants, until King James I sold the freehold in 1623. Fifty years later, by then known as Ebury, it was in the hands of the Grosvenor family, and today it covers Mayfair and Belgravia. Westminster Abbey held several thousand acres more including, of course, most of Westminster

itself, Chelsea, Hyde Park, Charing Cross and the Strand area, Paddington and Westbourne, Kilburn and Hampstead, and beyond, as far north as Hendon, as well as more distant manors in Surrey, Essex, Buckinghamshire, Berkshire, Oxfordshire and Gloucestershire. Second only to the abbey in wealth was the Priory of St John of Jerusalem, whose lands extended north from Clerkenwell through St Pancras as far as Hornsey. All these great tracts of land were secularised, and in time they became London.

The fate experienced by these many foundations varied in detail, but the pattern was always the same. In West Smithfield the priory of St Bartholomew the Great was destroyed and rebuilt by its new owner, the aptly named Sir Richard Rich, whose family kept it until the late nineteenth century, although the chapel was spared to become the parish church, and is now London's oldest. Across at Aldgate, the Priory of the Holy Trinity was granted to Sir Thomas Audley, the man who became the true ancestor of the later Grosvenor Estate, who destroyed the church and lived in the converted priory, which passed at his death to the Duke of Norfolk. The House of the Crutched ('crossed') Friars was granted to Sir Thomas Wyatt, famous among court circles as a highly original poet, and in place of the church he laid out leasehold workshops, and a tennis court for his own use. The priory and hospital of St Mary Spital, just outside Bishopsgate, was emptied and pulled down, leaving behind only the Spitalfields, which were covered with poor tenements by their seventeenth-century owners, principally John Balch. The Marquis of Winchester became the new owner of the Priory of Austin Friars, beside London Wall, and converted it into a large private house, which after his death was sold to John Swinnerton, a merchant, to be subdivided and leased. This process of sale and subdivision became more and more common as time passed, as London's wealthy and fashionable population moved westwards. Most of these properties had sizeable gardens, which offered further scope for their owners to build on, or sell or lease.

However, the conversion of a medieval priory to a private mansion was expensive, and so much property became available at one time that much of it lay untenanted, was used only for storage, or was demolished for its building stone. This was the fate of the land belonging to the Black Friars - the Dominicans - and the White Friars - the Carmelites - whose names survive on either side of the River Fleet. Perhaps the strangest story was that of the Priory of St John of Jerusalem in Clerkenwell, which King Edward VI granted

Opposite: the central part of pre-Reformation London, showing the extent of monastic properties (red) on the west side of the City: Blackfriars, St Paul's, Greyfriars, St Bartholomew's, and all the foundations in Clerkenwell. To the east of this map there were as many religious houses again, and to the west stood Westminster Abbey with all its vast properties. B.L. Maps Crace 1/7.

Above and opposite: two of London's rare monastic survivals: St John's Gate, Clerkenwell. B.L. Tab. 700.b.3, vol. 2. (above); and the cloister of the Charterhouse. B.L. Tab. 700.b.3, vol. 1. (*opposite*).

served as a store-room for the royal household until the time of the Civil War. By the eighteenth century all that remained of this once huge structure was the gateway, which still faces Clerkenwell Road. The manor belonging to this great religious house survived intact under secular ownership until the nineteenth century. The same was true of many other religious houses outside the City: in Southwark, Greenwich, Stratford, Barking, Walthamstow, Holborn, Kilburn, Syon and Sheen the monastic buildings were either converted or demolished, while the farmlands and manors passed into new hands.

Westminster Abbey survived the Dissolution as an edifice, but its vast landholdings were stripped away and a huge acreage later became Hyde Park, Kensington Gardens and St James's Park, which King Henry kept as a hunting-ground for himself. Another large part of the abbey's endowment, however - the entire Paddington district - soon returned to church hands, for it was granted to the Bishop of London by King Edward VI in recognition of his support for his religious reforms.

The social cost of the Dissolution was most obvious in the case of the hospitals, and three of the largest, St Bartholomew's, St Thomas's in Southwark, and the Bethlehem Hospital (the later Bedlam), were reopened under the direction of the City of London. The site and buildings of two monasteries - the Franciscan Greyfriars and the Carthusian House of Salutation - were formed by private acts of philanthropy into famous schools - Christ's Hospital and Charterhouse respectively - although this use had no connection with their earlier role.

These events of the 1530s and 1540s, many of them recorded by John Stow fifty years later, undoubtedly formed the greatest single transfer of property in the history of London. If we include lands outside the City itself, thousands of acres were involved and hundreds of buildings. In its scale and in the opportunities it presented for social change, good or ill, it must have been similar to the experience of the 1970s and 1980s, when thousands of acres of docklands were suddenly deserted and on the market. In both cases there was confusion, dislocation of communities, profiteering by individuals, physical destruction and rebuilding. Only the smallest traces of monastic London now survive, in stone or in pictures, and this is, in itself, a testimony to the suddenness and completeness with which the fabric of medieval London vanished in the 1530s.

to his sister, Mary Tudor. She used it as her palace before her accession to the throne, despite the fact that Lord Protector Somerset had already blown up part of the structure to obtain a supply of masonry to build his new house in the Strand. After Mary's death it

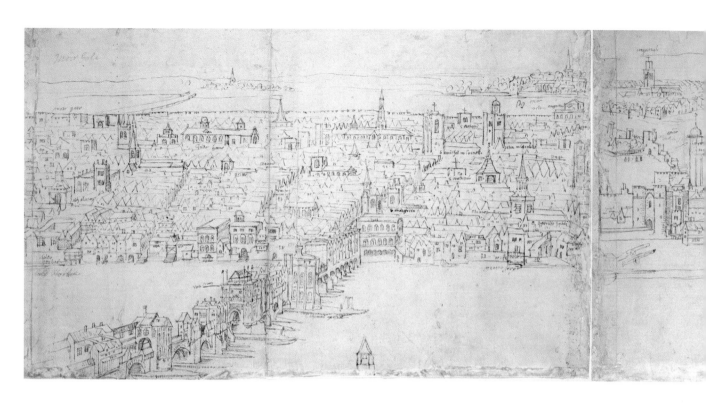

Renaissance London Revealed

Above and below: part of the Wyngaerde panorama, *c*.1544, the first comprehensive picture of London, almost certainly a royal commission drawn by a Flemish artist. The lower portion shows the old Greenwich Palace, birthplace of Henry VIII and Queen Elizabeth, where Wren's hospital now stands. Oxford, Ashmolean Museum.

Views of cities began to appear in Renaissance paintings in the late fifteenth century, often as backgrounds to religious subjects, or glimpsed through windows. Imaginary views of Jerusalem and Rome had long been common, but artists were evidently beginning to look with fresh eyes at the cities in which they actually lived, and by 1500 elaborate aerial views of Florence, Venice and Naples had appeared. It became fashionable for monarchs, and indeed for many wealthy citizens, to desire a picture, preferably a panoramic view, of their capital city, and Henry VIII is reported to have possessed such a picture of London. No trace of it has ever been found, but two important surviving pictures from the last years of his reign may give us some clues as to what it looked like, for after centuries in which no comprehensive image of London had existed, the 1540s saw the creation of two large and striking panoramas of the city.

The earliest by a few short years is the long panorama looking northwards across Southwark, the river and the whole city, drawn by the Flemish artist Anthonis van den Wyngaerde, datable from internal evidence to the year 1544. The Wyngaerde view sweeps impressively from Westminster to Shadwell, with an outlying view of Greenwich, in what is obviously a series of preparatory sketches – but sketches for what? Almost nothing is known about Wyngaerde, except that by 1558 he was employed by King Philip II of Spain to draw topographic pictures of the Hapsburg dominions. His presence in London in 1544 and the final purpose of these sketches are both unexplained. They must have been commissioned, but by whom? If a finished work emerged from them, to decorate a royal palace for example, it has not survived.

Wyngaerde's panorama originates from a viewpoint on the south bank, one high enough to show the walls and gates on the north side of London, and the hills of Hampstead beyond them. This viewpoint provides a perspective in which the landmark buildings rise above the sea of houses, but it is a viewpoint which required great ingenuity from Wyngaerde. Working without a city-plan to guide him, he must have taken sightings from church towers, primarily from St Saviour's in Southwark, and then have paced the streets in order to locate and study the buildings which he wished to portray. In reality, the viewpoint also shifts horizontally, for he has given a clear, frontal view of each section of the north bank from Westminster to the Tower, with none of the foreshortening that would actually result from a single viewpoint. The panorama gives an impression of great verisimilitude, but, in fact, there are a number of inaccuracies, in both location and architecture. The eastern arm of St Paul's Cathedral is far too small; the unmistakable tower of St Mary-le-Bow is misplaced to the west; the northward curve of the river is exaggerated and placed immediately beside the Tower, but in reality it is a mile to the east. Nevertheless, both the conception and the execution of Wyngaerde's panorama are hugely impressive, and if it was transformed into a finished work of art, it must have come as a revelation to its audience in Tudor England.

A Coronation Procession

A second image to offer a comprehensive view of London in the 1540s is the pictorial record of the coronation procession of King Edward VI. This picture has an unusual history, being a copy drawn and engraved from a mural which once adorned the house of Cowdray Park in Sussex. Six years after the copy was made, Cowdray Park and its contents, including this painting, were destroyed by fire, leaving us only this intriguing memorial of a magnificent Tudor panorama. The picture that we now have looks in some ways more like an eighteenth-century than a sixteenth-century image. The houses appear to be of stone and not of the timbers that would fuel the Great Fire, and Tudor Southwark here looks like a rather elegant suburb, with a neatly embanked riverside, which it certainly was not. The view is from the north, in contrast to almost every other view of London, which chose the panoramic riverside view from the south.

The events we are seeing took place on 19 February 1547, just three weeks after the death of King Henry VIII. The procession of his heir, the ten-year-old Edward VI, is seen leaving the Tower and winding its way through Cheapside, by way of St Paul's, Temple Bar and Charing Cross to Westminster Abbey. The boy king can be seen mounted on his horse beneath a canopy just east of Cheapside Cross. The buildings en route are hung with tapestries and the windows crowded with spectators. Six years later Edward would be dead, and his half-sister Mary, whom he had attempted to bar from the succession, would follow this same coronation route. It is the event which provides the subject matter here, but still this is the first fully finished picture of a city in English art, using an imaginary but natural viewpoint and showing distinct topographic detail.

Above: the Coronation Procession of Edward VI, 1547, an 18th-century copy of an original now destroyed. B.L. Maps 3 Tab. 24(4).

Left: King Edward VI, *c.* 1570, unknown artist. London, National Portrait Gallery.

Above: Moorgate and Bishopsgate around the year 1555. This surviving part of the lost 'Copperplate Map' shows the City still closely linked to the open countryside, with animals grazing and archers practising in the fields. Museum of London.

Copperplate: From Picture to Map

THE SPIT

A decade after the Wyngaerde panorama and the coronation view were drawn, an unknown artist was at work on a still more novel and impressive representation of London. Only a fragment of the 'Copperplate Map' exists, but its importance in the development of cartography in England is immense. The fragment owes its name to the fact that three of the original printing plates survive, but there are no contemporary printed copies.

The surviving sections of the map show the area around St Paul's and London Bridge, and then a long strip extending northwards from London Bridge through Bishopsgate to Shoreditch. A number of details point to a date in the mid 1550s, at the latest to 1559. Throughout the map houses, churches, gates, horses and ships are precisely drawn, but this is not a panorama or a bird's-eye view: despite its strongly pictorial character, this is a plan - the first street-plan of London. We seem to be above the city, but not at a single viewpoint, for there is no perspective or foreshortening: we are simultaneously above Thames Street, Leadenhall Street, Moorgate and Spitalfields. True, the buildings are pictured in elevation, but all are pictured at the same angle, so that we seem to see into each street equally, and moreover the streets are named, as they never are in purely artistic views.

This is then a fundamentally different type of image from a view or a panorama. The pictorial elements have been subjected to a deliberate rearrangement in order to serve an intellectual purpose. That purpose was to create a plan of London, a graphic model that would not simply delight the eye, but would enable the viewer to navigate his way through the streets as he studied it. What was depicted on the paper had to correspond in some way to what existed on the ground. True, there is no proof that a mathematically consistent scale was used (even if we had the whole map to examine), but the spatial relationships between the streets and the buildings show that whoever drew the plan had an instinctive grasp of importance of scale. This anonymous fragment is, therefore, a new and revolutionary type of topographic document - it is halfway to being a map. Where this concept came from is impossible to say, but parallel images from Europe show that the plan had been emerging from the perspective-view for some decades before the Copperplate Map was drawn, for comparable proto-maps exist for Venice, Amsterdam and a number of other cities.

We know nothing about the creator of this map, how many copies may have been printed, or how it was used, but we do know that it was widely copied and served as a model for other London maps during the next half-century. Some of the place names are contorted, as though the artist-writer were a foreigner, and, judging from 'Unsdiche', one of his local informants must have been a cockney who could not say his aitches.

Although only a fragment of the whole, this map piece can still tell us a great deal about London in the earliest years of Queen Elizabeth's reign. It was still a walled city whose gates were locked each night, and on those gates the heads and limbs of executed traitors were still displayed. Twenty years after the Reformation, there are clear signs of the transfer of the religious houses to private owners: between Moorgate and Bishopsgate is the former Augustinian priory which the Marquis of Winchester had bought and converted to a private mansion. The former hospital of St Mary Spital had been closed, but not yet demolished, and in its yard may be seen the open-air pulpit where sermons were still preached - the Queen herself attended one in 1559. The Spitalfields were not yet built over and inhabited by the nonconformist weavers who would later make the area famous for its silks. Just by Bishopsgate is the Bethlehem Hospital - 'Bedlam' - which would be removed to Lambeth two centuries later. The fields north of Moorgate were marshy and long deemed unsuitable for building, and here they are being used for archery practice and for drying linen. The 'Dogge hows' in Moorfields was the kennel for the lord mayor's pack of hounds. Perhaps the most striking feature of this plan, however, is the obvious spread of dwellings outside Bishopsgate. Where Liverpool Street station now stands, a succession of fine, large houses with sizeable gardens extend northwards, enjoying the space and air outside the confines of the City, almost foreshadowing the later growth of suburbia. This tantalising fragment of what must have been a large and immensely detailed work makes us long still more to see the lost original in its entirety.

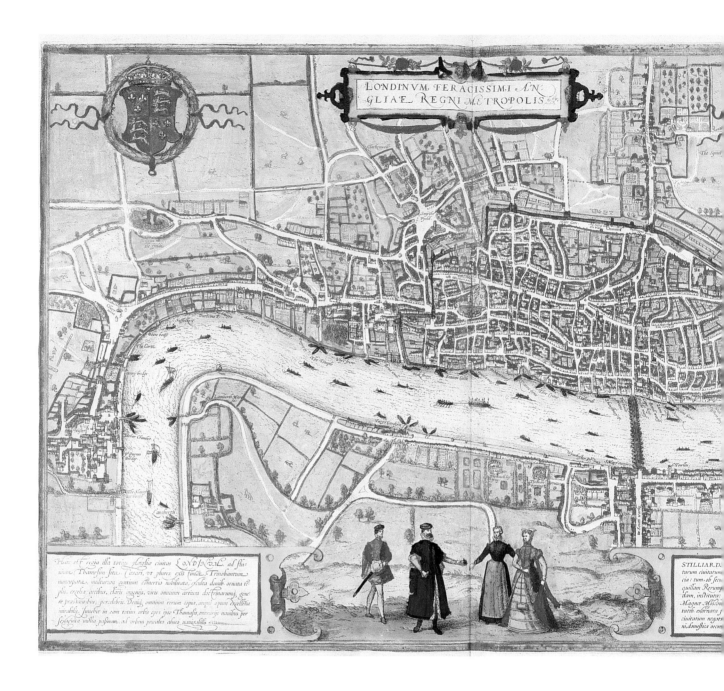

Braun and Hogenberg map of 1572, the first printed map of London that survives, it was undoubtedly a reduced copy of the Copperplate Map. The streets are shown in plan, the buildings pictorially. The figures in the foreground could almost be actors, and seem like a premonition of the theatres that would soon be built in Southwark. B.L. Maps 215.f.1.

Braun and Hogenberg

In 1572 there appeared, in Cologne, the first volume of a great atlas of city-plans entitled *Civitates Orbis Terrarum*, by Braun and Hogenberg. This was a landmark publication in the history of maps, for when it was completed many years later in six volumes, it brought together plans or views of more than 500 cities of the world, not only in Europe, but also in Asia, Africa and the Americas. It was obviously a response to the growing taste for topographic art, and it acted as an immense stimulus to the publication of further town plans. The 1572 volume included the first surviving printed map of the whole of London and Westminster. The publishers in Cologne clearly needed existing source material, or locally made drawings, on which to base their maps, and a study of the Bishopsgate area of their map reveals its strong similarity to the Copperplate Map, suggesting that the latter was their source. If this is so, it may be legitimate to regard the Braun and Hogenberg map as a reduced version of the lost Copperplate Map. This is reinforced by one significant detail, namely that the spire of St Paul's is shown by Braun and Hogenberg, although it was destroyed by fire in 1561, a fact which a well-informed editor might certainly have discovered by 1572. The probability is that this map represents London as it was some ten or twelve years before its publication date.

What then does this first complete plan of London tell us about the Elizabethan capital? The most striking feature is that London has clearly spread beyond its medieval walls. This was noted on the evidence of the Bishopsgate area on the Copperplate Map, and we see the same thing here outside Aldgate, Ludgate and Newgate. Above all, the Strand has emerged as a natural highway linking the City with Westminster. This was a thoroughfare of great houses – Arundel, Somerset, the Savoy, Suffolk – belonging to the nobility, whose properties faced the river, with landing stages or water-gates. The Thames, in fact, was the main highway from London to Westminster, as can be seen by the scores of small craft being rowed up or downstream, and the Strand was the back street. On the riverside by the City boundary, two famous vanished palaces can be seen: Bridewell, built for Henry VIII but already converted into a notorious prison, and Baynard's Castle, the Norman fortress which stood at the western approach to the City, and which was destroyed in the Great Fire. Westminster's

status as an extensive separate enclave is evident here, for around the court and the abbey there had grown up services, trades, shops and inns, and it even possessed its own gates. Perhaps surprisingly, the area had a bad reputation for squalor and crime, for many criminals claimed sanctuary in the abbey, while others preyed on courtiers, parliamentarians or pilgrims. Charing Cross already stands out as a pivotal point between London and Westminster. Southwark, the other detached settlement outside the City, had a bad reputation, too, for its low-life entertainment. One unsatisfactory feature of the map is that the Tower of London is quite poorly drawn: the shape of the White Tower is scarcely recognisable, and the ensemble of buildings around it do not relate to the known history of the Tower precincts. If the map is modelled on the Copperplate Map, it is possible that the artist, whoever he was, was denied access to make accurate drawings. Another defect is that rather few streets are named, even some major thoroughfares like the Strand. The number of gardens within the City, mainly attached to religious houses, had been remarkable during the Middle Ages, but here few are evident, the only large green space being the gardens of the great Augustinian priory just south of Moorgate, which had been acquired by the Marquis of Winchester. Far larger areas of garden and green fields lie to the west, north of Holborn and north of the Strand, waiting, as we now know, to be built upon in the next phase of London's growth.

For all its visual appeal, the Braun and Hogenberg map is a plan, for it shares the characteristics of the Copperplate Map on which was based. However, the artist has also taken considerable pains to produce a pictorial effect. The buildings are drawn in elevation, while the trees and animals cast shadows, as if the sun is shining on them from the west, and on the river the oarsmen are struggling with a very visible current. No human figures are to be seen in the streets, but instead four large figures dominate the foreground, as if to draw the viewer into the scene and remind him that this is a picture of a living community. Clearly both artist and publisher still saw the map as a picture: they were setting out to delight the eye by showing what London looked like, rather than providing a functional, impersonal document. This combination of map and picture would remain standard for another century.

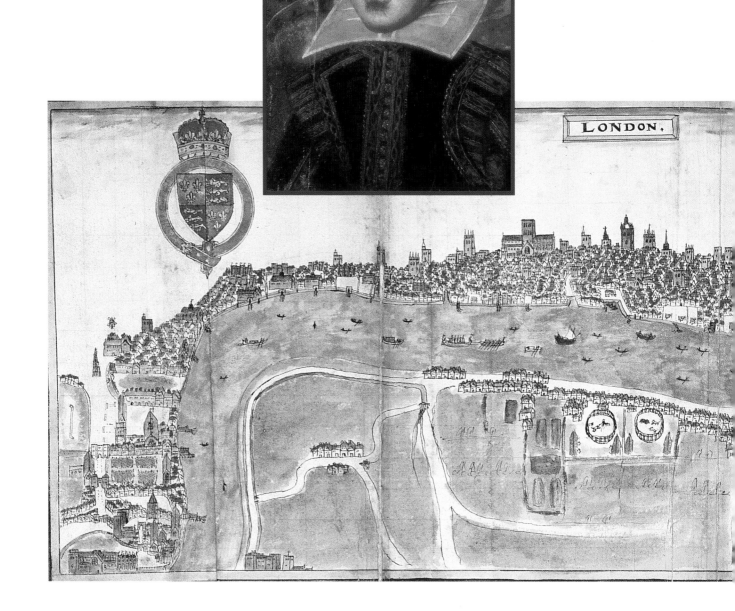

Shakespeare's London

In February 1585 the birth of Shakespeare's twin children, Hamnet and Judith, was registered in Stratford church. For seven years thereafter all trace of Shakespeare's life vanishes until 1592, when the first clear evidence of his career as a dramatist appears. Exactly how Shakespeare occupied those 'lost years' no one knows, but the one certain fact is that he left Stratford, came to London and established himself in the theatrical life of the capital. By chance, we have a rather precise image of London at exactly this time in the lively panorama painted by William Smith in 1588. The landmark buildings – the Tower, St Paul's (without its spire), Westminster Palace – ride above a sea of red-roofed common houses, whose extent shows the city's inexorable spread west and south. In this warren of streets, outbreaks of plague were frequent, causing 10,000 deaths in 1593 and driving Shakespeare out of London while the theatres were closed. In the centre foreground, in the open ground between Southwark and Lambeth, are the bull-baiting and bear-baiting arenas, close to the site where the Globe Theatre would be built in 1598. Shakespeare must have been very familiar with these cruel spectacles, for the image of the man tied to the stake and enduring humiliation and torment is a frequent one in his work, while in *The Winter's Tale* the bear which famously pursued Antigonus was surely borrowed from the nearby bear-pit.

Theatres were not permitted within the boundaries of the City itself, but were tolerated in outer districts like Shoreditch, where Shakespeare first worked with Burbage's company, and also in Southwark. Southwark was the focus of London's low-life, with its sports, taverns and brothels outside the jurisdiction of the City. We know that Shakespeare resided for many years in Cripplegate, lodging with a French Huguenot family named Mountjoy, so that when the Shoreditch theatre closed and moved across the river to become the Globe, he must often have walked over London Bridge, or have been rowed across by a waterman from Queenhithe. The majority of Shakespeare's plays are set far away from England, in remote times or kingdoms, but in the English historical plays London becomes a strong background presence. Political conflicts are played out in the Palace of Westminster and in the private houses of the warring nobles, while the shadow of death always hangs over the Tower. No doubt audiences delighted in references to Smithfield, Moorfields, the Guildhall, Limehouse, Greenwich, the Savoy, and the Temple, but Shakespeare's portrayal of his own contemporary London is found, above all, in the Eastcheap tavern scenes of *Henry IV*, where the young prince goes slumming with braggarts, drunkards, barmaids, whores, con men and thieves. Shakespeare must often have sat drinking with the prototypes of Falstaff, Pistol, Mistress Quickly, Doll Tearsheet and the others, but Falstaff's nemesis and death show that he had no illusions about their lives.

After twenty crowded and creative years, Shakespeare turned his back on the theatre and on the capital, and returned to Stratford and to silence.

Opposite, top: the so-called 'Flower Portrait' of Shakespeare, *c.* 1610–1750, unknown artist. Stratford, The Royal Shakespeare Theatre Collection.

Below: a panorama of London by the topographical artist William Smith, 1588, drawn at exactly the time when the young, unknown Shakespeare was living in the city. B.L. MS Sloane 2596, f.5.

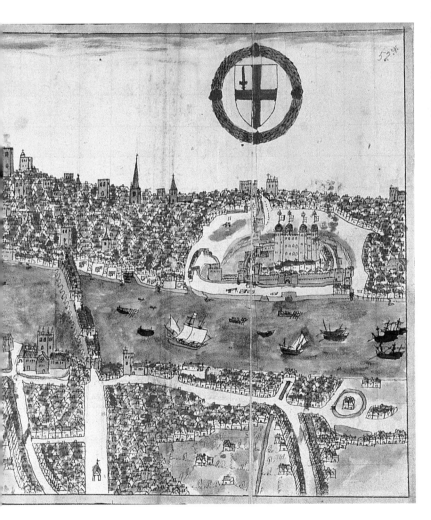

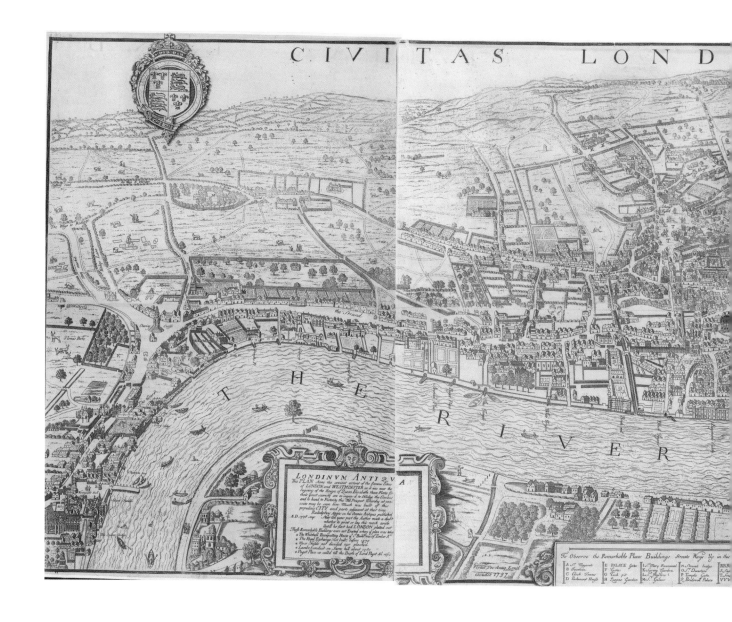

The Agas Map

There is a third map which gives us an impressive general picture of Elizabethan London, the so-called 'Agas Map'. There is no evidence at all to connect it with the surveyor Ralph Agas, but the name was applied long ago and it has stuck. It is a derivative of the Copperplate Map, but printed probably in the 1630s, and updated in some important details. The Royal Exchange, opened by Queen Elizabeth in 1570, is marked, and the spire of St Paul's is gone. The Stuart arms of King James I appear on the map, but the map-maker forgot to alter the Tudor arms on the state barge seen floating on the Thames. The Agas Map was copied again by the celebrated engraver George Vertue in 1737, and issued as a historical document, and this in turn served as the basis for still later versions which were promoted as maps of 'London in the Reign of Queen Elizabeth'. If the author had waited just five or six years longer after 1633, he would have been able to include the newly built Covent Garden piazza (completed 1639) and we should have had absolutely firm evidence of its date. In one sense, however, the date is fortunate, for the 1630s saw the beginning of the end of the official policy of resisting the growth of buildings outside the City walls, so that the Agas Map, printed just a few years before the Civil War, is the last glimpse of old London before the westward growth really began.

The Agas Map extends further north than the Braun and Hogenberg one, and there is a

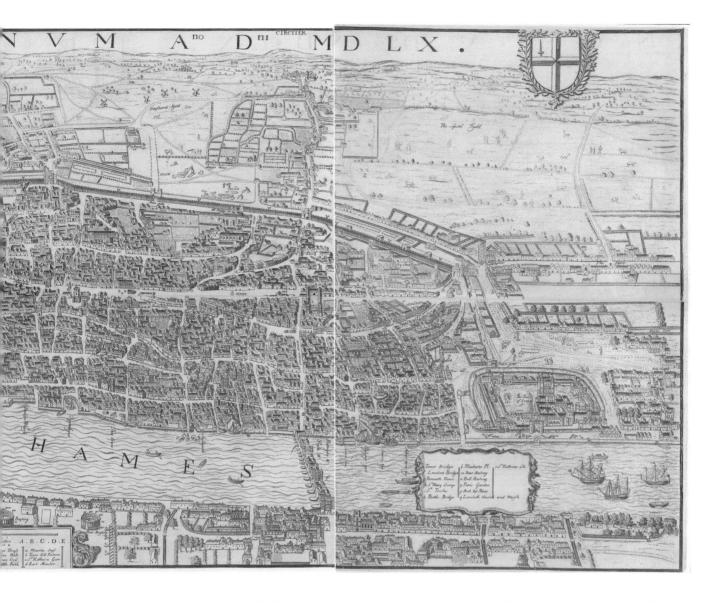

The Agas Map of 1633; essentially a copy of the lost Copperplate Map, slightly revised. The urban part of the map is drawn as a plan, but then in the background the hills of north London become more of a perspective. B.L. Maps 1/8.

spaciousness about it which displays very vividly London's rural hinterland. St Giles-in-the-Fields appears far beyond the built-up area as the self-contained hamlet that it was. Originally a medieval leper hospital named for St Giles, the patron saint of outcasts, the chapel became famous as the place where the 'cup of charity' was given to condemned prisoners on their way to execution at Tyburn. The hospital was closed in 1539, but it had already become the nucleus of a few houses and taverns at the western end of Holborn, which would eventually merge with those which were spreading west from Newgate. These houses backed onto the fields of Gray's Inn, the lawyers' college. Across these open fields, the River Fleet can be seen running

down from Hampstead through the modern Camden Town district. The other open-field site where cattle still graze is on the north-east, outside Aldgate, in the modern White-chapel. It is a pity that the eastern boundary of the Agas Map is at the Tower, and therefore we cannot study the riverside hamlets of Wapping, Shadwell and Deptford, which already in Henry VIII's reign had become centres of ship-building and maritime commerce.

Despite being printed in the 1630s, the importance of the Agas Map is that it almost certainly offers us a valuable copy of the lost Copperplate Map of seventy years earlier, that historic prototype of all London maps.

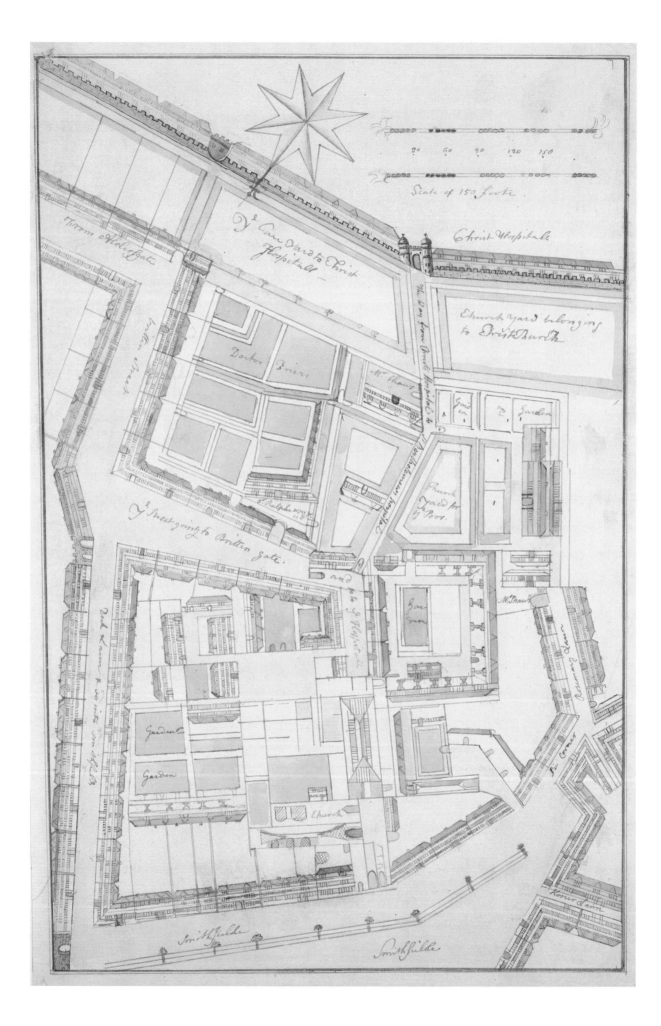

Scale of 150 foote

Yͤ Curr yard to Christ Hospitall

Throm Aldersgate

Doctor Priers

Mͬ Shaws

Christ Hospitale

Church yard belonging to Christ Church

Garden   Garden

S�* Ralphewins C.C.

Church yard for yͤ Poor

Yͤ Street going to Britten gate

and to yͤ Hospitall

Garden

Mͬ Shaw

Garden

Garden

Church

Smithfielde

Smithfielde

Smithfield and St Bartholomew's Hospital

The upsurge of Tudor topographic art expressed itself in many ways. In complete contrast to the sweeping, ambitious images of the entire city created by the panoramic artists and map-makers, Elizabethan London was also the setting for the first cadastral surveys (surveys of land defining ownership for administration – such as taxation – purposes), drawn by men like Ralph Treswell. For the first time private landowners, hospitals, schools and guilds began to realise the advantages of having large detailed plans of their properties, both for administration and in case of sale. The emergence of these plans indicates that a property market was developing in London, stemming partly from the Dissolution of the religious houses, which released many properties into private hands. Several dozen plans by Treswell survive, which offer detailed snapshots of individual streets, such as this one commissioned by Christ's Hospital School. It was characteristic of Treswell's work that he used the form of the strict plan, with scale and compass points, but he showed pictures of the buildings in frontal elevation.

When this plan was drawn in 1617, Christ's Hospital was but three decades old, having been founded by Edward VI as a refuge for the city's orphans. It soon became known by its alternative name of the Bluecoat School, and it broadened its intake from orphans to gentry. It was given the land and buildings of the former Greyfriars – the Franciscan Monastery – against the City wall in Newgate Street. The buildings drawn here were severely damaged in the Great Fire, and were rebuilt by Wren.

Christ's Hospital's neighbour to the north was the much older charity of St Bartholomew's Hospital, founded in 1123 and staffed by Augustinians. After the Dissolution it was re-endowed by the monarch and by the City of London, and it prospered, despite the execution of its chief physician, Rodrigo Lopez, for conspiracy to poison Queen Elizabeth. It was not touched by the Fire, but it was extensively rebuilt in the eighteenth century. Smithfield, in which the hospital stood, was the centre of a large and distinct district outside the City walls, whose reputation was pretty unpleasant on a number of counts. The field itself was the site of the annual Bartholomew Fair, which had begun as a medieval cloth fair, to which a cattle market was added; the tolls from the fair supported first the priory and then the hospital. The fair later became famous for its theatricals and street entertainments, so riotous and disreputable that they were finally suppressed in 1855. Smithfield had also been a place of public execution before the gallows was moved to Tyburn. Common criminals, traitors and heretics were butchered or burned here as late as 1652, and it was long associated with the Protestant martyrs of Mary Tudor's reign. The cattle market was also a place of open slaughter, noise and stench, which Dickens described in the 1840s as being ankle-deep in filth and mire. This, too, was finally swept away when the sale of live cattle and horses was moved to Islington, and a market for meat and poultry took its place in 1868. Centuries of slaughter, of both humans and animals, gave the very word Smithfield a sinister overtone, which time has not altogether erased.

Opposite: plan of St Bartholomew's Hospital in 1617 by Ralph Treswell; south is at the top where the site is bounded by Christ's Hospital. Treswell made many such large-scale plans of London properties, with the buildings characteristically still pictured in frontal elevation.
B.L. Maps Crace VIII/92

Right: a view of Smithfield in 1811.
B.L. K.Top. 22.35b.

The Norden Panorama

The outburst of topographic art and publishing in Elizabethan England throws up famous names such as Christopher Saxton and John Speed, who made their first, landmark maps of the country. The creator of this unusual London panorama, John Norden, also planned to map all of England but, unlike his two great rivals, he failed to find the necessary patronage, and his grand schemes came to nothing. This London image of 1600, with its cavalcade of mounted aldermen, survives in only one unique copy in Stockholm's Royal Library. In addition to the vivid Thames-side view which it offers, it has several idiosyncratic features which are all its own. Above the church

of St Mary Overy in Southwark appear the words *Statio prospective* - the point from which the prospect was drawn. The tiny human figure just visible on the church tower may therefore be Norden's own whimsical self-portrait. He must have somehow contrived to reverse the sketches which he made of Southwark itself, in order to incorporate them into a north-facing panorama.

The most unusual feature of the picture is the curving horizon to the east and west, a distinctly odd way of making the townscape fade into the distance. The adoption of a single perspective point has presented Norden with the problem of how to represent Westminster,

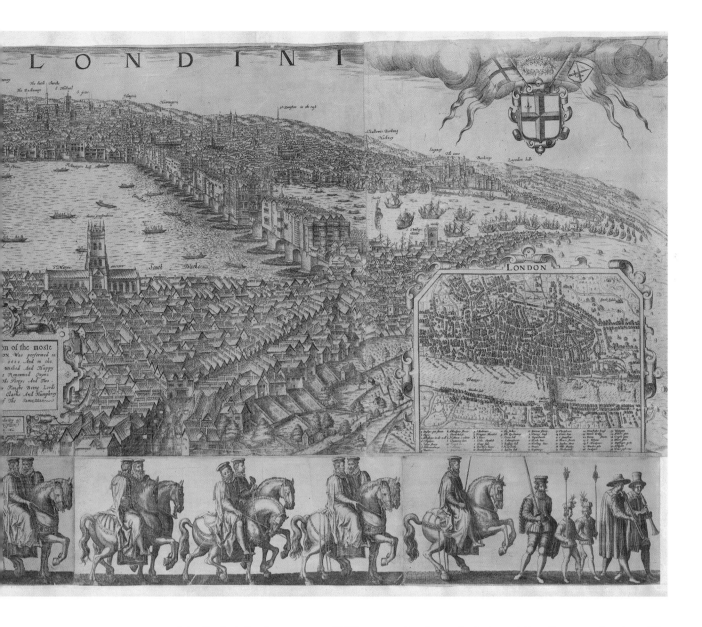

John Norden's London panorama, 1600, a comprehensive work of art, consisting of a perspective view of the whole city from an imaginary point in the air above Southwark, with Norden's own two detailed plans of London and Westminster set into it. Stockholm, Royal Library.

a mile away upstream and virtually hidden around the river's bend. His solution is to place a quite separate view of Westminster in the empty marshes of Lambeth. He has drawn the ground peeled back like folds of cloth, to reveal the whole area west from the Temple to the Houses of Parliament, from a high viewpoint which enables him to draw all the great Thames-side houses and their gardens in some detail. This strange visual conceit is balanced on the right-hand side by a functional plan of the City, complete with street index. This panorama is remarkable for showing three distinct approaches to the problem of depicting London, or any city for that matter: the plan, the profile from a relatively low viewpoint, and the bird's-eye view from high above. It is almost a compendium of Tudor topographic art. One puzzle in Norden's picture is the appearance of two tall, three-masted ships which could never have passed London Bridge, and which would never have been built upstream of it for the same reason. There was a drawbridge in Old London Bridge, at the southern end, which could be raised to cut off access to the City, but whether craft of any size could pass through the gap is very doubtful.

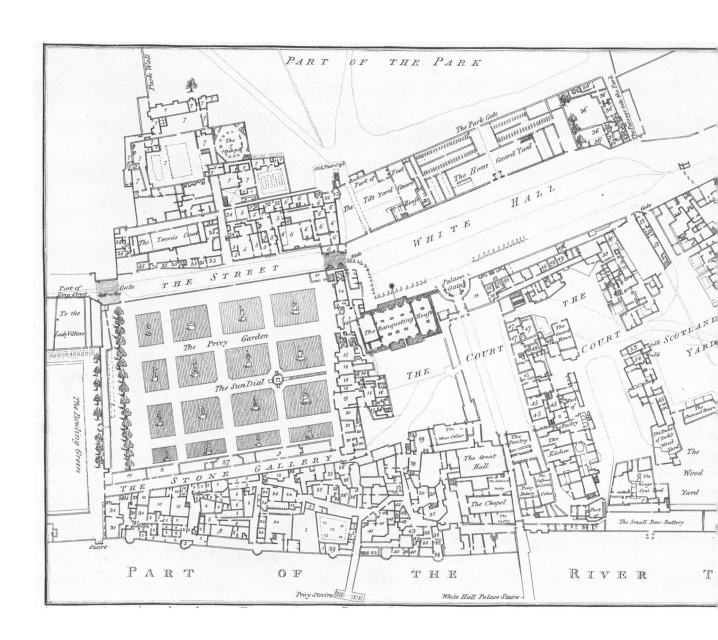

PART OF THE PARK

Park Wall

WHITE HALL

The Park Gate

The Horse Guard Yard

Old Stair Case

Part of the Tilt Yard Guard

Foot Guard House

The Entrance into the Park

Gate

The Gallery into the Park

THE STREET

Part of King Street

To the Lady Villiers

Gate

Gate

The Banqueting House

Palace Gate

THE COURT

THE COURT

SCOTLAND YARD

The Guard House

The Charcoal House

The Duke of York's Wood Yard

The Wood Yard

The Privy Garden

The Sun Dial

The Bowling Green

The Tennis Court

The Wine Cellar

The Pantry

The Pantry

The Kitchen

The Pastry

The Kings Coal Yard

The Great Hall

The Chapel

The Vestry

The Coffee

The Small Beer Buttery

THE STONE GALLERY

Stairs

PART OF THE RIVER T

Privy Stairs

White Hall Palace Stairs

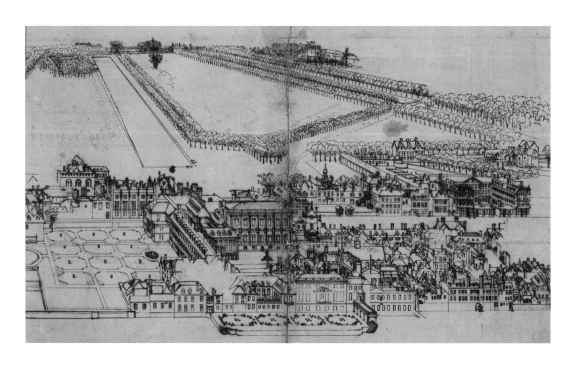

Whitehall Palace

Whitehall is now the name of a broad street in central London, and it is a shorthand term for the British government; but originally it was the name of one of the largest palaces ever seen in England, now entirely vanished from public view, except for one graceful fragment - the Banqueting House. The historic embryo of Whitehall Palace was York House, residence of the Archbishops of York, which Thomas Wolsey, holder of that office, expanded and rebuilt, only to lose it to his royal master, Henry VIII:

> You must no more call it York Place,
>   that's past;
> For since the cardinal fell, that title's lost;
> Tis now the king's and called Whitehall.
>   Shakespeare, *Henry VIII*

Never a single unified structure, the palace grew into a rambling maze of apartments, grand halls, and courtyards, which was said to contain at its height almost 2,000 rooms. On one side it fronted the river, while the other parts of the palace awkwardly straddled the road between Charing Cross and Westminster, and two large gatehouses, the Holbein Gate and King Street Gate, were positioned so as to be able to close the road. The reason for Whitehall Palace's name is obscure, for it was built mainly of Tudor red-brick and must have resembled Hampton Court, another unwilling gift from Wolsey to his king. One of the few features built of white stone was the later Banqueting House, designed by Inigo Jones in 1620, with its ceiling paintings by Rubens. On a specially built platform outside this hall, Charles I was beheaded in 1649 and here, eleven years later, Charles II celebrated his return to the throne, having landed at the palace by boat from the Thames.

Whitehall Palace was wholly associated with the Tudor and Stuart monarchs, who entertained themselves here with tournaments, tennis courts, bowling greens and bear-baiting. Here Henry VIII was married - several times - and here he died. Elizabeth and James I witnessed plays performed privately, including those of Shakespeare and Ben Jonson. Charles I built up his collection of paintings to adorn the palace - Titians, Raphaels and van Dycks - which was dispersed when Cromwell moved in during the Commonwealth years.

The last great events in the history of the palace were the flight of James II by river in 1688, and the offering of the crown to William and Mary in the Banqueting Hall shortly afterwards. King William never cared for the place, believing that its proximity to the river aggravated his asthma, and he removed to Kensington Palace in 1690. In 1698 a massive fire left most of Whitehall Palace a ruin, destroying hundreds of Tudor documents and artefacts, including - to give just one example - Drake's map of his circumnavigation of the world, which he had presented to Elizabeth I. The Banqueting House survived, as did the two gatehouses, although the latter fell victim to the increase in London's wheeled traffic, and they were demolished in the eighteenth century, just as the City gates were. Vanburgh called the Holbein Gate 'one of the greatest curiosities in London', and there was talk of re-erecting it in Windsor. On the ruins of the palace, various houses and alleys were built in the eighteenth century, which were in their turn swept away by the empire-building of the Victorian governmental machine.

Opposite, top: the plan of Whitehall Palace by John Thomas Smith, published in 1680, shows the exceedingly complex layout of the place. The black dot by the Banqueting House marks the spot of Charles I's execution. B.L. Maps Crace XI/66.

Opposite, bottom and below: a view of the Palace by Knyff, drawn perhaps ten years before its destruction in 1698. British Museum, Dept of Prints and Drawings.

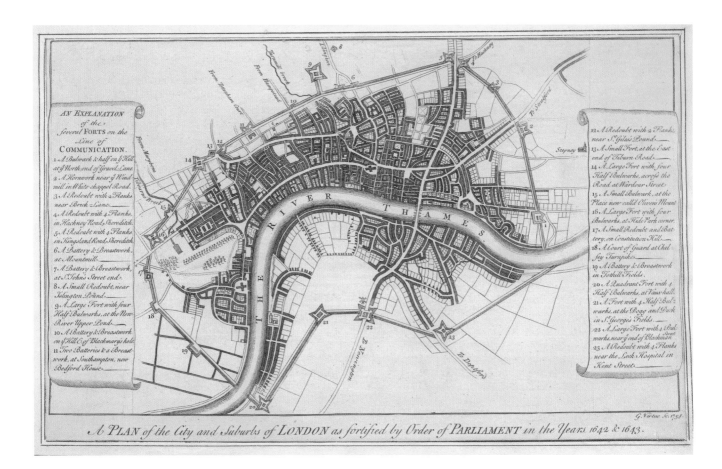

A PLAN of the City and Suburbs of LONDON as fortified by Order of PARLIAMENT in the Years 1642 & 1643.

A. Seine Kön: May: an dem Block. B. Doctor Juxon. C. Colonell Tomlinson. D. Colonell Hacker. E. F. die 2. Executorn. C. R. V. N. 1649

Civil War London

'The sink of all the ill humour in the kingdom', a city whose 'unruly and mutinous spirit' overturned the throne: these were the words used by Clarendon, the royalist his-

torian to describe London and its role in the build-up to the Civil War. Events in London were indeed crucial, and King Charles I's decision to abandon his capital early in 1642 was fatal to his cause. He had alienated the City's financial elite through his oppressive taxes, and the common people through his religious policy, which appeared to be Catholicism by another name. In the years preceding the war, angry crowds from the City had frequently marched to Westminster to air their grievances, and in 1642 the entire House of Commons had taken refuge from Charles's soldiers by shifting en masse to the Guildhall.

After the king had raised his standard at Nottingham in August 1642, his first strategic objective was to retake London and re-establish his authority. The nearest he came was in November, when his army reached Brentford, where his way was blocked by a 20,000-strong force of volunteer Londoners. The king hesitated, and turned back without giving battle, but the city was convinced that the threat would recur, and turned its energies to fortifying the capital. For six months thousands of unpaid citizens, men and women, rich and poor, laboured to construct a series of 24 forts, linked by miles of earthwork ramparts which encircled the city. The line of these ramparts lay well outside the old walls, and took in the whole of Westminster, St James's, Shoreditch, Whitechapel, Wapping, Bermondsey and the South Bank to Vauxhall. In the event, these defences were never tested, and they were demolished after a couple of years. They have left no permanent traces behind, although people have claimed to identify certain fragments here and there. The king's final return to his capital was to face trial and execution in Whitehall, where the struggle had begun.

Cromwellian London has often been portrayed as a city tyrannised by puritan dictators. It is true that the theatres were closed, and supposedly pagan festivals such as Christmas and May Day were suppressed, but witnesses such as Samuel Pepys and John Evelyn make it clear that normal social life and pleasures went on much as before. Taverns, pleasure-gardens, music concerts, dances – none of these were curtailed, and it was during the Commonwealth that the first coffee-houses were opened in the city. In 1655 Cromwell ended almost four centuries of exclusion when he permitted Jews to settle and worship in the city once again, and the first Jewish businesses and synagogues soon appeared.

Only one comprehensive map of London was published during the Commonwealth period, drawn by Richard Newcourt and engraved in 1658 by William Faithorne. It is drawn in the traditional picture style, like the Agas Map. Its scale is quite large at fourteen inches to the mile, and it presents a last snapshot of the crowded warren of city streets before the Great Fire.

Opposite, top: plan of the fortifications built by order of Parliament in 1642–43. B.L. Crace I/ 39.

Opposite, bottom: the execution of King Charles I in Whitehall. B.L. Crace. I. Tab. 4.c.1(18).

Above: King Charles II returns in triumph to London. British Museum, Dept of Prints and Drawings.

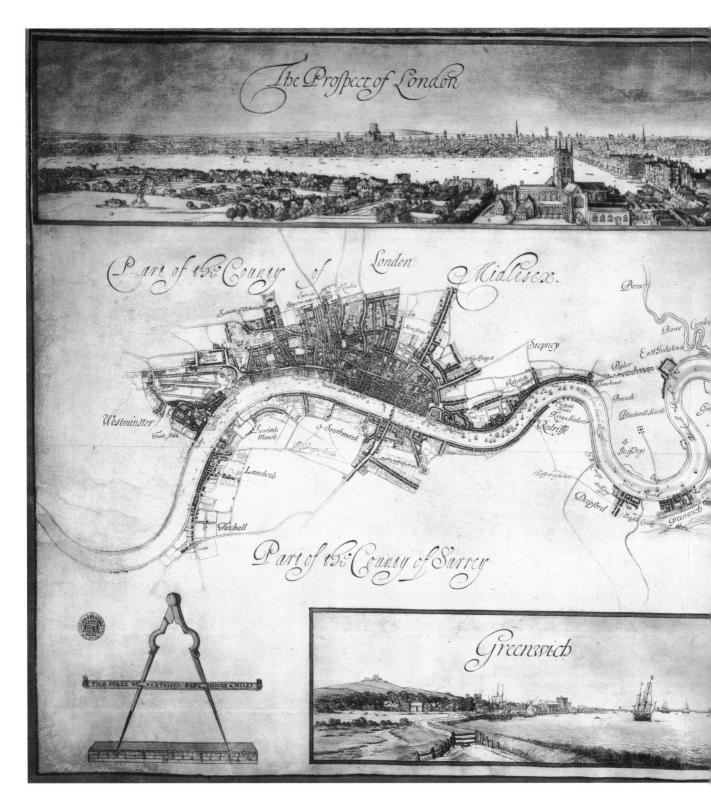

Above: part of the chart of London and the Thames by Jonas Moore, *c.*1662, commissioned by the Navy Office. London Topographical Society/B.L. Maps 188.h.1(1).

Opposite: Howland Great Dock, the large privately-built dock completed around 1700, and later absorbed into the Surrey Commercial Docks. B.L. Maps 458.f.2.

Maritime London

The River Thames, now almost empty of commercial traffic, was for nearly 2,000 years London's link with Europe and the wider world. The wool trade, on which so much of medieval England's prosperity was founded, was dispatched to the Flemish ports from the city's wharfs, while fish, wine, furs, timber, grain and many other imported wares were landed. Not embanked in the modern sense, the river's edge was punctuated by timber quays where boats could moor, especially at inlets such as Queenhithe. As craft increased in size, however, London Bridge became a barrier, and it was natural that the loading and repair of ships should move down river, and hence the sixteenth century saw the growth of the riverside hamlets of Wapping, Ratcliff and Shadwell. It was from the quays of Shadwell and Ratcliff that many Elizabethan explorers embarked on their voyages of discovery – Willoughby and Chancellor for the North Cape and Russia, Frobisher for the North-West Passage and Raleigh in search of El Dorado.

It is often said that the story of London's docks dates from around 1800 when the West India and other great docks were begun, but there is a dockland prehistory stretching back several centuries before that date, on both the north and south banks. As early as 1513 two royal docks and shipyards were excavated at Deptford and at Woolwich, where Henry VIII's navy would be built and maintained.

The huge Tudor warship *The Great Harry* was built at Woolwich, as was Charles I's *Sovereign of the Seas*, whose enormous cost contributed not a little to the build-up to the Civil War. It was at the Deptford yard that Queen Elizabeth came aboard the *Golden Hind* to knight Francis Drake, amid riotous scenes, after his circumnavigation of the world. Another Tudor shipyard and dock lay at Blackwall, a natural mooring point which avoided the long detour around Greenwich Reach past the Isle of Dogs. In 1606 the Virginia settlers under Captain John Smith set sail from Blackwall to found the first permanent colony in America.

This fine manuscript chart, which places London in its maritime context, was drawn around the year 1662 by Jonas Moore, mathematician and surveyor. It was commissioned by the Navy Office, and was certainly seen and studied by Pepys himself. It shows the riverside settlements stretching eastwards from the Tower, and the fine views of London, Greenwich and Woolwich may have been drawn by Hollar. Some thirty years after this chart was made, the largest of all the pre-modern docks, the Howland Great Dock, was built just upstream from the Royal Dock at Deptford. It could accommodate 130 ships and was protected from the tides by a lock. It was later renamed Greenland Dock, for the whalers which berthed there, and eventually became part of the Surrey Docks group.

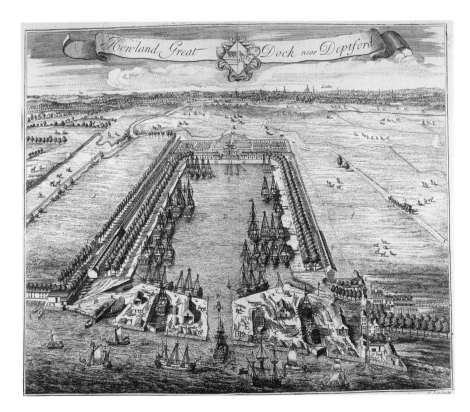

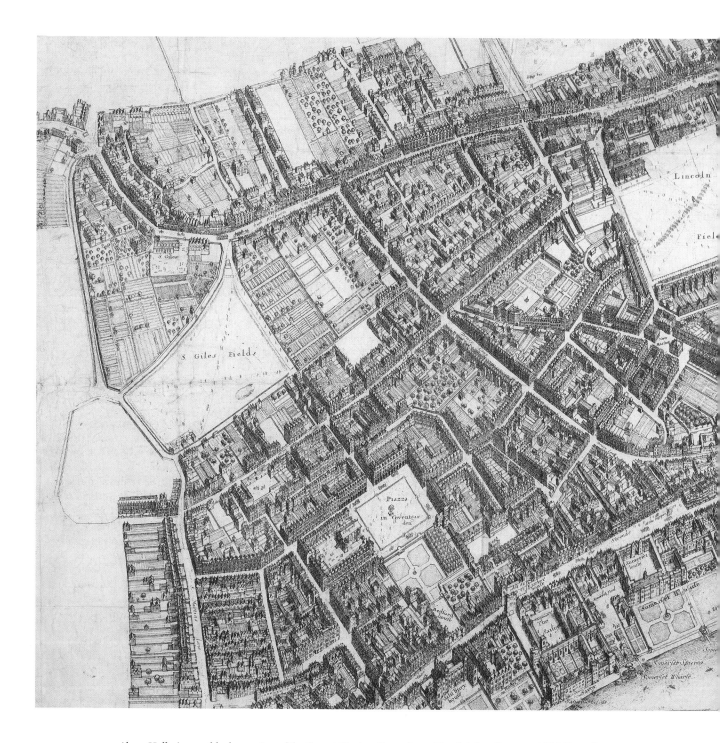

Above: Hollar's superbly drawn view of the Covent Garden–Drury Lane–Lincoln's Inn district, *c.*1658. Part of a great map-view of the whole of London which Hollar projected, but which was pre-empted by the Great Fire, and never completed. British Museum, Dept of Prints and Drawings.

Opposite: Detail from Hollar's view showing Covent Garden's piazza.

London was a city with two physical centres, two identities. The City was the commercial centre to the east, while less than a mile away Westminster was the seat of the court and the government. A physical merging of these two communities was inevitable, and in the Middle Ages the Strand was already the link-road between the two. But the City authorities and the Crown had long struggled to limit London's growth beyond the walls, a policy which sprang from fear: fear of plague, famine and social disorder which might spread in communities not subject to the strict laws which ruled the City. Licences were supposed to be obtained for all new extra-mural building, but bribery and disregard of the rules led to piecemeal and sometimes shoddy developments outside all the City's gates. Demographic pressure finally made this policy unworkable, and landowners such as the Earl of Bedford persuaded the authorities that licensed, high-quality housing development was the answer. The decisive moment in London's westward growth came between 1630 and 1640, with the extensive building that took place on the fields north of the Strand. The development of Lincoln's Inn Fields and Covent Garden, with Drury Lane running between them, created the large, new, elegant residential district that is captured on this 1658 engraving by Hollar, the Czech-born artist who mapped so much of Stuart London. Much of this land had once been gardens or pasturage owned by the religious houses. A century later, after the Dissolution of the religious houses, the westward pull of the court and the seat of government gave their new secular owners the chance to build there, and in so doing they altered the social geography of London.

Lincoln's Inn was the larger site, but there was a demand for some of it to be left as open fields, and houses were built only on the northern and western sides. Covent Garden, however, was planned by Inigo Jones as a unity, and on more innovative lines. It was modelled on the open piazzas which Jones had seen in Italy, open to the south, with a church on the west, and rows of fine houses around the square. The tall stone town-houses opened into vaulted arcades; no originals remain of these, since those now on the north side are nineteenth-century replacements.

The experiment was an architectural and social success: wealthy buyers quickly took every available house, and by 1655 additional streets had filled almost the entire area between the Strand and Holborn, leaving only St Giles Fields open for a further twenty years. For the first time London had a fashionable residential suburb, equidistant between court and City, with new, Italianate houses, where artists, politicians, country gentlemen and foreign visitors could live in style outside the City's close-packed lanes. Commercially, too, Covent Garden was a milestone, making a handsome profit for its owner, the Earl of Bedford, and inspiring others to develop their London estates in the same way. It was the beginning of a property boom in London which has never ceased. Yet the pattern of social change is never controllable, and the second wave of development in St James's and the West End soon drew fashionable tenants still further west, leaving Covent Garden and Drury Lane to decline into the raffish, low-life area of taverns, coffee-houses, theatres and brothels depicted by Hogarth – the *Beggar's Opera* ethos which it has kept almost to this day. This superb engraving by Hollar shows this bridgehead of London's westward growth when it was new, centred around the first and most innovative of London's many squares.

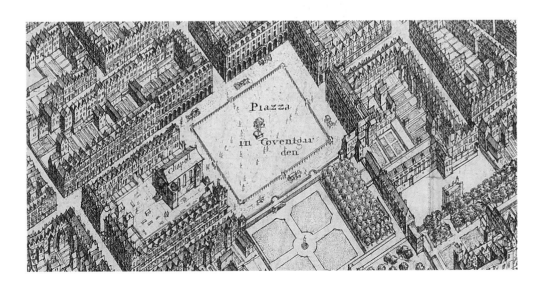

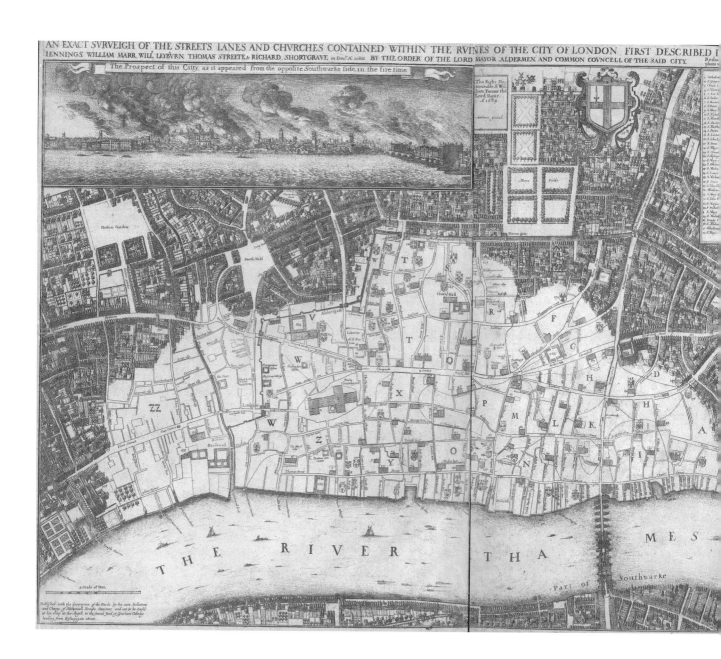

AN EXACT SVRVEIGH OF THE STREETS LANES AND CHVRCHES CONTAINED WITHIN THE RVINES OF THE CITY OF LONDON. FIRST DESCRIBED I
IENNINGS. WILLIAM MARR, WILL LEYBVRN, THOMAS STREETE & RICHARD SHORTGRAVE in Decr A. 1666. BY THE ORDER OF THE LORD MAYOR ALDERMEN AND COMMON COVNCELL OF THE SAID CITY.

The Prospect of this Citty, as it appeared from the opposite Southwarke side, in the fire time.

THE RIVER THAMES

The Great Fire

The summer of 1666 was exceptionally hot and dry, and as the weeks passed in the narrow, filthy alleys of London, the citizens went in fear of a new outbreak of the plague that had attacked the city in the previous year, killing 100,000 people. Instead, as the summer was ending, it was not plague but fire which ravaged the city, the most destructive fire in English history. In three days, the timber-and-thatch London of the Middle Ages, of the Tudors and of Shakespeare, was wiped off the

map, preparing the way for a new, more modern, city of brick and stone to rise in its place.

It was in the early morning of 2 September, a Sunday, that the news began to spread that several buildings were ablaze near London Bridge. Few regarded the matter as serious, least of all the lord mayor, Sir Thomas Bloodworth, whose scornful remark that 'a woman might piss it out', has given him his niche in the history of incompetence. Inaction in these first few hours proved disastrous, and by noon that day 300 houses had already been devoured, along with half of London Bridge. By evening, people were leaving their homes in their thousands, many escaping by boat. Samuel Pepys was one of those who crossed over to Bankside and saw with horror that the City was 'crowned with one entire arch of flame'. Fanned by a fierce east wind, the flames drove westward, leaping across the narrow streets, creating a firestorm which no

defences could stop. The Guildhall, the Royal Exchange and St Paul's were all destroyed, and the lead from the cathedral roof ran down Ludgate Hill like a river. In addition to the heat and flames, the noises of the fire were overwhelming, 'like iron chariot wheels beating on stones', joined every few minutes with the crash of falling buildings and the cries of the terrified people. The Fleet River failed to act as a barrier, and Bridewell and Baynard's Castle were both engulfed. Naval officers saved the Tower by blowing up houses in the streets around it. The destruction continued for three days, until miraculously the wind dropped, which at last halted the fire's progress. The catastrophe was over, but the ashes were still dangerous and several deaths were caused when people ventured too soon into the smouldering ruins. Within the City walls, 400 acres had been laid waste, destroying 13,000 houses and 87 churches. Incredibly, only nine lives had been lost.

It was soon established that the source of the fire had been a baker's shop called Farriners, in Pudding Lane, but how had it started? Coming so soon after the upheavals of the Civil War, the Commonwealth and the Restoration, many voices were raised to proclaim that the plague and the fire were acts of divine vengeance. People recalled the religious madman, Solomon Eagles, who the year before had run half naked through the streets with a pan of burning brimstone on his head, prophesying that London would be consumed by divine fire. Rumours of foreign plots and Catholic conspiracies spread just as rapidly, and a Frenchman named Robert Hubert was hanged at Tyburn as the perpetrator of the catastrophe. When Wren's monument to the event was completed in 1677, an inscription around its base explicitly blamed 'Popish frenzy' for the fire - words that were removed only in 1830. No evidence of any conspiracy was ever found, and the verdict of history is that the fire was a mere accident.

In the aftermath, the most amazing thing is the speed with which rebuilding took place. Grand schemes for a newly designed Italianate city were put aside, and the old street lines were retained, although they were made wider, and the buildings were of brick or stone. The only completely new street was the King Street -Queen Street line which led from the Guildhall to the river. By 1676, a decade after the city's devastation, published views of London 'now rebuilt after the late dreadful fire' showed how completely all traces of the terrible event had been erased, and how a new and more elegant London had arisen from the ashes.

Above: the destruction wrought by the Fire is graphically illustrated on this contemporary map by John Leake. B.L. Maps Crace I/50.

Left: Londoners escape from the Fire with their belongings by river. British Museum, Dept of Prints and Drawings.

Above right: Solomon Eagles, the religious fanatic said to have prophesied London's destruction by fire, drawn by Cruikshank. Private collection.

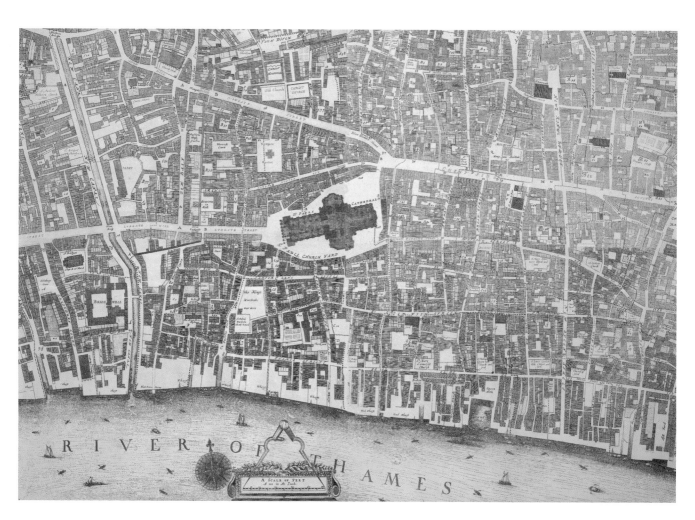

The Great Fire and the Map of London

One of the incidental effects of the Great Fire was to hasten a cartographic revolution in England. The rebuilding of the city street by street and house by house obviously called for accurate scaled maps, and the city authorities immediately awoke to the fact that no such thing existed. The concept of scale had been around in map-making for at least a hundred years before 1666, but the great aim of all urban maps was to give, quite literally, a *picture* of a city, to show its streets and its buildings as if seen from above. This is easily seen in the last large-scale map of London made before the Fire, which was published by Newcourt and Faithorne in 1658. This contains elements of a plan, for one can see into all the streets equally, and the map has obviously been planned on a generally consistent scale, although this is nowhere stated. But most of the area of the map is filled up with pictures of thousands of little houses, drawn in elevation, and these elevations conflict with and obscure the horizontal scale. For this reason it is not the kind of map that can be used for measurement or to establish boundary lines; indeed it has an almost medieval appearance - as did the city which the Fire destroyed.

After the Fire, the lord mayor and the city aldermen quickly commissioned a survey from technical experts including John Leake and William Leyburn. Their depiction of the fire-devastated area was engraved by Hollar, and published before the year was out. This plan served as the basis of the many maps which were printed and sold throughout Europe as broadsheets giving news of the Fire. The really intriguing thing about the Leake map (see page 52) is that it appears to combine both the old and the new forms of mapping. Around the edge of the burnt-out area we see exactly the same swarms of little house pictures which appear in the Newcourt and Faithorne map; but inside the Fire area these have been wiped away, leaving quite simply a plan of the streets. This map is surely the key transitional document which provided the model for a new form of urban mapping. This approach was extended in a great new map of the City published in 1676 by John Ogilby and his grandson William Morgan. These two must have been thoroughly familiar with the Leake map, and, if they did not know it already, it must have shown them instantly the precision and the clarity that could be achieved when the pictorial element was abandoned. The Ogilby and Morgan map was drawn at a scale of 1:1200, and on its publication it was at once recognised as opening a new era in the mapping of London. It was a functional diagram, a form of map eminently suited to the new scientific age, even if this was achieved by sacrificing the charm of the traditional pictorial map. Views and perspectives of London's streets and buildings would continue to be drawn, and often they were published as part of a map, but - and this is the crucial difference - they were placed in its margins or blank spaces: the scaled plan and the pictorial view were now two separate entities.

Opposite, top and bottom: sections from the maps by Newcourt and Faithorne, 1658, *top*, and by Ogilby and Morgan, 1676, *bottom*. The earlier map uses the traditional pictorial style, the later one is a precise scaled plan.
B.L.Maps Crace I/35 and Maps Crace II/61.

Right: the Fire Monument designed by Wren.
B.L. Maps Crace II/68.

The Age of Elegance

The restoration of the monarchy in 1660 brought about a huge change in the life of the capital, for the presence of the court acted as a magnet for the return of the aristocracy and gentry to London, all seeking houses in which to live, and seeking the social entertainments which had been severely curtailed for almost two decades. This, in turn, acted as the spur for a dramatic new phase of urban growth which was to transform the character of London. 'The beauty of this great town and the convenience of the Court', wrote the Earl of St Albans in 1663, 'are defective in point of houses fit for the dwellings of noblemen and other persons of quality,' and the earl was one of an energetic group of men who were determined to set this right. The westward growth of London had taken a vital step forward in the 1630s, when the Earls of Bedford and Southampton decided to build on their estates, and create the districts of Covent Garden, Lincoln's Inn and Drury Lane - the districts shown on Hollar's fine engraved view of 1658 (see page 50). They retained ownership of the land while covering what had previously been open fields with fine houses, made available to wealthy tenants on leases of, at

this stage, thirty years. This process of building and leasing of the aristocratic estates was to become the fundamental pattern which would shape London's growth for virtually two centuries.

The phases of this growth, the building of the individual squares, were carefully planned: the landowners, architects and builders reflected the taste of their time, and created the Georgian streets and squares which are now so highly prized. But the development as a whole was not planned in the modern sense, for there was no controlling hand: it was a triumph of private initiative, private money and private taste. It was in this way that the great districts and squares were born, which merged to become the 'West End': St James's Square, Grosvenor, Berkeley, Cavendish, Hanover, Portman, Bedford and Russell, many of them preserving the names of their aristocratic landlords. One of the crucial strengths of the leasehold estate system was that the landowner was able, in most cases, to manage and control the buildings and the tenants over a long period of time, and to ensure that both were kept up to a high standard; it was, after all, essential to the success of the schemes

A portion of the long riverside view by Samuel and Nathaniel Buck, 1749, showing the new and more elegant city that arose from the ashes of the Fire.
B.L. K.Top. 21.43.

that they should remain desirable places to live, and attract tenants able to pay good rents. In certain other areas, however, there was no single patron and no central control, and here there tended to be piecemeal rebuilding, sub-letting, and a steady decline in the social tone. This is what happened in Soho Square, Golden Square, Leicester Square and, most disastrously, in Seven Dials, where the houses were subdivided and neglected and became the crime-infested slums known in Victorian times as the 'Rookeries'. There were some exceptions to the leasing system: the Earl of St Albans found he could not attract tenants to St James's Square on the usual thirty-year leases, and was obliged to sell individual free-hold plots, and this explains why rebuilding took place even before the end of the eighteenth century, destroying the square's unity.

Most landowners were reluctant to involve themselves in the business of developing their properties, and worked through agents or through builders, whose task it was to put up the houses and find the tenants. Perhaps the most celebrated of the early middlemen was Nicholas Barbon, physician, Member of Parliament, and daring entrepreneur, who between 1670 and 1690 built street after street of new houses in the area between Holborn and the river, demolishing in the process some of the great mansions south of the

Strand, such as York House, Arundel House and Essex House. The owner of York House, the Duke of Buckingham, insisted on having his memory perpetuated in the names of the new streets: George, Villiers, Duke and Buckingham. Typical Barbon houses may be seen today in Red Lion Square and Bedford Row. Barbon was probably the first entrepreneur to clearly identify and exploit the market for London property in this way. The name of this brash empire-builder is recorded only in one tiny close off Great Ormond Street, but he had many followers, for this form of enterprise was the fulfilment of the process which had been foreshadowed with the secularisation of the religious houses. Barbon's career signalled the emergence of a property market, and London's growth would henceforth lie in the hands of an endless stream of financiers and builders who made the market grow, and made fortunes for themselves.

The growth of the West End was the decisive sign of a new form of social differentiation in London's geography - the creation of districts that were exclusive and superior, and with them the sense that to live there flattered people's image of themselves. In the Tudor city, the inheritance of the Middle Ages had persisted, with rich and poor, master and man, living cheek by jowl in the same street. There were certain natural reasons why the

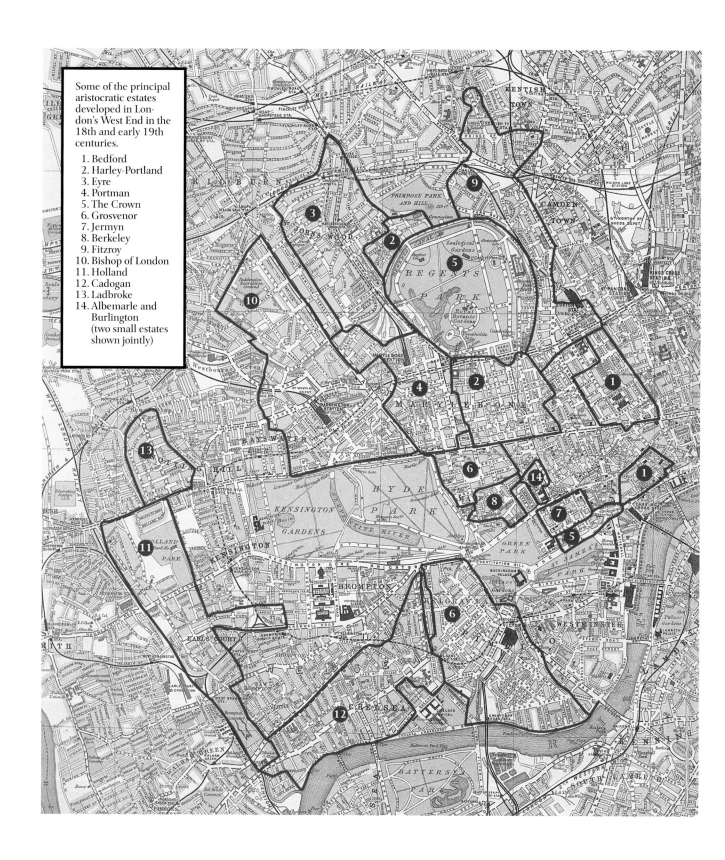

Some of the principal aristocratic estates developed in London's West End in the 18th and early 19th centuries.

1. Bedford
2. Harley-Portland
3. Eyre
4. Portman
5. The Crown
6. Grosvenor
7. Jermyn
8. Berkeley
9. Fitzroy
10. Bishop of London
11. Holland
12. Cadogan
13. Ladbroke
14. Albemarle and Burlington (two small estates shown jointly)

West End developed as it did. In addition to the presence of the court, the western side of London was upwind and upstream of the City and the East End. The rest of London was smelly, and darkened, as John Evelyn wrote, by a 'hellish and dismal cloud of pernicious smoke', caused by the ever-increasing use of coal as fuel, some half a million tons of it by 1700, brought by sea from Newcastle. Moreover, the flow of the river from west to east was a providential blessing in carrying away the sewage and rubbish from the West End, down past the East End. The West End happened also to border the Temple and the Inns of Court, whose legal services were greatly in demand by London's aristocracy, and this land

Right: Mayfair as part of the ancient manor of Ebury, a manuscript map drawn in 1664 when the area was still open fields, with Park Lane on the left.
B.L. Add. MS 38104.

Below: the same area by the 1790s, built by the Grosvenor and other families.
B.L. Maps Crace X/19

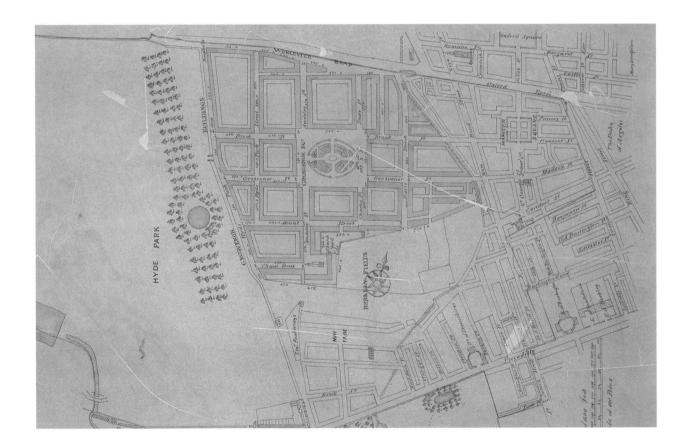

of lawyers was probably the first identifiable professional or trading quarter in London.

One significant pointer to the future was that the new West End streets were built wide enough for wheeled carriages. Traditionally all movement in the narrow streets of the City had been on foot or horseback, but the use of wheeled transport was another novel and unmistakable sign of social class: the early eighteenth century marks the emergence of traffic as a major factor in London's life. An ominous sign of its impact was the demolition in the 1720s of all London's ancient gateways, because they impeded traffic, although perhaps there was also a recognition that they no longer defined the city's real boundaries.

Traffic problems, road building and road widening would increasingly become a force for change in the fabric of London. The Marylebone Road was laid out in the 1750s, financed by a consortium of London businessmen, to provide an entry into the City which avoided the congested St Giles–Holborn–Newgate route; it was London's first by-pass. It was only in 1750 that Westminster Bridge was opened, London's second crossing of the Thames to be built since Roman times, and it was followed just twenty years later by Blackfriars Bridge, whose purpose again was to by-pass the City. Together these two bridges opened new prospects for Lambeth and Southwark: a network of roads to connect them became essential, and the building over of St George's Fields followed in the 1790s. Socially and economically south London was now integrated with the rest of the metropolis, at least as integrated as it would ever be.

The people of the West End, many of them renting second houses in town while their main residence was in the country, fuelled London's expanding economy, an economy now based not on primary production, but on services and 'conspicuous consumption'. For it was not only the rich who prospered in London, but also the army of servants, retailers, clothiers, food and wine merchants, suppliers, artists and craftsmen of all kinds, doctors and lawyers, who danced attendance on them. Entertainment, although limited by modern standards, also flourished in the form of theatres, pleasure-gardens, music and literature. And, of course, building itself became one of London's most important industries, and has remained so ever since. In essence, London acquired an energy, a momentum, and an urban style which acted as the motor, not only for its own economy but also for that of the nation as a whole, a momentum for change and diversification which has never slowed.

The residential growth sparked by the Restoration in 1660 was in no way halted by the most destructive event in London's history - the Great Fire of 1666, whose devastation was confined to the old City. In fact, the Fire served merely to stimulate the growth of the West End, for a number of those made homeless and driven out by it did not return but settled permanently in the western districts, including many professionals, shopkeepers and merchants. The City as rebuilt after the Fire was, in part, modelled on the new West End, with wider streets, stone or brick houses, and neoclassical churches, thus giving the two halves of London a more unified look. Grandiose schemes for the total replanning of the City - the most famous being Christopher Wren's - never had much

serious chance of success, for the speediest and cheapest course was to reconstruct the old street lines. The only significant new thoroughfare was New King Street, linking the Guildhall to the river. The Guildhall itself, the Royal Exchange, the Custom House and the livery company halls were all rebuilt, with the new St Paul's as the overarching achievement and symbol of the City's post-Fire rebirth.

One incidental effect of the Great Fire was the stimulus it gave to the emergence of the scaled urban plan. Within days of the Fire, as soon as rebuilding was considered, the need for detailed scale plans of the City was felt, and of course none existed, only the semi-pictorial views which had been evolving for more than a century. The last great pre-Fire map of London was that by Newcourt and Faithorne, published in 1658, in which the streets were lined with pictures of row upon row of identical little houses, like those on a Monopoly board. This map showed the layout of London in a picturesque way, but it was not a functional diagram which could be used to distinguish precise street lines and boundaries. The City authorities immediately commissioned new surveys of the devastated area, and two of the surveyors, John Ogilby and William Morgan, went on to publish in 1676 their great map of the City, effectively the first accurate scaled plan of London ever printed. It was a strictly functional plan, from which all the old pictorial elements had now been banished, save for a few ships placed on the river, and it heralded a new era of urban mapping in Britain, one suited to the new age of science and town planning. In 1682 William Morgan published an equally impressive map of London, Westminster and Southwark, which gives a comprehensive picture of all the development in the west-central district and in St James's. This work restored the ornate, graphic dimension to maps, but all the decorative elements were now placed around the borders, and not in the streets: the separation between functional plan and work of art was maintained. These two works were the first of a small group of monumental maps of post-Fire London, drawn from original and accurate surveys, which offered periodic summaries of the city's continual growth. In 1745 John Rocque published his large-scale map of London and Westminster, in which the formal street patterns of the West End estates appear so strikingly, as well as the more random growth in the east.

The latent wealth of the City was demonstrated by the speed with which the post-Fire rebuild was completed and, in fact, the City went on swiftly to develop ever-greater sophistication in the financial markets. The

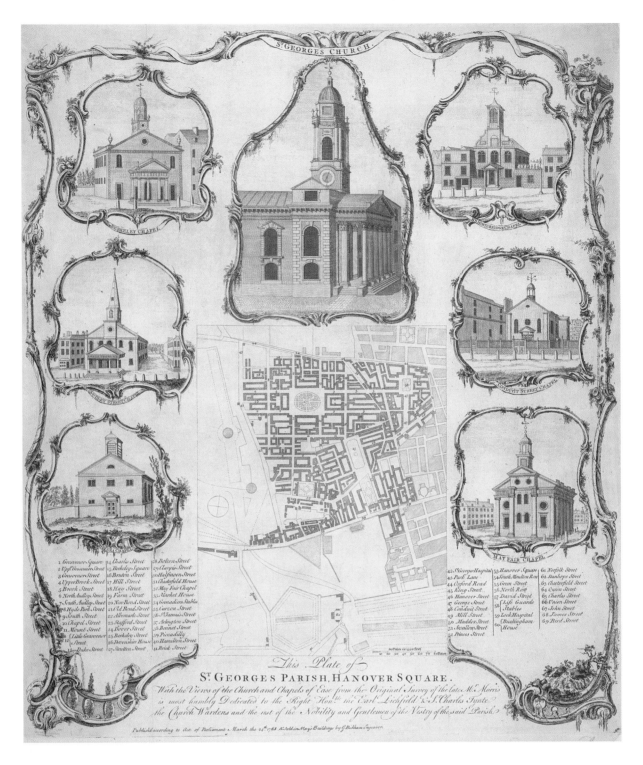

The Parish of St George's Hanover Square, the parish created for the new West End residents, showing the impact which London's expansion had on church building, both in the West End and the East. B.L. Maps Crace X/17.

Bank of England was founded in 1694 in order to finance the government, its loans being secured upon future tax duties. The Fire itself gave a great impetus to the business of insurance, while the market in company stocks was first regulated in 1696. These activities soon acquired their own headquarters, and became cornerstones of the City's identity. The government too was developing its own institutions, not in the City but in Westminster: the Admiralty and the Treasury were the first administrative buildings completed in Whitehall, while the new

Somerset House was built to accommodate various government and royal offices, from the Inland Revenue to the Royal Academy. In a sense these buildings were London's first office blocks, although they were effectively disguised as Palladian palaces. Private palaces in their own right were built throughout the West End by the leading architects of the age of elegance: Burlington House, Marlborough House, Devonshire House, Spencer House and so on, which were the country mansions of the aristocracy transferred to London, to be used for a part of the year only. An exceptional

John Rocque's great map of London, Westminster and Southwark, 1745, at the scale of 26 inches to one mile. The first comprehensive new survey of London for over half a century, this map shows the new West End, and the equally visible eastward growth in Whitechapel and along the riverside. B.L. Maps Crace III/107.

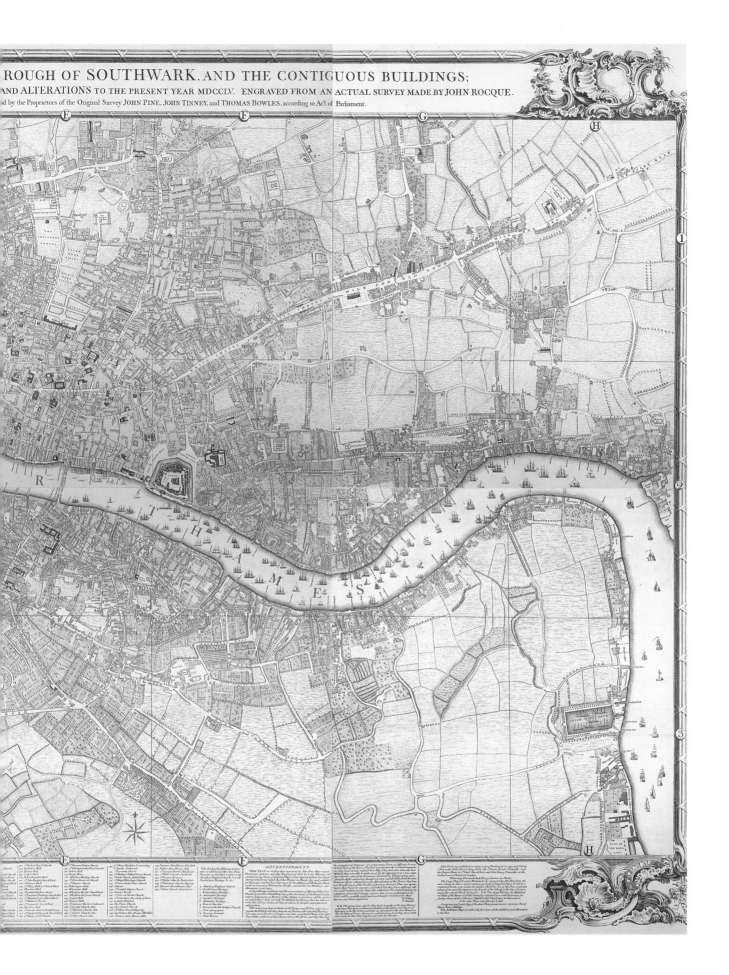

ROUGH OF SOUTHWARK, AND THE CONTIGUOUS BUILDINGS;
AND ALTERATIONS TO THE PRESENT YEAR MDCCLV. ENGRAVED FROM AN ACTUAL SURVEY MADE BY JOHN ROCQUE.
d by the Proprietors of the Original Survey JOHN PINE., JOHN TINNEY, and THOMAS BOWLES, according to Act of Parliament.

experiment in urban design was the Adelphi, a huge palace-like terrace on the very edge of the river, which was actually twenty-four very extensive houses, but given the façade of a unified structure; the Adelphi almost foreshadows the blocks of luxury flats of a much later age. The spiritual needs of the new population in London's western and eastern suburbs were recognised in the building of a new generation of superb churches, commanded by an Act of Parliament of 1712. Hawksmoor, Archer and Gibbs were the architects whose genius found expression through these com-

Tyburn. Mainstream English painting was largely based in the countryside of the aristocracy, the idyllic world portrayed by Reynolds, Gainsborough or Zoffany, but Hogarth's was the art of the city. The two Londons, the world of elegance and wealth and that of the underclass, occasionally collided in the street riots that punctuated the calm of Georgian London, and, above all, during the Gordon Riots of 1780, when the mob ruled the capital unchallenged for nearly a week.

Hogarth was not alone in his concerns, and there were serious responses to urban misery.

Above: Somerset House, completed in 1780, by the architect Sir William Chambers. The neoclassical façade conceals the first ever purpose-built government offices, housing the Inland Revenue, the Navy Office and many other departments, as well as the Royal Academy and the Royal Society in their early days.
B.L. K.Top. 25.6.D

missions, in St John's Smith Square, the new St Giles in the Fields, St Mary Woolnoth, Christ Church Spitalfields, and a dozen others. So much of Georgian London has vanished, but these glorious churches remain, some unfortunately islanded now in the roaring ocean of traffic.

The world of Georgian London was officially one of elegance, fashion, show and laughter; but there was an underside, the *Beggar's-Opera* world of slums, crime, brothels, gaming-dens, prisons and madhouses. This was the London which Hogarth depicted so unforgettably, the London of those who failed to keep up with the fashionable crowd, those who gambled and lost, those betrayed by greed and pleasure. Hogarth's simpler, sterner morality reminds us of the hollowness of much of the surface glitter of the age of elegance. Any man, like Hogarth's rake or Fielding's Tom Jones, could crash through that surface into a much grimmer world, and find himself reviled, imprisoned, or on his way to

There was a huge outpouring of philanthropy, most notably in the founding of a new generation of hospitals and schools, maintained by private donation. But for many, the teeming London of Hogarth had become a place to escape from. Street crime and robbery were endemic, while the mortality rate due to poor sanitation was still astronomical. Many who could afford to do so removed their families to the green villages which lay in a ring around London: Chelsea, Ealing, Richmond, Harrow, Hampstead, Highgate, Wanstead, Greenwich, and others, where the unpolluted river or the higher ground offered healthier air. These were the elegant villages, often with an aristocratic mansion nearby, which are shown on Rocque's delightful map of 'London and the country near ten miles around', published in 1746. They still retained their own distinct and unspoiled identity, and it would be many years before London's tide would begin lapping towards them, to transform them eventually into suburbs.

The growth of eighteenth-century London seems to reflect a deep-rooted characteristic of the age - that this was an unregulated society, controlled by a network of powers that was informal, indeed almost invisible. Wealth and poverty, health and disease, justice and injustice, pleasure and suffering - all these things were seen as matters of providence or chance. It was a society in which the forces of private influence reigned supreme, and those of government were virtually nowhere. In terms of London's physical growth, no one discussed or approved or vetoed what the oligarchy wished to do. Enlightened self-interest ruled, and in creating the West End it did indeed create a framework for urban living that was appealing, lasting, and architecturally beautiful, although obviously inequitable. Large parts of London were remodelled by a social elite on new and elegant lines which reflected the aesthetic tastes of the time. The London of the following century would face a number of profound challenges to this simple - but simply undemocratic - way of doing things.

A PERSPECTIVE VIEW OF THE FOUNDLING HOSPITAL, WITH EMBLEMATIC FIGURES.

Above: the Foundling Hospital, the archetypal 18th-century charity, founded in 1742 by Captain Thomas Coram, and supported by the great and the good of the time. B.L. K.Top. 25.23

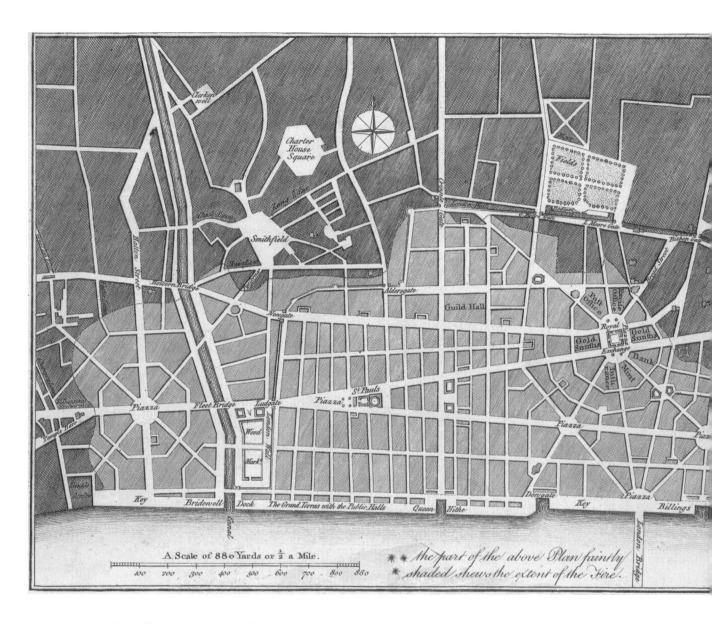

Above: Wren's plan for the post-Fire city, rapidly produced within days of the catastrophe. B.L. Maps Crace XVII/3.

Opposite: Wren's dream city, reconstructed by the artist Paul Draper, with its Venetian-style quaysides and avenues radiating from the great monument by the bridge; the other focal points are the Royal Exchange and St Paul's. Paul Draper.

The London that Wren Never Saw

The embers of the Great Fire had scarcely cooled before the question of rebuilding the city was being urgently discussed. The possibility of laying out an entirely new, modern city on the ruins of the old excited the imagination of artists, scientists and intellectuals, and they rushed to submit their plans to the city authorities and to the king. For one man in particular, the destruction wrought by the Fire seemed a heaven-sent opportunity to find an outlet for his genius. Christopher Wren was thirty-four years old, a mathematician, Professor of Astronomy at Oxford, one of the founders of the Royal Society, and now turning his attention increasingly to the science of architecture. He had already designed the Sheldonian Theatre in Oxford, and had been consulted by Gilbert Sheldon, Archbishop of

Popes. Wren's London was to be a baroque capital, fit for a great European monarch. Wide boulevards running east to west would obliterate the old medieval street lines, and these avenues would be intersected by open piazzas, of a kind never seen before in England. The riverfront would be rebuilt with raised stone quaysides, and the Fleet River would become a canal to supply the capital's markets. The focus of the city's commercial life would be an ensemble of public buildings around the Royal Exchange, and a mile to the west a magnificent baroque cathedral would replace the ruins of the medieval one.

To carry out such a plan, however, two things were essential - finance on a huge scale, and the will of an autocratic ruler; sadly for Wren, and perhaps for London,

Canterbury, about rebuilding the crumbling fabric of St Paul's Cathedral. Wren had also visited Paris and Versailles to study the reshaping of the French capital undertaken by Louis XIV.

On hearing of the fire, Wren hastened to London to survey the extent of the devastation. By 11 September, just four days after the last remnants of the blaze had been extinguished, Wren had delivered his plan for the new London to Charles II, and was assured that the king favoured its adoption. The plan showed the influence of Wren's visit to Paris, and of his study of the plans of Rome as it had been rebuilt by the Renaissance

neither of these existed. The immediate, practical problems of accommodating the homeless, removing the debris, surveying the land, apportioning property, and rebuilding at the basic level would absorb all the city's energies. To override existing street lines and property boundaries would have required political powers that simply did not exist in Restoration England. Wren's new city was never built, and London was not transformed into a baroque capital. Yet, thanks to the overwhelming presence of his new cathedral, Wren has always been seen as the presiding genius of post-Fire London.

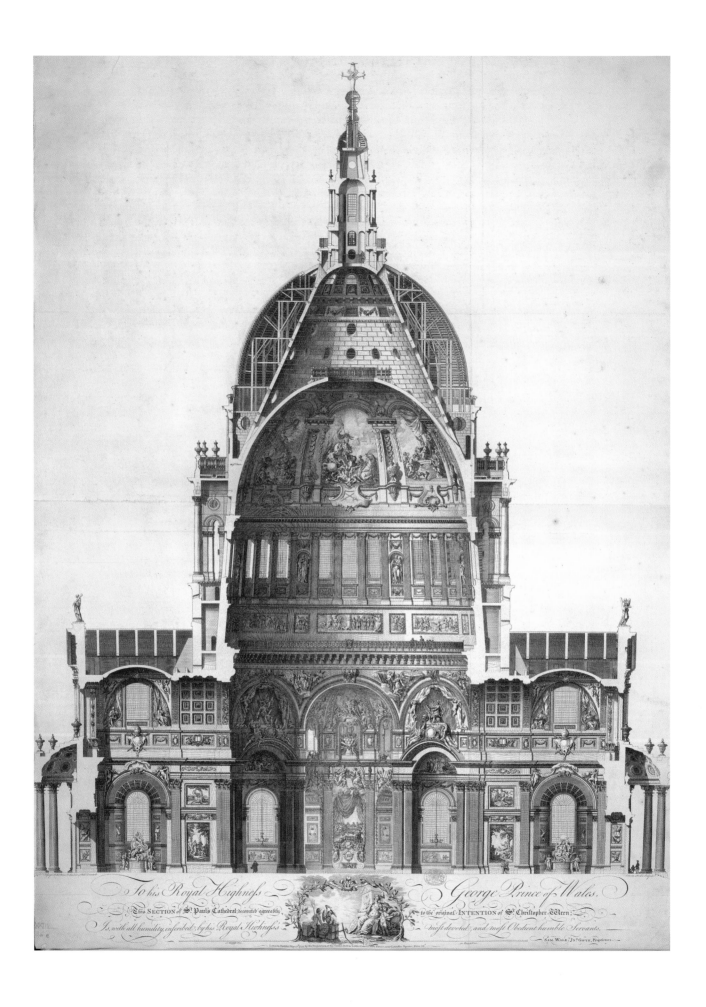

To his Royal Highness George Prince of Wales.

This SECTION of St. Paul's Cathedral, decorated agreeably to the original INTENTION of St. Christopher Wren; Is, with all humility, inscribed, by his Royal Highness's most devoted, and most Obedient humble Servants.

Sam. Wale, Jno. Gwyn, Proprietors.

St Paul's

The Gothic cathedral which was destroyed in the Great Fire stood on the site of an even older Saxon church, which in turn had replaced a Roman temple to Diana. This medieval cathedral was a massive structure – its spire was taller than Wren's dome – and it was central to London's social life. The cathedral was the focus of great ceremonial events, secular as well as religious, while St Paul's Cross, the covered pulpit in the precincts, became a place where proclamations, civil and religious, were read, and a place of public penance and punishment; Carlyle called St Paul's Cross the 'Times newspaper of the Middle Ages'. By the year 1600, however, the fabric of the cathedral was in a critical state; as early as 1561 the steeple had actually been destroyed by lightning and not replaced. Charles I had commissioned Inigo Jones to commence major restoration work, but this was interrupted by the Civil War. During the war, the nave was used by Cromwell's army as a cavalry barracks, and the interior was comprehensively vandalised by the fierce puritan soldiery. Soon after the Restoration, Wren was asked to draw up plans to save the cathedral, but his frank opinion was that it should be demolished and built afresh. This advice was rejected, and more modest plans were being prepared when the Fire intervened – a miraculous opportunity for Wren to design his new cathedral after all. In the weeks after the Fire, Pepys reported wandering in the ruins and seeing the mummified remains of bodies in the broken tombs.

The only monument to survive the Fire was that of the poet John Donne, a former Dean, and this was re-erected in the new building.

Wren's concept of a great new cathedral in the classical style went through three distinct phases, the last of which was finally accepted by his masters in 1675, yet the structure which finally emerged did not correspond precisely to any of the three. The 'Great Model' which is now preserved in St Paul's Cathedral lacks the twin western towers, while the design of the dome is quite different. The dome, always regarded as the unique distinguishing feature of St Paul's, represented Wren's second thoughts, his first idea being a spire. The most extraordinary thing about this dome is that it is actually two domes, one inside the other. Wren's exterior vision of the dome would have looked impossibly tall and misshapen from the inside, while his interior plan would have appeared squat and ugly from the outside. His solution was to build two vaults, separated by an empty, sixty-foot-high space, invisible from inside or out. There was just one master builder, Thomas Strong, with whom Wren worked for a full thirty-five years to raise the cathedral. In 1697, after twenty-two of those years had passed, Parliament became so exasperated by the delays that it halved Wren's salary of £200; not until the final completion in 1710 did Wren receive his arrears. Although he lived to the age of ninety-one and designed so many other superb buildings, much of Wren's energy and genius was concentrated in this one glorious structure.

Opposite: a cross-section through St Paul's showing the structural secret of the double-dome, and the beauty of the interior decorations by Thornhill.
B.L. K.Top. 23.36.E.

Right: the South elevation of the cathedral.
B.L. Maps Crace XIX/61.

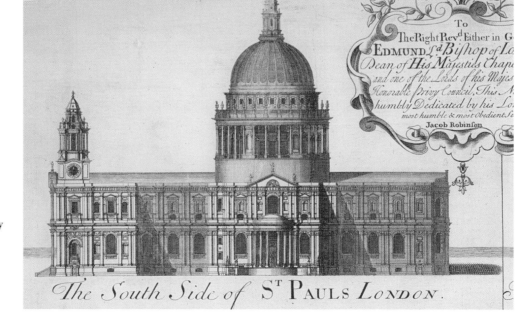

The South Side of St Pauls London.

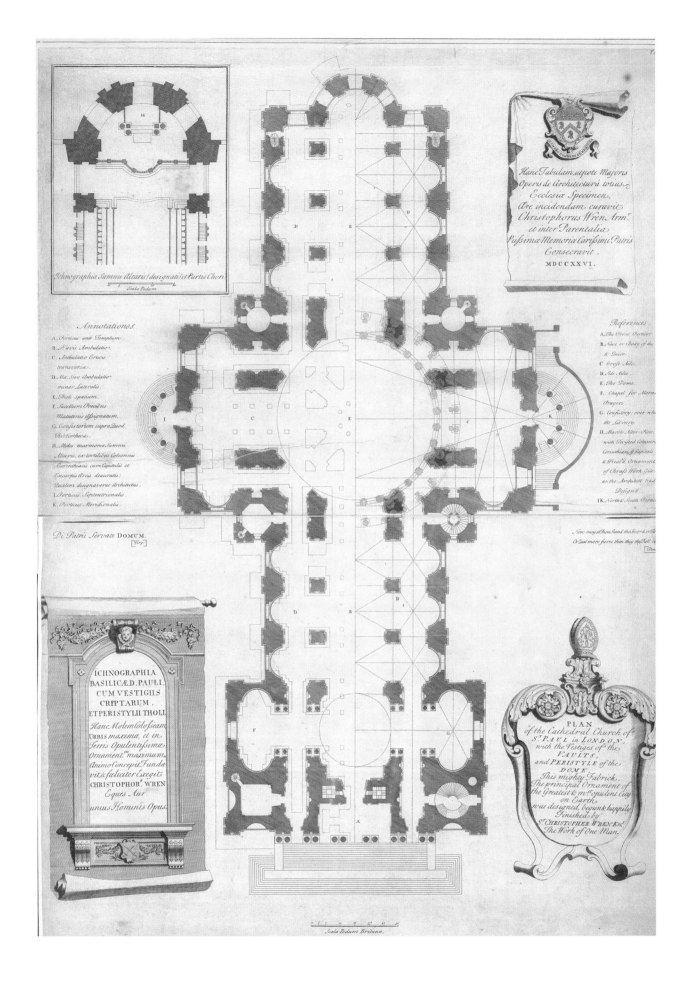

Perhaps the unique beauty of St Paul's lies in the fact that it is classical in its overall symmetry, but baroque in its detail. The nave and the choir are exactly proportional, as are the north and south transepts, but within, the magnificent carvings by Grinling Gibbons, the ironwork by Jean Tijou and the painted dome by Thornhill all bring the classical form vividly to life. Equally delightful is the wealth of exterior carving by Gibbons and others on the fine white Portland stone, much of it revealed afresh by recent cleaning. The mosaics in the choir are later, nineteenth-century additions. It is this grandeur of con-

ception combined with the perfection of detail that makes this structure reminiscent of that other product of England in the 1680s – Newton's physics. To Londoners, it seemed both miraculous and fitting that St Paul's should be preserved almost undamaged during the Blitz, when so much of the surrounding city was reduced to ruins. The post-war history of St Paul's was less inspired: first flanked then overshadowed by modern buildings of terrifying awfulness. One longs to see this cathedral as earlier generations saw it, dominating the city's skyline as Wren intended.

Opposite: Wren's ground-plan of St Paul's, engraved and printed from his papers in 1726, three years after his death. B.L. Maps Crace VIII/88.

Above: the west front and the north elevation of the cathedral. B.L. Maps Crace XIX /61.

AN
Exact and lively Mapp or
REPRESENTATION
Of Booths and all the varieties of showes and
Humours upon the ICE on the River of
THAMES by LONDON
During that memorable Frost in the 35th yeare
of the Reigne of his sacred Majty
King CHARLES the 2d
Anno Dni MDCLXXXIII.

With an Alphabetical Explanation of the
most remarkeable Figures

Frost Fairs on the Thames

The original London Bridge - the medieval bridge that was encrusted with shops and houses - rested on no fewer than nineteen arches, which were built on foundation piers so wide that even small boats found it difficult to pass between them. The bridge acted, in effect, like a partial dam, holding back the waters of the river. One of the curious side-effects of this was that, in exceptionally severe winters, the Thames could actually freeze over above the bridge. This was further helped by the fact that in the unembanked river the current at the edges was much weaker than it is now, permitting ice to form in the slack water and spread outwards.

These two factors explain the many paintings and engravings from the seventeenth and eighteenth centuries which - incredibly to our eyes - show Londoners merry-making on a Thames frozen over by ice several feet thick. Half a dozen great frosts occurred between 1564 and 1814, during which impromptu fairs were organised on the ice; presumably there were earlier ones, too, which were not recorded. Market stalls were put up, carriages were driven across the river, and there was dancing, archery and ox-roasting. A favourite trick was to set up printing presses on the ice, and sell souvenir broadsheets and pictures of the scene, with the eye-catching imprint 'Printed on the River Thames'.

Perhaps the best-known of these frost fairs took place in the memorable winter of 1683/4, during a prolonged and severe frost which held England in its grip from December to February. A whole street of stalls extended from the Temple across to Southwark, and King Charles II and his court paid a visit to the scene. There were three frost fairs in the eighteenth century, in 1715, 1739 and again in 1789. The last of these events took place in 1813/14, and was the source of an unexpected profit to the Thames watermen: deprived of their usual livelihood, they cut channels in the ice and charged people to be carried over to the fair. This fair was the subject of many pictures and souvenir notices, with proclamations such as 'Jack Frost, having taken possession of the river by force and violence, is hereby given notice to quit by Mr. Thaw'.

Old London Bridge was demolished in 1831, and replaced by a bridge of more modern design resting on only five arches, while the embanked river became faster-moving. Since that date the Thames has never been known to freeze over, and frost fairs, like horse-drawn carriages and public executions, are gone forever from London.

Opposite, top: the frost fair of 1683/4, with its street of stalls. B.L. K.Top. 27.39.

Opposite, and below: two pictures of the frost fair of 1813/14, the last before the demolition of Old London Bridge consigned the frost fairs to history. British Museum, Dept of Prints and Drawings and B.L. K.Top. 27.41.3.

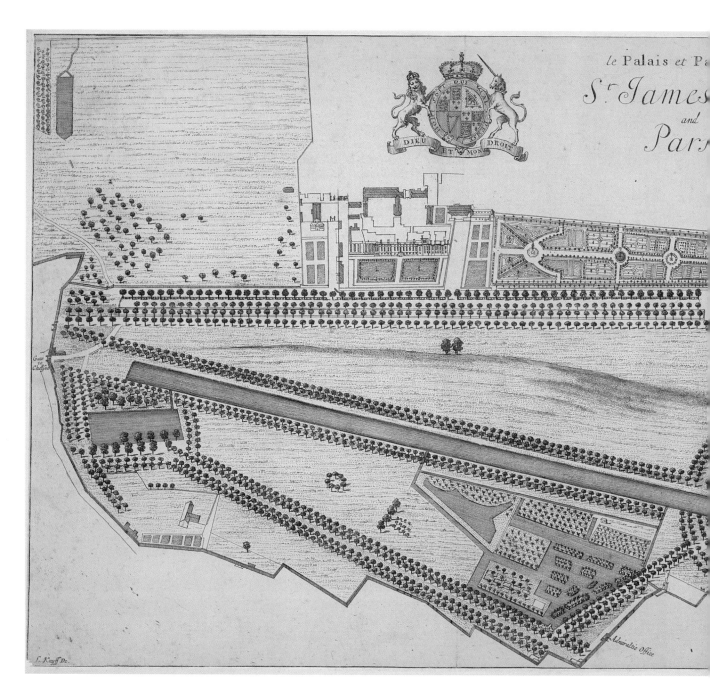

le Palais et Pa

St James

and

Par

Above: view of St James's Park and Palace by Kip, 1710; supposedly designed by Le Nôtre, the long, straight central canal was remodelled by Nash and King George IV in the 1820s. B.L. Maps Crace XIII/30.

Opposite: the new St James's Square and its surrounding streets, laid out as a business speculation by the Earl of St Albans in 1680. B.L. Maps Crace II/58.

St James's

When Henry VIII acquired the old hospital of St James's and rebuilt it as St James's Palace, he created a third centre of gravity in London to add to the City and Westminster. This act would later have an enormous impact on London's westward growth. The palace was a typical red brick Tudor structure of halls and apartments, with the great gatehouse, a landmark at the western end of Pall Mall for over four centuries, now black with time. For 150 years it was one of many royal palaces, and its function *vis-à-vis* Whitehall and the others is hard to define. After the Whitehall Palace fire of 1698 it became, for a time, the principal royal residence, and the scene of formal court occasions. Between St James's and Whitehall lay a stretch of marshy land which the king had drained and turned into a deer park, to which his descendants added a menagerie of exotic birds and animals, including crocodiles and ostriches. It was Charles II who had the park more formally landscaped, advised by André Le Nôtre, the designer of Versailles, combining several ponds into one long central lake (this was remodelled into its present shape in the early nineteenth century). In the winter of 1662, Samuel Pepys went onto the ice in the park, 'sliding on his skeates' with the Duke of York, the future King James II. Although always a royal park, the public was never barred from entering, and it was a place where the royal family frequently mingled with the people.

When Whitehall Palace was destroyed by fire in 1698, St James's Palace became the principal residence of Queen Anne and her Hanoverian successors, until it was supplanted by Buckingham Palace. On the north side of the park, Charles II had an alley laid out between rows of elm trees where he and his companions would play a game resembling croquet. This game had apparently originated in Italy, where it was known as *pallo a maglio* ('ball and mallet'). This alley soon gave its name to the road immediately beside it – Pall Mall.

The presence of the Restoration court in Whitehall and St James's created a need for housing for the courtiers, diplomats and royal hangers-on, and the army of tradesmen who served them. The development of Covent Garden in the 1640s had been London's first significant westward movement, and the moment had come for another migration to the west of Charing Cross. In 1665 Henry Jermyn, Earl of St Albans, followed the Duke of Bedford's pioneering example in leasing his land north of Pall Mall to builders for the construction of aristocratic houses around a central piazza, which was to have four symmetrical exits to the north, south, east and west. St James's Square was completed by 1680, and at the same time houses were built to the south in Pall Mall itself, and to the north in Jermyn Street and Portugal Street – the latter soon known for uncertain reasons as Piccadilly. Thus the district of St James's was defined and its parish church consecrated in 1684 – the only Wren church to be built on an entirely new site. St James's long remained the most exclusive address in London, where the aristocracy chose their London residences, alongside foreign ambassadors, while the shops of jewellers, tailors, furnishers and wine merchants sprang up in Jermyn Street and St James's Street, where they remain to this day.

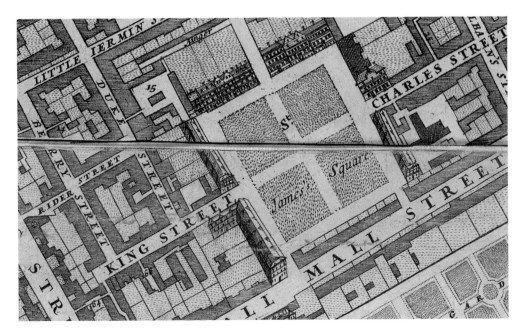

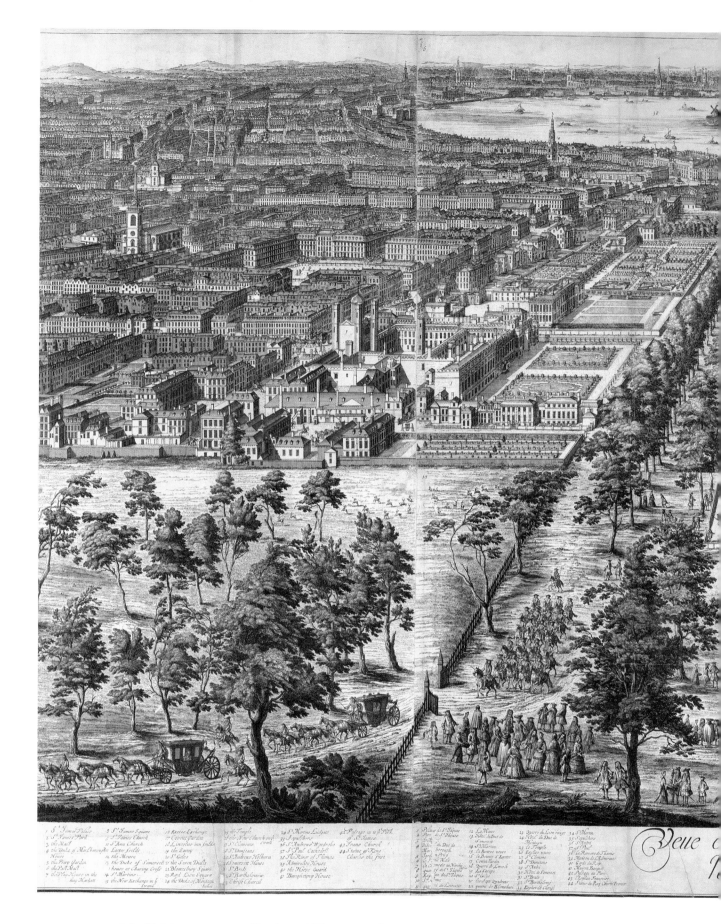

Veue

John Kip's large panorama of London and Westminster of 1720 gives greatest prominence to the court of St James's and the newly built West End, while fashionable parties drive or promenade in the park. This view shows a significant shift of social emphasis away from the commercial City, now seen only on the distant horizon. B.L. Maps 3518(9).

pective ... de la Ville de Londre
...nster et ... Parc S.t Jacques

The West End

At exactly the same time that St James's was being constructed, another large area west of St Giles was being reclaimed from the fields and built over with fine houses. This district was constituted into the parish of St Ann's Soho, and it was bounded by the three squares Leicester, Soho and Golden, which were built during the 1670s and 1680s, and were soon colonised by princes, dukes and other aristocrats. Yet the district enjoyed its fashionable status for little more than fifty years. It was perhaps too far from the court, and it later became home to physicians, artists and craftsmen, many of them immigrants. By 1740 an observer could write that 'Many parts of the parish so greatly abound with French that it is an easy matter for a stranger to imagine himself in France.' This cosmopolitanism made it the natural centre for foreign restaurants, when the fashion for eating out began to grow in the nineteenth century. All three squares have been extensively rebuilt, so that the symmetry we expect from Georgian streets is completely lacking. They are filled, instead, with offices or places of entertainment, so that Soho remains the Bohemian West End. Some form of collective identity has strengthened year by year, making it still the centre of theatres, restaurants and media companies.

But Soho's loss was Mayfair's gain, the next development which acted as a magnet to draw wealthy tenants westward. Already in the 1660s along the north side of Piccadilly, a handful of great houses had been built – Burlington, Berkeley and Clarendon. Behind these mansions lay open ground as far as Tyburn Way (soon to become Oxford Street), much of it in the hands of a small group of owners, who, by the 1720s, had realised that the time was ripe to spin these acres into gold; they succeeded so well that their descendants are now the wealthiest families in England. Their family names and titles are perpetuated all over this district – Grosvenor, Davies, Albemarle, Dover, Curzon and Grafton. Of these the most important was Sir Richard Grosvenor who owned the ancient Manor of Ebury, which included much of what would later become Mayfair, and all of Belgravia. In exchange for ground rents, Grosvenor and the others sold fifty- or hundred-year leases to builders, who agreed to erect high-quality town-houses, the ultimate ownership of the land being retained. Rigid architectural rules were not imposed, but the post-Fire building regulations together with the neoclassical taste of the time ensured a general uniformity of style, thus creating what we now think of as Georgian London. Contemporary observers saw it as virtually a new town, and they were

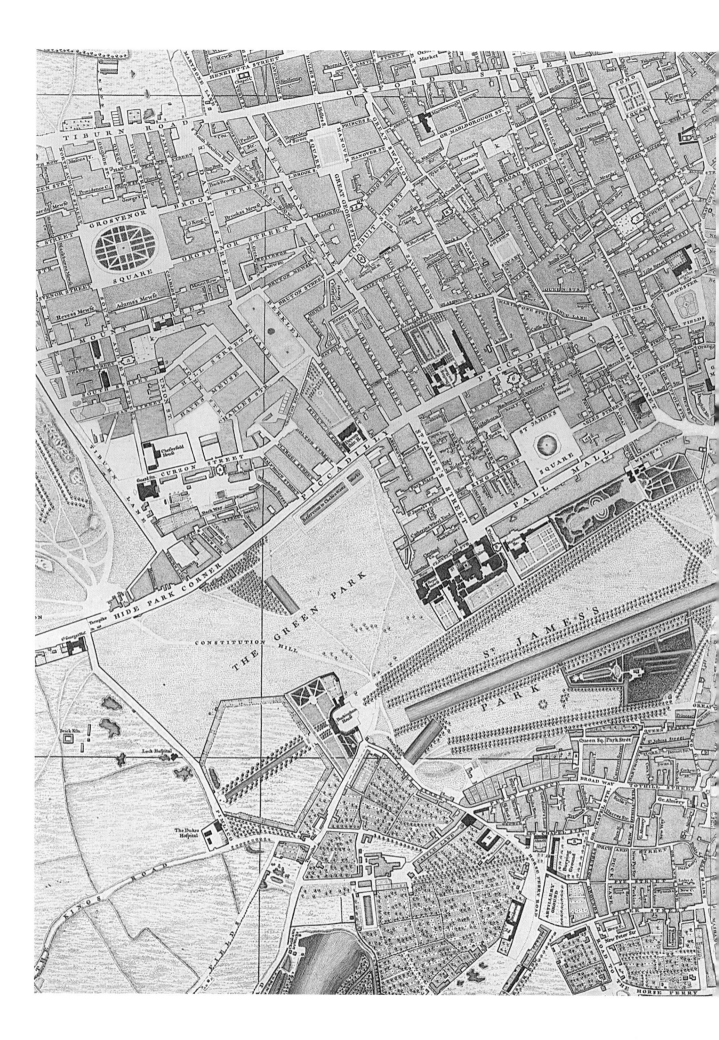

right, except that this was no overnight development. The Grosvenors steadily opened land to developers, until by 1780 around 1,300 new houses had appeared on their estate, with Grosvenor Square as the centrepiece. The great difference between the West End proper and the earlier building east of the Regent Street line is that the latter lacked a single aristocratic landowner. There was no central control in Soho, Golden Square or Leicester Square: leases changed hands rapidly, there was rebuilding of individual plots, architectural and social unity was lost, and the district went downhill.

Park Lane formed a natural western boundary to Mayfair, so the development process eventually leapt over Oxford Street in the period between 1760 and 1780, when the Portman, Portland and Cavendish estates repeated the pattern. The aristocratic developer would often order his own mansion to be built in the centre, and the Duke of Manchester's house in Manchester Square – now home to the Wallace Collection – gives an excellent idea of what these great town mansions were like. In the years between 1780 and 1800, the process turned back on itself to the east this time, as the Russell family developed its Bloomsbury estates; Bedford Square is the only intact Georgian square left in London.

One important consequence of the growth of the West End was the building of new churches. In some cases new parishes were formed within the boundaries of the old, as happened with St James's Piccadilly and St George's Hanover Square, while others were rebuilt on the site of older churches, as had already happened with St Mary le Strand and St Clement Danes. The rapid growth in London's new districts was recognised in an Act of Parliament of 1711, which called for the building of fifty new churches in the city. The commissioners who put this Act into effect called into being some magnificent post-Wren baroque churches by Hawksmoor, Gibbs and Archer, among them St John's Smith Square, St George's Bloomsbury and the new St Giles and St Martin's-in-the-Fields.

The social significance of the West End was that London districts were now plainly differentiated according to wealth and social position. In the old City of London itself this seems not to have been true: there were no exclusive streets or quarters reserved for the rich and barred to the poor. By the eighteenth century, however, London's economy had become more complex and diverse: trade, especially overseas trade, financial speculation, the professions, the arts – all these were capable of producing new fortunes … fortunes which sought to proclaim themselves in the possession of smart new properties out of the ruck of the City. As a centre of social display, the West End acquired a life of its own and, as early as 1712, Addison could write that London was now subdivided into enclaves both geographic and social; the city was now 'an aggregate of various nations, distinguished from one another by their respective customs, manners and interests … the inhabitants of St James's are a distinct people from those of Cheapside, who are likewise removed from those of the Temple on the one hand and those of Smithfield on the other by several climates and degrees in their way of thinking and conversing.'

Of course the West End was not inhabited exclusively by the rich, for they called into being an army of servants and tradesmen, from boot-makers to physicians, who would dwell in the interstices between the elegant houses. When too many of these people came together in one street, it could easily slip down and become disreputable, and the path back up was often impossible. So, life in Mayfair did have its drawbacks: the proximity to the crime-infested Hyde Park, the riotous mobs who flocked to Tyburn on execution days, and the fair-time crowds, would all continue to try the patience of Mayfair-dwellers for some years to come. But the West End was firmly established as one of the three faces of London life, that of court and society, balanced by the City for finance and the East End for manufacturing.

Opposite: Westminster and the West End from the Rocque map of 1745. The Royal Parks plainly acted as a buffer to the residential development of West London; had they passed into private hands during the 17th century, they too would certainly have been built over. The area in the south-west of this map would eventually become Belgravia, while the top of the Chelsea Waterworks reservoir is where Victoria Station would be built.
B.L. Maps Crace III/104.

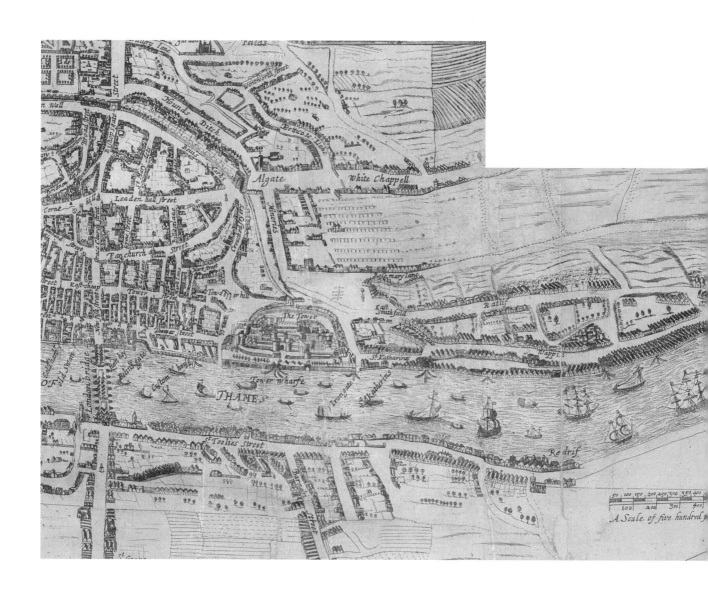

Whitechapel and the East End

In the year 1600 London had pushed a few slender fingers eastwards beyond the city walls - beside the river and along the Whitechapel road. By 1700, these strands had lengthened enormously and had become linked by the mass of houses and work-places which formed, in embryo, the developing East End. Unlike the simultaneous growth of the West End, there are no fine squares, no elegant streets or terraces whose erection can be precisely dated, and no royal court to provide a social focus and a reason for growth. Instead, there were half a dozen factors which stimulated this eastward surge of population and housing into an area which had, for centuries, been arable and pastureland, supplying London's food.

First and most obvious was the extension of the wharfs along the riverside which supported England's growing maritime activity - both merchant and military. The building and servicing of ships called into being a wealth of subsidiary trades - the supply of rope, timber, sails, barrels, weapons, charts, food and so on, and all these trades filled the workshops and warehouses of Wapping High Street. This was a curved road following the line of the river, and it was natural that a second road should cut directly across this loop. This road became the Ratcliff Highway. Immediately north of this highway lay Goodman's Fields, an area of predominantly Jewish settlement, which was greatly expanded by the Cromwellian tolerance of Jews in London after centuries of official exclusion. In turn Goodman's Fields was adjacent to Whitechapel High Street, just outside Aldgate, and the main highway to Essex and Cambridge. Here arose the innumerable inns, blacksmiths and provisions shops which catered for the traveller to and from East Anglia. Along Whitechapel High Street were located many of the trades which were not wanted in the City itself by reason of their noise or nuisance value: brick-making, lime-making, metal foundries, leather-tanning, soap-making and so on. Here also were markets which flourished outside the City's jurisdiction, the most famous being the garment market that was well established by 1600 and which became Petticoat Lane. Just to the north of Whitechapel was the distinctive area of Spitalfields, where weavers had settled from 1600 onwards and where nonconformist religion flourished; this tradition was enriched by the influx of French Protestant silk weavers in the 1680s and 1690s.

In other words, this whole warren of mean streets and poor housing came into being as a hive of labour - skilled and unskilled, native and immigrant - which had no place in the City itself. As the West End was the place of fashion and political influence, the East End was the place of work, and for many, anonymous poverty. Thus, more than a century before the Industrial Revolution arrived in London, the character of the East End was already established, based on the proximity of the river and the separation from polite society. In this east-west structure, the City lay strategically in the centre, providing much of the finance which underpinned both districts.

As in the new West End of the eighteenth century, the growing population needed new churches in which to worship, and the commissioners who took charge of this task bequeathed some magnificent structures to the East End, notably those by Hawksmoor. His St George's in the East, St Anne's Limehouse and Christ Church Spitalfields have, for three centuries, towered rather improbably over their mean surroundings.

Opposite, top: the Porter-Walton map of 1654, the first printed map to recognise the existence and importance of the East End; all other maps of London at this time halted at the Tower, and continued to to do so for many years afterwards. B.L. Maps Crace I/34.

Opposite, bottom: riverside scene at Rotherhithe, with St Mary's church, surrounded by tenements and warehouses. Private collection

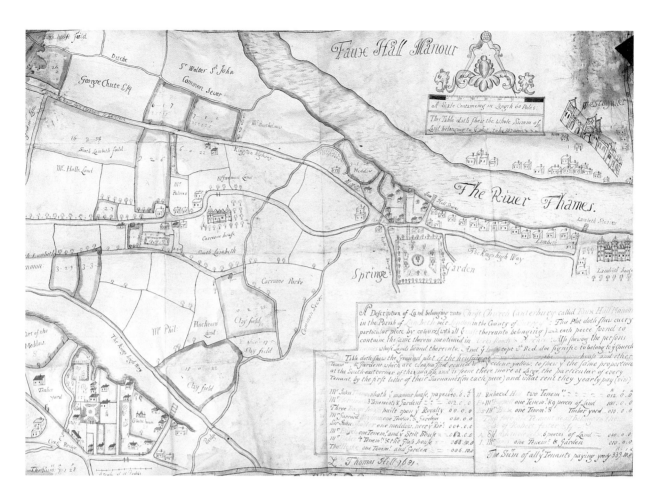

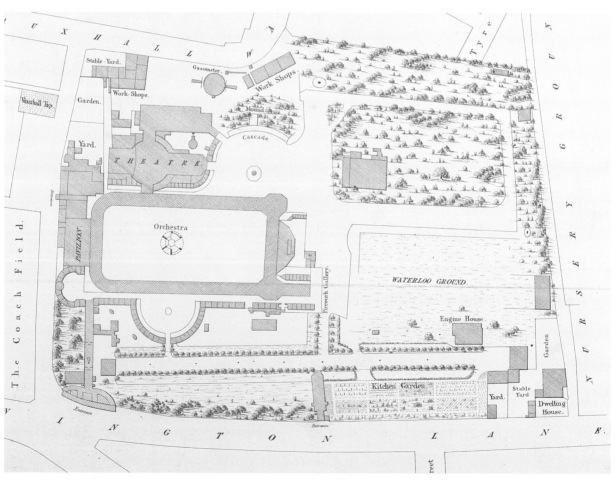

Vauxhall and Ranelagh Gardens

The leisured elite of eighteenth-century London desired, above all, places where they could see and be seen, places where both sexes could relax and mingle, dine and be entertained, match-make and pursue courtships, and would be able to do all these things not in private houses, but on neutral ground, where etiquette was relaxed or, better still, non-existent. These wishes were satisfied by the 'pleasure-gardens', which added a kind of opulent vulgarity to London's social life.

The original pleasure-garden was probably Spring Gardens at Charing Cross, which were well established by 1610, and where it was usual 'to find some of the young company till midnight' and where arbours 'seemed contrived to all advantages of gallantry'. Soon after the Restoration the land was required for building, and their place was taken by the New Spring Garden, later known as Vauxhall Gardens. Before the building of Westminster Bridge, Vauxhall was accessible from the West End only by river, and each evening in summer would see a stream of boats ferrying their parties to Vauxhall. It was laid out as a formalised woodland, with arbours and long walks lit by hundreds of lanterns hung in the

Opposite, top: the Manor of Faux Hall, 1681, with Lambeth Palace on the right, and 'Springe Gardens' in the centre, the original of Vauxhall Gardens. B.L. Add. MS 34790.

Opposite, bottom: a plan of Vauxhall Gardens drawn up for its final sale in 1859. B.L. Maps Crace XVI/66.

Below: Ranelagh Gardens, rival to Vauxhall, with its central rotunda. B.L. K.Top. 840.m.28.

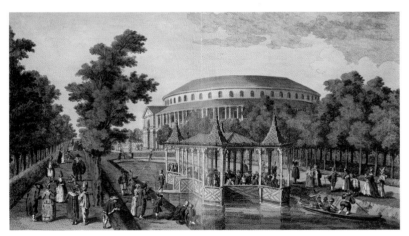

trees; the darker fringes, however, were 'adopted to all species of gallantry or vice', and there is no doubt that part of the excitement of these gardens was their sexual freedom, which shocked even Samuel Pepys. Vauxhall enjoyed its heyday between the 1720s and the 1760s, under the management of Jonathan Tyers, who greatly enlarged the facilities. There were pavilions for music and dining, fountains, statues and picturesque bowers. In these years it reached the height of fashion, visited equally by royalty, intellectuals and socialites. Addison pointedly compared it to a Mahometan paradise (full of available women), while

even Swift and Johnson did not despise its delights. Both its patrons and its pleasures seem to have been distinctly two-tiered: in the front, around the music pavilion and the supper boxes, it was fashionable, vivacious but respectable. Beyond the brilliant lamplight, however, in the darker walks and arbours, it was a place of secret meetings, and of prostitution. Perhaps it was this social permeability that made it so attractive to visitors. In the Regency years, Vauxhall experienced a second golden age, with the patronage of the Prince, and fireworks shows with balloon ascents for the victory celebrations after Waterloo. From Vanbrugh and Fielding to Byron and Thackeray, Vauxhall is depicted as a meeting place of high and low life, a place for 'the great, the rich, the gay, the happy and the fair', but also a place of potential risks and scandal. By the 1840s, social attitudes were beginning to change and there were other opportunities for entertainment; Vauxhall came to look tawdry, like a rather ornate slum. After a series of closures and re-launches, it finally vanished beneath the rows of bourgeois houses in 1859, and its site was for many years untraceable somewhere between Vauxhall Walk and Kennington Lane. However, it is now a park again, albeit a lifeless one in comparison with its predecessor.

Such a brilliant success as Vauxhall naturally produced its imitators, and its greatest rival was Ranelagh Gardens in Chelsea, immediately east of the Royal Hospital. Soon after its opening in 1742, Horace Walpole wrote, 'Everybody that loves eating, drinking, staring or crowding is admitted for twelvepence ... Ranelagh has totally beaten Vauxhall ... you can't set your foot without treading on a Prince or Duke.' The centrepiece was a great rotunda which functioned as a concert hall, dining salon and assembly rooms, and the ornamental lake beside it, painted by Canaletto. Beneath all the music, the dancing and the promenading, once again it was clearly the relaxed sexual ambience of the gardens that was foremost: 'the women came swimming by you like swans', said one contemporary, and even the scholarly Gibbon considered it 'the most convenient place for courtships of every kind - the best market we have in England'. In the 1750s, the road from St James's to Ranelagh was so attractive to footpads that it had to be both lit with lamps and patrolled by watchmen. But for reasons no one can now explain, it was Vauxhall which survived and prospered into the new century, while Ranelagh was closed in 1803. The rotunda was demolished and the gardens are now part of the grounds of Chelsea Hospital.

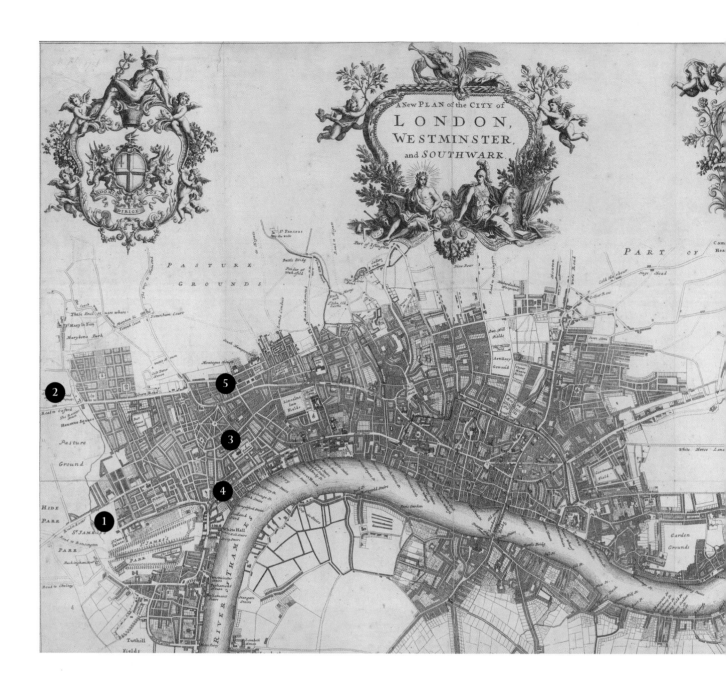

1

2

Hogarth's London

Many artists, English and foreign, have painted London or have been associated with the city: Canaletto, Blake, Turner, Pissarro, Whistler have all captured something of London's form and spirit. But the artist whose work is utterly inseparable from London's streets and London's social life is William Hogarth. He was born in Smithfield in 1697 and lived and worked in Covent Garden, St Martin's Lane and Leicester Fields. He rarely travelled further from London than Chiswick, save for one short trip to France, and he never painted any other part of England. He achieved success as a historical and portrait painter, but above all he sought to put his art before a wider audience through the medium of printing. His work was narrative and satirical, his images of vice and folly closely paralleling the social comedies of his novelist friend Henry Fielding. London is the stage for all these narratives: the slums and alleyways, the fashionable houses, the theatres, prisons, churches, taverns and fairs.

But Hogarth was not a topographical artist in the usual sense, and the number of identifiable London scenes in his pictures is probably not more than a dozen. He did not set out to capture in paint a view of St James's or Covent Garden or London Bridge for its own sake; instead his interest was always in the human drama enacted there. Hogarth used London's social topography as symbols in the journeys which his characters make through life. The Rake begins his career in a respectable house in the city where his father made his money, but quickly moves to an ostentatious house somewhere in the newly built West End, probably Mayfair. He frequents the gaming houses and brothels of Covent Garden or Southwark, and is then arrested for debt just as he seeks preferment at the court of St James. He descends through the debtors' prison, undoubtedly the Marshalsea or the King's Bench, to the final degradation of Bedlam, the lunatics' hospital at Moorfields. Hogarth's other famous sequences, *The Harlot's Progress*, *Marriage à la Mode*, and *Industry and Idleness*, are likewise moral journeys through life and at the same time topographical journeys across London. They resemble secularised versions of *A Pilgrim's Progress*, which end, however, not in any kind of celestial city, but in London's lowest depths – Newgate prison, or still worse on the gallows at Tyburn. The sense of life as a theatre is everywhere in Hogarth's work, and the backdrop is the neoclassical architecture or the affluent interiors of Georgian London. On the surface there is wealth and pleasure, but tragedy or retribution waits around the street corner or at the half-open door. Hogarth was a ceaseless critic of the vanities of social life, and there is no sharper record of eighteenth-century London than his brilliant engravings.

Opposite, top: map of London by Strype, 1720. B.L. Maps Crace II/85.

Opposite and left: London scenes by Hogarth (from bottom left):
1. Arrested for debt at St James's.
2. The Idle Apprentice at Tyburn.
3. Morning at Covent Garden.
4. Night at Charing Cross.
5. Gin Lane.
British Museum, Dept of Prints and Drawings.

3

4

5

Above: Chelsea from Rocque's 1746 map of London's environs. B.L. Maps Crace XIX/18.

Above right: a view of 18th-century Chelsea. B.L. K.Top. 28.4.BB.2.

Below: Richmond on Rocque's map. B.L. Maps Crace XIX/18.

Centre right: a view of old Richmond Palace, B.L. K.Top. 41.17.

Below right: a fashionable party at Richmond Ferry. B.L. K.Top. 41.17.g.

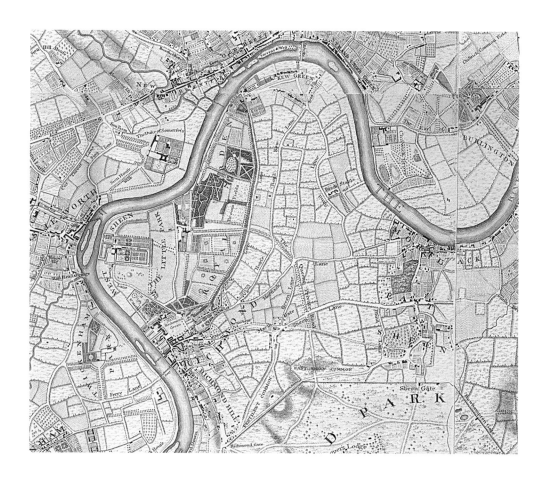

Fashionable Suburbs

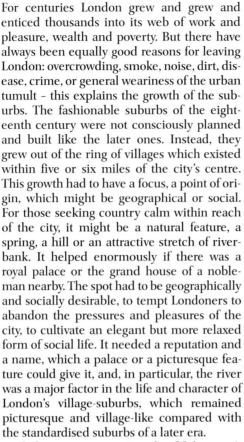

For centuries London grew and grew and enticed thousands into its web of work and pleasure, wealth and poverty. But there have always been equally good reasons for leaving London: overcrowding, smoke, noise, dirt, disease, crime, or general weariness of the urban tumult – this explains the growth of the suburbs. The fashionable suburbs of the eighteenth century were not consciously planned and built like the later ones. Instead, they grew out of the ring of villages which existed within five or six miles of the city's centre. This growth had to have a focus, a point of origin, which might be geographical or social. For those seeking country calm within reach of the city, it might be a natural feature, a spring, a hill or an attractive stretch of riverbank. It helped enormously if there was a royal palace or the grand house of a nobleman nearby. The spot had to be geographically and socially desirable, to tempt Londoners to abandon the pressures and pleasures of the city, to cultivate an elegant but more relaxed form of social life. It needed a reputation and a name, which a palace or a picturesque feature could give it, and, in particular, the river was a major factor in the life and character of London's village-suburbs, which remained picturesque and village-like compared with the standardised suburbs of a later era.

Chelsea was a mere straggle of fishermen's cottages until Sir Thomas More built himself a country house there in 1520, to be followed by Henry VIII and by so many noblemen that it became known as 'the village of palaces', in one of which Queen Elizabeth I passed her childhood. It boasted a horse ferry exactly where Battersea Bridge now stands, and was an admirable site for Wren's Royal Hospital. The palaces were replaced in the early eighteenth century by the Queen Anne houses of Cheyne Walk, which immediately drew residents from London – so close to the West End yet distinct enough to acquire its own reputation for chic. With its river sunsets, its elegance, its shops and its village atmosphere, it prospered and became famous, attracting a seemingly endless stream of writers and artists, among them Swift, Addison, Turner, Whistler, Carlyle, George Eliot, Swinburne and Henry James. Chelsea soon lost its status as a suburb and became an essential part of the urban fabric, adding probably more to the lexicon of London life than any other district – buns, porcelain, flower shows, pensioners, and art schools.

Five miles up-river another fishing village, then called Sheen, began its process of transformation when the late medieval kings began to use the manor house as a country retreat. In 1510 Henry VII rebuilt the burned-down house, and renamed it Richmond Palace, after his earldom in Yorkshire. It stood facing the river, west of the green, and became a favourite residence of the Tudors. It was largely destroyed during the Commonwealth years, but not before the presence of the palace had induced courtiers and gentlemen to build themselves houses around the green or on Richmond Hill, with its superb views over the river, while businesses supplying the palace formed the core of what became the shops in George Street and Hill Street. Long after all traces of the palace had vanished, Dickens wrote of the green as a place 'where hoops and powder and patches, embroidered coats, rolled stockings, ruffles and swords had had their court days many a time'. When Disraeli visited the ageing Metternich here in 1849, he was so enchanted with the green that he wanted to abandon London and move there. Richmond Bridge was built in 1777, without wholly killing off the ferries of the district, while the riverside walks and boat hire around the bridge made Richmond a favourite place for a day out from the city.

To the east of London the river is much broader – its banks are of interminable mud and marshland, and there would be little reason to anticipate the appearance of a fashionable suburb here. Yet the steep hill rising abruptly above the stretch of firm, chalk riverbank at Greenwich offered a natural setting for the palace and park built by Humphrey, Duke of Gloucester, in the 1420s. The turreted palace rose directly above the water's edge, with hamlets on both sides, while its grounds extended south to the summit of the hill and beyond. Here Henry VIII, Mary Tudor and Queen Elizabeth were born, and here they witnessed tournaments, practised archery, hawked and hunted. The great advantage of the east river was that the monarch could watch the large merchant ships sailing up to London, or go aboard the men-of-war of the Tudor navy, as they moored at Greenwich. In the reign of William and Mary, the palace was demolished and replaced by Wren's seamen's hospital. At the same time, the park was opened to the public and the Easter and Whitsun fairs held there were magnets for crowds of Londoners throughout the eighteenth and nineteenth centuries. Greenwich Hill was suggested as the site for the new Royal Observatory by Wren, who designed the original house. The Naval Hospital and Observatory gave Greenwich a fame and importance in national life, while the charm of its setting encouraged residential building. To the west of the park, Croom's Hill and Gloucester Place were laid out with fine houses, while large taverns appeared on the

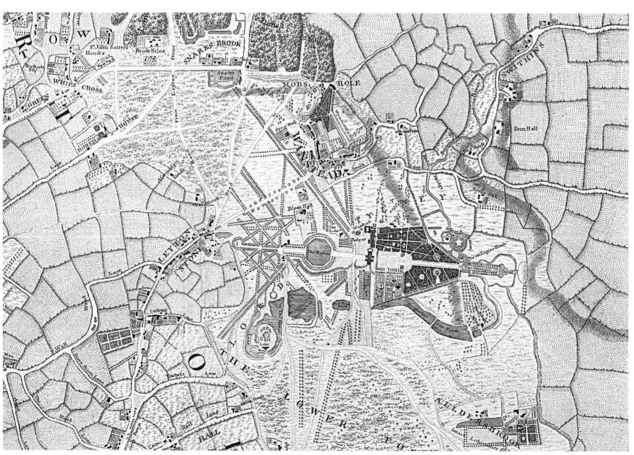

riverside to offer whitebait suppers to the visitors. In the nineteenth century, house-building crossed the heath to the south and created the new neighbouring suburb of Blackheath. With the open heathland, the broad, tidal river and the magnificent classical buildings of the hospital and the museum, Greenwich is grander in scale than the riverside playgrounds of Chelsea and Richmond, but somehow it never found favour with artists and writers as they had.

Opposite: details of Greenwich, (*top*), and Wanstead, (*bottom*), from the Rocque map, 1746.
B.L. Maps Crace XIX/18.

Above: views of Greenwich, (*top*), and Wanstead, (*bottom*), in the 18th century.
B.L. K.Top. 17.1.3.D.2 and K.Top. 13.30.D.

To the north of London, the slopes of Hampstead Heath provided a natural setting for a village to develop around the coaching inns and blacksmiths' shops on the roads into Hertfordshire. The village and the heathland had been a refuge for Londoners during the Black Death of 1349 and the Plague of 1665, and on more than one occasion when the end of the world was predicted. But Hampstead's fortunes were transformed in the 1690s by its promotion as a spa on London's very doorstep: Hampstead spring water was proclaimed to be 'of the same nature and equal in virtue with that of Tunbridge Wells'. A pump room was built, coffee-houses, bowling greens and a racecourse, and Hampstead became a cockney Bath, which rather quickly declined in tone and became raffish. Belsize Pleasure-Gardens, south of the heath, was built over with elegant houses in the mid-nineteenth century, and it became a magnet for writers, artists and intellectuals - from Blake, Keats and Constable to Wells, Lawrence and Freud - that surpassed even Chelsea. Somehow the presence of Freud in the last year of his life seemed to set the seal on Hampstead's intellectual reputation, and the home of critical, progressive chic.

It was sometimes possible for a village to become fashionable without either a royal palace or a setting of great natural charm, provided it had some other social focus. The original Wanstead House was owned by the Earl of Leicester, Queen Elizabeth I's favourite, but it passed to the Tilney family, who in the 1720s commissioned a vast Palladian mansion that rivalled Holkham or Blenheim in size and splendour. In Wanstead village and in Leytonstone to the east, communities of suppliers and servants to the big house developed, and gentlemen built their villas. But Wanstead House soon became a disreputable place, a kind of Essex branch of the Hell Fire Club, with nameless orgies supposed to have taken place in the garden grottoes. It is not impossible that this reputation suggested the use of the Tilney name to Jane Austen when she was writing her pseudo-gothic romance, *Northanger Abbey*. The Tilney family became involved in debt and disgrace, and in the 1820s this great house was pulled down and sold for building stone. However, the lines of its avenues are still clearly to be seen in the suburban streets which now stand on the site, and remnants of its gardens and lakes survive as a public park. On the fringes of Epping Forest, Wanstead is still a green, village-like suburb, but not famous in London history as Chelsea, Richmond and Greenwich are.

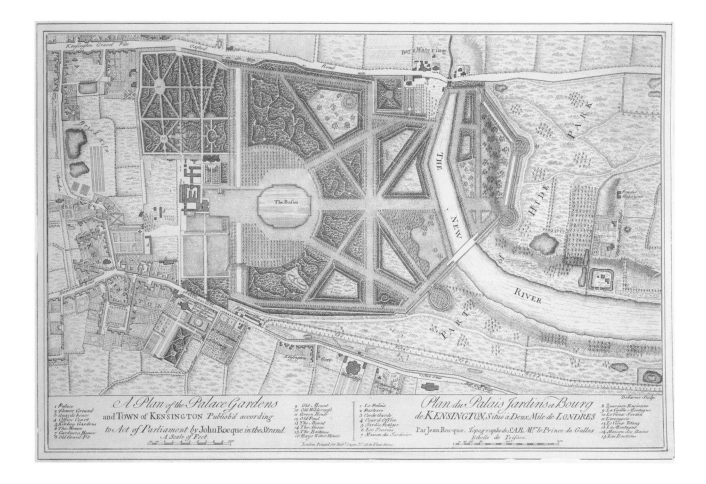

A Plan of the Palace Gardens
and Town of KENSINGTON Publish'd according
to Act of Parliament by John Rocque in the Strand.
A Scale of Feet.

1. Palace
2. Flower Ground
3. Guards house
4. Office Court
5. Kitchen Gardens
6. The House
7. Gardeners House
8. Old Gravel Pit

9. Old Mount
10. Old Wilderness
11. Green House
12. Old Pond
13. The Mount
14. The House
15. The Bastions
16. Bays Water House

1. Le Palais
2. Parterre
3. Corle Garde
4. Cour d'Office
5. Jardin Potager
6. Les Fournes
7. Maison du Jardinier

Plan du Palais Jardins et Bourg
de KENSINGTON, Situé à Deux Mile de LONDRES
Par Jean Rocque, Topographe de S.A.R. M. le Prince de Galles
Echelle de Toises.

8. Quarrere Encienne
9. La Veille Montagne
10. Le Vieux Jardin
11. L'orangerie
12. Le Vieux Etang
13. La Montagne
14. Maison des Bains
15. Les Bastions

London, Printed for Rob.t Sayer N.o 53 in Fleet Street.

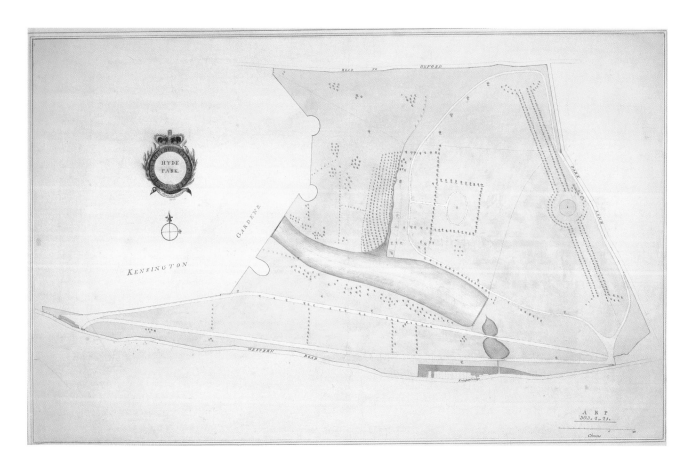

HYDE PARK

KENSINGTON GARDENS

Hyde Park and Kensington Gardens

West of St James's Park lay further tracts of open land that were seized by Henry VIII from their former monastic owners and designated as royal hunting grounds. In the process of time, this act of royal greed preserved many hundreds of acres of green parkland in the heart of London's growing expanse of brick, dust and noise. By the seventeenth century, the deer and boar had been more or less hunted out, and St James's Park was opened to the public, becoming a favourite place for May Day and other festivities. During the years of the Interregnum, from 1649 to 1660, it was sold to a private owner who charged for admission, but during the Restoration it returned to royal hands. It became, and always remained, a place for riding and social display, which in the nineteenth century became concentrated on Rotten Row, where endless lines of aristocratic carriages and social celebrities would parade each afternoon, watched by their admirers and their enemies.

The major event in the park's history came in 1689 when William III and Queen Mary, unhappy with Whitehall Palace, bought Nottingham House on the north-western edge of the park, and began transforming it into Kensington Palace. At the outset, thirty acres

that Queen Caroline once asked Walpole what it would cost to enclose the entire park for private royal use, to which he replied that it would cost her her crown. She contented herself therefore with the slightly smaller portion, and with damming the Westbourne Stream to create the Serpentine Lake - which flowed through both the gardens and park - and placing two royal yachts on its water.

Both halves of the park were walled or fenced, and their public/private status was never easy to define. Both became notorious as the haunt of footpads and highwaymen, and George II himself was robbed while walking beside the Round Pond. No sensible person would cross the park after dusk, except in a large group. The Hyde Park side was also the favourite duelling ground for London's gentry - Wilkes, Sheridan and Fox are among those who fought there. Fairs large and small were held in Hyde Park, including the huge but slightly premature peace celebrations of 1814, when a mock Battle of Trafalgar was enacted on the Serpentine. The park was the natural choice for the Great Exhibition of 1851, and the original site of the Crystal Palace was beside the South Carriage Drive opposite Prince of Wales Gate. Kensington Gardens had become recognised as the tranquil, semi-private domain, richly planted with trees and flowers, and the correct site for Prince Albert's brooding memorial. Hyde Park had always been arid and sandy, trampled by feet and hooves, more like a heath than a park, and this only began to be remedied by the first plantings in the 1870s. Its reputation for prostitutes was also an enduring one: as one diplomatic guidebook of the 1920s remarked, 'Many public and well-known men have ruined their careers through falling victim to a pretty face in Hyde Park after dark.' Another distinction between the two parks was that by the mid-nineteenth century a definite belief had grown up in the right of public assembly in Hyde Park. This belief was vindicated by an extraordinary battle, in July 1866, between around 50,000 people supporting political reform and the troops sent to eject them. Today's pop festivals are a legacy of the rights established then.

The two parks now seem essentially similar, for the society carriages and the duellists and most of the prostitutes have departed. But they have had rather different histories, and it is useful to remember why it would have been impossible for J. M. Barrie to set *Peter Pan* in Hyde Park, with its raffish reputation; Kensington Gardens with its formality and period charm was exactly right.

were set aside for the palace grounds, but in the 1720s a further 200 acres were added at the request of Queen Caroline, wife of George II. The whole area was landscaped to the design of Henry Wise and George Bridgeman, with the Round Pond, the Broad Walk and the many tree-lined avenues. It is said

NEWGATE.

A. The Keeper's House
B. Lodges for the Turnkeys
C. Tap Rooms
D. The Arcade under the Chapel
E. Closets
F. Stair Cases

G. Cells for the Refractory
H. Passage to the Condemned Cells
I. Passage to the Sessions House
K. Wards
L. Bed-Rooms for Turnkeys
M. Cellar-Stairs
N. Passages. a Area on the Cellar Floor.

Men Felons Quadrangle.

Debtors Quadrangle.

Women Felons Quadrangle.

Bedlam and Newgate

As well as new houses and renovated palaces, the third element in the post-Fire reconstruction of London was the renewal of public buildings. Churches most obviously, but also schools, hospitals, prisons and places of business were rebuilt in the newer architectural styles, replacing the Tudor or medieval piles that had stood for centuries, and this fashion for rebuilding spread to institutions and to parts of London that had not been touched by the Fire. Two of London's grimmest institutions - Bethlehem Hospital for the insane and Newgate Prison - were housed in imposing new structures, and throughout the eighteenth century they played an important role in London's social life and in the city's psychology.

As early as the fourteenth century, Bethlehem Hospital outside Bishopsgate was spoken of as caring for 'distracted' patients, that is, they were kept locked up, and were whipped or ducked if they proved troublesome. In 1675-6 the hospital was moved to a new site in Moorfields, to a new building designed by the scientist Robert Hooke. This was a magnificent structure, said to be modelled on the Tuileries in Paris, with an ornate façade and long galleries within, all set in a large formal garden. It seems like a bizarre joke to have placed lunatics in such a setting, but one of its side effects was to make the place attractive to visitors, and Bedlam became one of the sights of London. Patients were exhibited like creatures in a human zoo, to be laughed at by the visitors, who paid well for their entertainment. This practice was finally stopped in 1770, and some first steps towards the reform of mental health care had begun with the work of John Howard. By 1800 the

Opposite, top: George Dance's 1780 plan for Newgate - 'large, strong and beautiful'. B.L. Maps Crace VIII/84.

Opposite, bottom: Bethlehem Hospital, the design by Robert Hooke that resembled a palace. B.L. K.Top. 25.22.

Right: Execution day at Newgate, early 19th century. B.L. 010348.g.9.

building had become unsafe, and a new building in a new location was proposed. James Lewis designed a new hospital in Lambeth, completed in 1815 in the classical style. A few years later a dome was added, and a fine portico which looked remarkably like that of the British Museum - not surprising since both were the work of the same architects, Sydney and Robert Smirke. Like Hooke's hospital, it too had the appearance of a palace, and it is now the Imperial War Museum; perhaps there was a certain symmetry in designing structures that might be palaces, lunatic asylums or war museums.

Bethlehem in its corrupted form 'Bedlam' added a new word to the English language. Newgate did not quite do that, but the symbolic force of the name as another London purgatory was just as strong. A prison had existed on the site since the twelfth century, but the old edifice was destroyed in the Great Fire, and a new building 'of great magnificence' soon replaced it. Behind the magnificent façade, however, it was a prototype of hell. In the penal system of the eighteenth century, the only long-term inmates were the debtors; all the others were in transit, awaiting trial or execution. Newgate was insanitary and fever-ridden, and the prisoners were brutalised by both their fellow prisoners and the keepers. A semblance of civilised treatment could only be obtained by payment, so that Fielding remarked that although Newgate was a hellish place, it was also the most expensive place in London to live. One of Howard's reform measures was to pay the gaolers a salary so that they need not extort money from the prisoners. Jonathan Wild and Jack Sheppard were among the underworld figures held here, and these celebrities awaiting death were visited by celebrities from the outside, for a fee paid to the gaoler, and had their portraits painted by Hogarth and others. For eighteenth-century London, Newgate was one end of a fatal public procession, with Tyburn waiting at the other end.

In the 1770s the prison was rebuilt by the architect George Dance, and the new structure was described by the poet Crabbe as 'very large, strong and beautiful', but it was this new building which was burned and destroyed by the Gordon Rioters in 1780, freeing some 400 prisoners. Some days afterwards the public could wander through the smouldering ruins, and, strangest of all, some of the liberated prisoners returned too, having nowhere else to go. It was rebuilt to the same design, and here Lord George Gordon himself died in 1793, imprisoned for debt. The opportunity was then taken to end the riotous processions to Tyburn, and to move the place of execution to the street outside Newgate itself. Here for almost ninety years, enormous crowds would gather to see the public hangings, until the practice was halted in 1868 after loud protests about its brutalising effects by Dickens and many others. Newgate was finally demolished in 1902 to make way for the new court buildings of the Old Bailey.

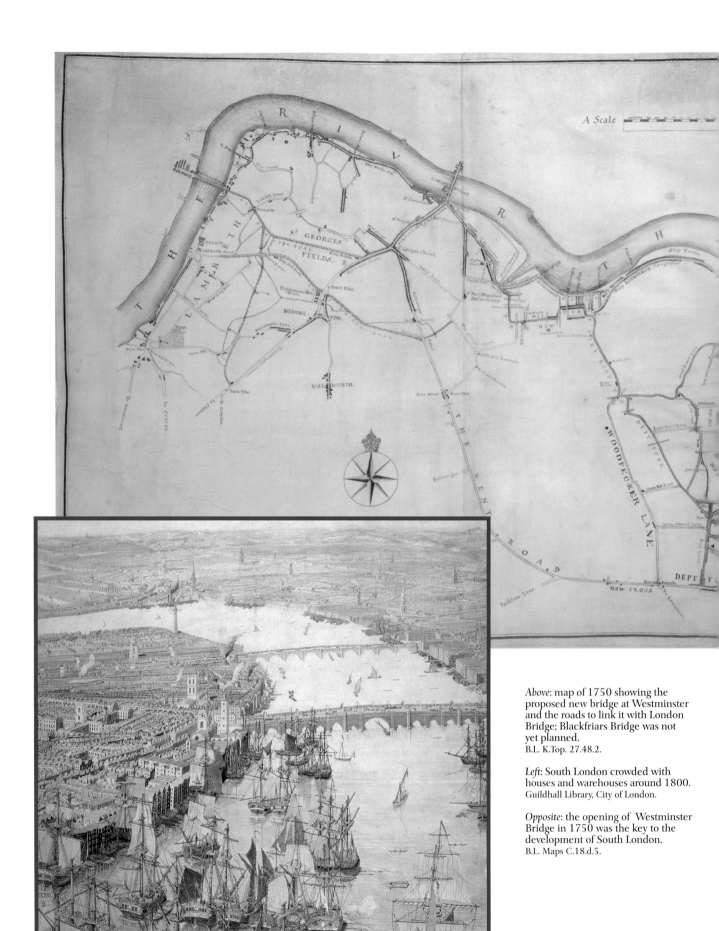

Above: map of 1750 showing the proposed new bridge at Westminster and the roads to link it with London Bridge; Blackfriars Bridge was not yet planned.
B.L. K.Top. 27.48.2.

Left: South London crowded with houses and warehouses around 1800.
Guildhall Library, City of London.

Opposite: the opening of Westminster Bridge in 1750 was the key to the development of South London.
B.L. Maps C.18.d.5.

South London: New Bridges, New Roads

The geographical spread of London, the wider streets and people's desire to be part of fashionable society, all contributed to the increase of wheeled transport: traffic jams and road rage became features of London life. In 1660 Pepys noted 'In King Street, there being a great stop of coaches, there was a falling-out between a drayman and my Lord Chesterfield's coachman, and one of his footmen killed.' In the 1720s, the City's historic gates were all demolished because they hindered the traffic so badly.

By far the greater part of this growth was north of the river, but the empty fields on the southern side could not long resist being drawn into London's grasp. In 1700 the only place still of national importance south of the Thames was Lambeth Palace. The two great obstacles were the large tract of marshy ground in Lambeth and St George's Fields, and the lack of bridges connecting north and south London. The first problem yielded to piecemeal drainage, but the second involved great cost and decisive planning. Almost twenty years of proposal and counter proposal preceded the start of work on a new bridge at Westminster in 1738, and the construction itself took another twelve years. London's resentful watermen, who controlled all passenger traffic on the Thames, were compensated by a grant of £25,000, while the Archbishop of Canterbury, who owned the Lambeth–Westminster ferry for horse traffic and carriages, was awarded a further £21,000. This, only the second bridge to be built over the Thames in more than a thousand years, received its grand opening in 1750, when it became immediately obvious that new road links to Southwark and London Bridge would be needed.

Before these could be planned and built, however, a new factor entered the equation, with the decision to build a third bridge over the Thames, from a point near the mouth of the Fleet River, so that all traffic to and from London Bridge would not be compelled to pass through the City. Blackfriars Bridge was opened in 1769, and its architect, Robert Mylne, also proposed a road plan for the south bank, a modified version of which did emerge some twenty years later. On this map of Mylne's ideas, there are two key road intersections. The northern one, with link roads to Westminster and London Bridges, was never built. The southern one, where the north- south road crosses the east–west route, became St George's Circus, with its obelisk by George Dance designed to be the focal point of South London, with roads radiating east and west from it. But this role soon passed to the junction which can be seen clearly to the south-east, which became the Elephant and Castle (a place name which has never been properly explained). The new bridges represented a turning-point in London's development, and the south side was soon built over. As one contemporary wrote in 1810:

> Saint George's Fields are fields no more;
> The trowel supersedes the plough;
> Swamps huge and inundate of yore
> Are changed to civic villas now.

But neither Lambeth nor the south bank generally ever became another West End, and the district retained a character of its own, a place of small industries, warehouses, taverns, markets and prisons, which consistently refused to turn its back on its tradition of raucous beggary. In the 1770s Smollett wrote of the Old Kent Road: 'It would be to the honour of the kingdom to improve the avenue to London by way of Kent Street, which is a most disgraceful entrance to such an opulent city. A foreigner, in passing this beggarly and ruinous suburb, conceives such an idea of misery and meanness as all the wealth and magnificence of London and Westminster are afterwards unable to destroy.'

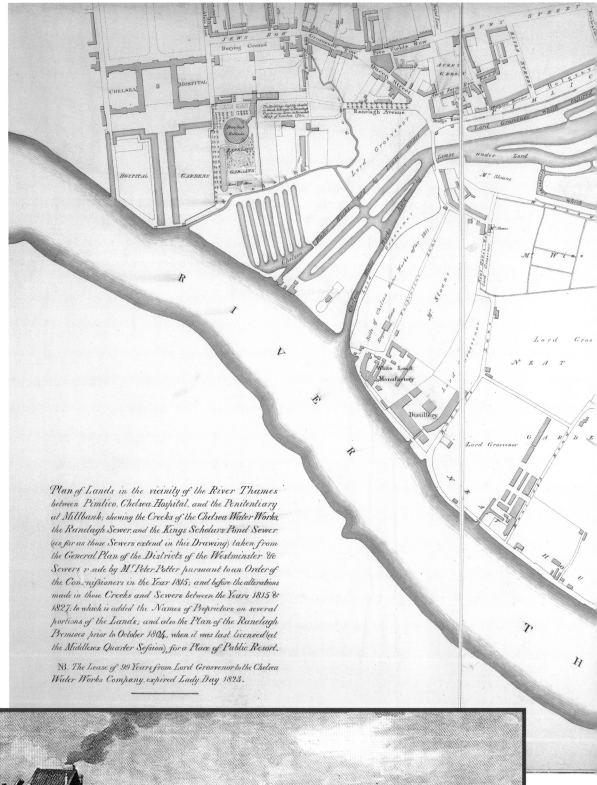

Plan of Lands in the vicinity of the River Thames between Pimlico, Chelsea Hospital, and the Penitentiary at Millbank; shewing the Creeks of the Chelsea Water Works, the Ranelagh Sewer, and the Kings Scholars Pond Sewer (as far as those Sewers extend in this Drawing) taken from the General Plan of the Districts of the Westminster &c Sewers made by M.r Peter Potter pursuant to an Order of the Commissioners in the Year 1815; and before the alterations made in those Creeks and Sewers between the Years 1815 & 1827, to which is added the Names of Proprietors on several portions of the Lands; and also the Plan of the Ranelagh Premises prior to October 1804, when it was last licensed (at the Middlesex Quarter Sefsion) for a Place of Public Resort.

N.B. The Lease of 99 Years from Lord Grosvenor to the Chelsea Water Works Company, expired Lady Day 1823.

Chelsea Waterworks

The innumerable wells which had supplied medieval London with water soon proved inadequate, and they were supplemented by conduits bringing water from rivers and streams north of the City, especially the Tybourne, which were built and paid for by the City authorities. These pipes issued at fountainheads like the one in Cheapside, which was made to run with wine on coronation days. By the late Tudor period these sources, too, were unable to supply the needs of the growing city, and a succession of private-enterprise engineering schemes were devised over the next two centuries. As early as 1581, a great waterwheel was installed under one of the arches of London Bridge which pumped water to the City - for cleaning rather than drinking, since it was too saline. More radical was the New River Scheme of 1608-13, by which a channel - effectively a man-made river almost forty miles long - was dug to bring fresh water from springs in Hertfordshire. It was gathered in a large reservoir in Islington from where it was distributed to the City, after 1760 by steam pumps.

The rapid growth of the West End demanded yet another new water source, and in 1723 the Chelsea Waterworks Company was founded, which drew water directly from the Thames into a great network of channels. Windmills and horse-mills, and after 1750 steam engines, pumped the water to the slightly higher ground of the West End via reservoirs in Hyde Park and St James's Park. The cuts and channels eventually covered almost 100 acres and pumped nearly 2,000 tons of water a day to the new houses of St James's and Mayfair. Much of Pimlico was turned into a strange suburban fenland, with creeks, sluice gates and footbridges, frequented by waterbirds and anglers. The intake was exactly where Grosvenor Road railway bridge now stands, and the steam pump stood on the site of Victoria Station.

How clean was this water? For centuries the Thames had been London's primary sewer and the water at Chelsea, less saline than at London Bridge, was still not intended for drinking, but inevitably some of it was consumed, and by the early nineteenth century the medical implications were becoming clear. In 1827 the radical politician Sir Francis Burdett complained to Parliament that 'The water taken from the River Thames at Chelsea for the use of the inhabitants of the western part of the metropolis, being charged with the contents of the great common sewers, the drainings from dunghills and laystalls, the refuse of hospitals and slaughter houses, colour lead and soap works, drug mills and manufactories, and with all sorts of decomposed animal and vegetable substances, rendering the said water offensive and destructive to health, ought no longer to be taken up by any of the water companies from so foul a source.' This complaint spurred the company into experiments with filtration through sand and gravel, and this certainly improved the water, so that by 1835 two million gallons a day were being pumped to 13,000 houses in the West End. But it could only be a temporary expedient since the waters of the Thames were becoming more polluted each year, and the cholera outbreaks of the 1840s forced a complete rethink of London's water system. At the same time, east Chelsea became attractive to developers, and the Water Company decided to build new works in Putney and to draw its water at Walton, several miles upstream. The maze of channels and reservoirs were drained, and their site vanished beneath the streets of Pimlico.

Above: Chelsea Waterworks from the Horwood map of 1799; the intake from the river and the reservoirs are where the railway lines now run to Victoria Station. B.L. Maps Crace X/23.

Left: view of the waterworks. B.L. K.Top. 28.4.dd.1.

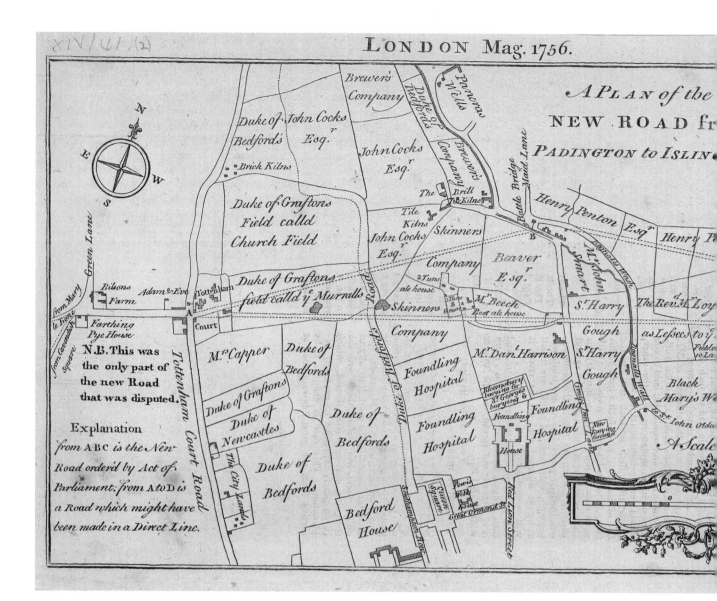

XIV/41.(2)

A PLAN of the
NEW ROAD fr
PADINGTON to ISLIN

Brewer's
Company

Duke of John Cocks
Bedford's Esq.r

Duke of
Bedfords

Duke of Bedfords

Panaras
Wells

Brewer's Company

Battle Bridge

Maid Lane

Henry Penton Esq.r

Henry P

Duke of Graftons
Field call'd
Church Field

• Brick Kilns

John Cocks
Esq.r

The
Brill

Tile Kilns

Skinners

Tile
Kilns

John Cocks
Esq.r

Company

Beaver
Esq.r

Mr John
Smart

St. Harry

The Rev.d Mr Loy

Green Lane

from Mary le Bone

from Cavendish Square

Bilsons
Farm

Adam & Eve

Tottenham
Court

Duke of Graftons
field call'd ỹ Murralls

3 Tuns
ale house

Skinners
Company

Mr Beech
Root ale house

Gough

as Lessees to ỹ

Fields
to La

Road
Duke of Bedford's

Farthing
Pye House

N.B. This was
the only part of
the new Road
that was disputed.

Explanation
from A B C is the New
Road order'd by Act of
Parliament: from A to D is
a Road which might have
been made in a Direct Line.

Mrs Capper

Duke of
Bedfords

Duke of Graftons

Duke of
Newcastles

The City Lands

Duke of
Bedfords

Duke of
Bedfords

Bedford
House

Foundling
Hospital

Foundling
Hospital

Foundling
Hospital

Mr Dan.l Harrison

Bloomsbury
burying Gr
St Georges
burying G

Foundling
House

Foundling
House

St. Harry
Gough

Black
Mary's W

to St John of Ld

A Scale

New
burying
Ground

Tottenham Court Road

Powis
Well
house
Great Ormond St.

Queens
Square

Red Lion Post Office

Southampton Row

Bagnigge Wash

Gray's Inn

Above: Part of the Marylebone Road, London's first planned road, bringing traffic into the City from the west, skirting the new residential areas and the St Giles district. This section east of Tottenham Court Road had to take a northerly tack, because of landowners' arguments. B.L. Maps Crace XIV/41b.

Opposite: traffic congestion, 18th-century style. British Museum, Dept of Prints and Drawings.

Marylebone Road

For centuries the only approach route into London from the north-west – in other words from most of the rest of England – was via St Giles, High Holborn and Newgate. The eighteenth century saw an enormous increase in wheeled traffic and, at the same time, droves of cattle, sheep and pigs still passed this way en route to Smithfield and other markets. A coach journey through the narrow, crowded streets from Grosvenor Square to the Bank of England could take two hours. These were the same pressures that had led to the building of the roads and bridges of south London. The situation became intolerable to the residents of the new West End, and in 1755 a group of north London gentlemen and traders petitioned Parliament to build a relief road well to the north of St Giles. It was to run from Paddington Green to Islington, with a south-easterly extension towards Moorgate and the City. It would be built over open pasture land, much of it owned by the Portman, Portland and Bedford Estates. Any objections these landowners may have felt soon faded as they realised the lucrative opportunities to develop their property that would follow. The plan was quickly approved, and the road built in 1756, the first new road in London's history deliberately planned to relieve traffic congestion. It was known for a hundred years simply as the New Road, until others appeared to confuse things and it was renamed Marylebone, Euston and Pentonville. The initial cost of the road was recouped through tolls, and to guard against the obvious danger of footpads and highwaymen on a road bordering open country, watchmen were employed.

Inevitably this road became, for a time, London's northern boundary, enticing the neighbouring estates to build on their land north of Oxford Street and High Holborn, thus creating the Marylebone and Bloomsbury districts which we know today. When Somers Town and Pentonville were built beyond the New Road in the 1780s and later, it was a sign that London's growth had leapt forward once again. The building of Regent Street and the park also had the effect of drawing people northwards. Originally envisaged as a traffic route only, the New Road was soon edged with houses, although it was not until 1828 that Sir John Soane's Holy Trinity Church was built to provide a place of worship for the residents of Fitzroy Square and Portland Place.

One incidental effect of London's growth and the switch to wheeled traffic was the death of the sedan chair, for the distances were now too great. In 1791 Horace Walpole observed that 'Hercules and Atlas together could not carry anybody from one end of this enormous capital to the other,' and he noted that when travelling by coach from the West End to the Strand, he was halted over and over again, 'for the tides of coaches, chariots, curricles, phaetons etc. are quite endless'. The New Road, like its many hundreds of successors, was not destined to solve London's traffic problems.

Above: the heart of the City: the Mansion House, the Bank of England, the Royal Exchange, the Stock Exchange. B.L. Maps 3480(260).

Opposite: the ceremonial installation of the Lord Mayor in the Guildhall. B.L. K.Top. 24.13.e.

The City and its Institutions

The City's earliest role was as home to the guilds - the bodies which regulated London's trades: butchers, barbers, goldsmiths, glovers, saddlers, salters and a multitude of others. The standards set by the guilds guaranteed quality, and they became trusted institutions at the heart of urban life. As such, they were central to the wider government of the city, electing the mayor and sheriffs. The mainstay of the English economy from the Middle Ages onwards was the trade in cloth, at home and abroad. Then as now, any large-scale trade, especially if it was international, required a financial infrastructure - investment, banking and credit. This structure was founded on trust, on probity, and on a network of personal contacts within the City, but also much further afield - in France, the Netherlands, the Baltic and so on. Investment, loans and international credit all became central in the age of maritime expansion, when merchant adventurers set out from London to found colonies or to open trade routes with America, Asia and Africa. It soon became evident that, in addition to material goods, there was a strong market for money itself, that in fact the flow of money was an essential precondition of all other trades. To raise and invest money

successfully, to connect those requiring money with those willing to invest it, became the major new role of the City, a role formally embodied in the institutions of the Royal Exchange, the Bank of England, Lloyd's and the Stock Exchange, founded respectively in the sixteenth, seventeenth and eighteenth centuries.

John Stow, London's great chronicler, reported on the defects of the Elizabethan way of business: 'The merchants and tradesmen, as well English as strangers, for their general making of bargains, contracts and commerce, did usually meet twice every day. But these meetings were unpleasant and troublesome, by reason of walking and talking in the open street, being there constrained to endure all extremes of weather, or else to shelter themselves in shops.' It was Thomas Gresham who determined that London must possess a copy of the bourse which he had seen in Antwerp. The building, which he conceived, was opened by Queen Elizabeth I in 1570, and she so admired it that she proclaimed that it must henceforth always be known as 'The Royal Exchange'. Destroyed in the Great Fire, it was rebuilt in the baroque style, only to perish in flames again in 1838. The third, surviving

Above: traditional City men flood
Threadneedle Street.
Private collection.

Right: a printed copy of Sir John
Soane's master plan for the Bank of
England drawn up in *c.*1790.
B.L. Maps Crace III/75.

GROUND PLAN

OF THE

BANK

OF

ENGLAND.

*Copied from a
Drawing in Sir
John Soane's
Museum.*

BY

JOHN WEALE,

1851.

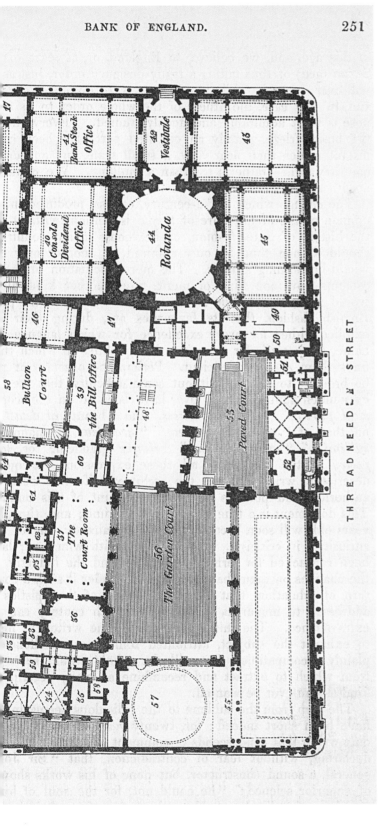

Exchange, with its classical portico, was opened by Queen Victoria in 1844, and she also renewed its royal title. Lloyd's had no building of its own until the 1920s and it, too, was housed in the Royal Exchange.

The Bank of England was conceived in the 1690s, to advance funds to the government upon the security of future taxation – in other words to formalise and manage the National Debt. It issued banknotes which it guaranteed to redeem for gold; notes which soon began to circulate as a convenient medium of exchange. Although governed by statute, it was, until 1946, a private enterprise whose funds were raised and managed privately. It received its own premises in Threadneedle Street in 1734, a site magnificently remodelled by Sir John Soane in the 1790s, with a classical façade uniquely without windows.

Lloyd's originally dealt principally with marine insurance, and was founded in Lloyd's coffee-shop in Lombard Street, frequented by seamen and ship-owners. Fire insurance was the other main sphere of business, greatly stimulated by the experience of the Great Fire. It was in the nineteenth century that wider concepts such as life insurance began to emerge, as well as liability, accident and theft. All these have grown until insurance has come to be one of the dominant sectors of the entire financial market, symbolised in Lloyd's new (1980s) headquarters, probably the brashest and most criticised modern building in London.

The City's attraction as a money market has always been founded on trust and confidence, but the system has occasionally gone out of control and sparked off a series of crises and crashes, from the South Sea Bubble of 1720 onwards. Yet the system has always survived, and it expanded hugely in the nineteenth century, funding new colonial and industrial activity. It has been open to criticism in its fostering of 'gentlemanly capitalism', in which a social elite can manipulate money without first-hand involvement in trade and industry, and the divorce between the City's prosperity and that of the nation as a whole is real enough. To outsiders, what goes on there – especially in the Stock Exchange – is a complete mystery, but it seems to work, for as an engine of wealth-creation its effect on London has been incalculable. The oak-panelled boardrooms of the Edwardian banks and insurance offices have given way to today's City of glass towers and electronics. With its manic architecture and its manic electronic trading, the modern City remains true to its role of farming money – sowing it, cultivating it and harvesting it.

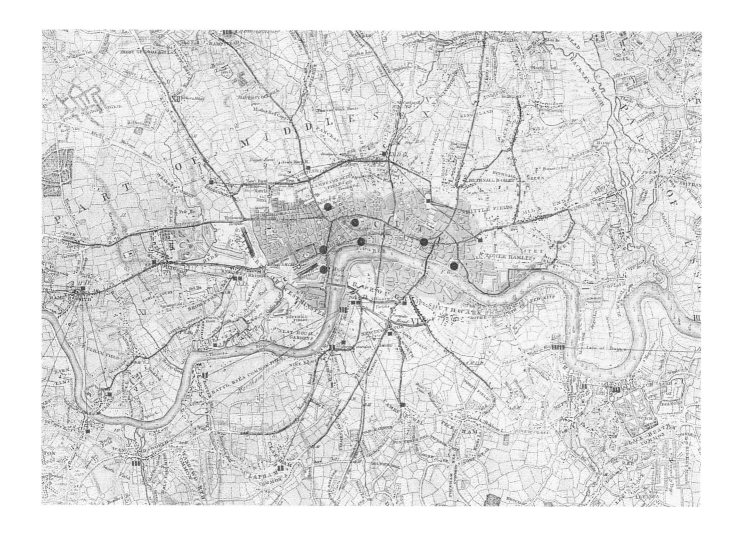

The Gordon Riots

The summer of 1780 witnessed the most violent outbreak of civic disorder in London's entire history - the Gordon Riots. If this episode had occurred after 1789, it would surely have seemed that England was on the verge of a revolution as dramatic as that in France, but, occurring when it did, it remained merely an isolated riot, triggered by one specific cause and having no lasting consequences. The events began as a protest against the government's proposal to repeal some of the anti-Catholic laws which were a legacy of the preceding century. A turbulent young Member of Parliament, Lord George Gordon, assembled a great crowd of some 50,000 supporters at St George's Fields, intending to march to Westminster to protest against the bill. The mob spent the first day surging around Westminster, then ranged further afield and began to burn Catholic chapels. Far from dispersing that night, the mob split into a number of commands, and began to attack wider targets - the private houses of certain government figures, Catholic shops and foreign embassies. Most serious of all, London's prisons were stormed one by one and the prisoners released: Newgate, Bridewell, the Fleet and the King's Bench were opened and burned. Distilleries were looted and the mob became ever wilder. The Bank of England had to be defended by its staff firing from the roof and windows.

After several days of apparent paralysis, the authorities were at last goaded into action: 11,000 troops were brought into London and encamped at St James's Park, Lincoln's Inn Fields and the Tower. They began patrolling the streets and they had orders to shoot the rioters, which they did. After a day facing the armed troops, the mob finally dispersed, leaving several hundred of their number dead, and several hundred more under arrest, of whom twenty-five were later hanged. Gordon was seized and tried for treason, but it was apparent that he had not planned or even foreseen the riot, and he was acquitted.

Historians have never reached a unanimous verdict about the Gordon Riots, about the details of what happened or about their significance. Some accounts give the number of dead - that is the rioters shot by the soldiers - as a little over 200, while others claim almost 1,000. Some have portrayed the rioters as looting and burning everything in sight; this was the picture Dickens drew in *Barnaby Rudge*, a foretaste of his description of the murdering mob in *A Tale of Two Cities*. Others have pointed out that for almost a week London had been at the mercy of the vast mob, yet the targets and the destruction were undoubtedly limited. Did the rioters have genuine radical ideals which they were pursuing? The presence of William Blake among those who stormed Newgate suggests that this was a conscious and symbolic act of liberation. It is certainly striking that in an anti-Catholic riot lasting five days, not a single Catholic was reported to have been killed. But if the targets were carefully chosen, what had the Bank of England or Newgate prison to do with Catholic laws? The questions remain unanswered.

The Gordon riots had surprisingly little permanent impact on London's fabric or on its collective memory. Catholic emancipation was postponed for a generation, but the prisons were quickly rebuilt. Lord George Gordon died in Newgate, sentenced on an entirely unrelated matter, and even St George's Fields where it had all begun was built over with middle-class houses, in one of which, strangely enough, Blake was to live.

Opposite, top: map with contemporary overdrawing to show troop concentrations placed at strategic points during the riots.
B.L. Add. MS 15533, f. 39.

Opposite, bottom: soldiers face the rioters.
B.L. K.Top. 22.9.

Right: Sir George Gordon, famous forever for the riots he caused but never planned.
London, National Portrait Gallery.

The Victorian Metropolis

London ... takes a lot of understanding. It's a great place. Immense. The richest town in the world, the biggest port, the greatest manufacturing town, the Imperial city, the centre of civilisation, the heart of the world. It's a wonderful place ... a whirlpool, a maelstrom! It whirls you up and it whirls you down.

H.G. Wells: *Tono-Bungay*

All contemporary observers, from William Cobbett to William Morris, agreed that there was something awe-inspiring about nineteenth-century London. By any objective measure it was the largest city in the world, unique in its scale, energy and diversity. The history of Victorian London has innumerable facets – social, industrial, architectural, moral, political, artistic, and many more. But, between 1800 and 1900, the central fact about the city was the growing awareness on all sides that it presented a series of urgent challenges, each of which demanded a response if the fabric of society was to hold together. The dramatic growth of the nine-teenth-century city meant that the old-style laissez-faire informality would no longer serve, and London had to be directed, governed and planned in a way that it had never been in the past.

The first and most obvious challenge was the population explosion, and this in a sense underlay all the others. In the year 1800 approximately one million people lived within ten miles of Westminster. By 1881 it was 4.5 million, and by 1911 it would be 7 million. By the end of this period, part of this increase was due to better health and lower mortality rates, but until around 1860, it was still being fuelled by immigration from the English countryside, from Ireland and Scotland, and from continental Europe. London's population was greater than that of Switzerland, or Greece, or Australia. There were more Irish in London than in Dublin, and more Roman Catholics than in Rome. And these statistics are in spite of the high levels of emigration – 250,000 people *left* the capital in the 1870s. The consequences of this surge of population into the city were visible everywhere: overcrowding, squalid housing, relentless competition for work, starvation wages, crime, disease, prostitution, drunkenness and disorder.

The second challenge was a very different one: the pursuit of wealth through new industries, and through an intensified spirit of commercialism. Population growth throughout the nation, and access to markets throughout the world, meant greater commercial opportunities than had ever existed before. It did not matter what your social origins were, wealth was open to anyone with the energy and imagination to become an entrepreneur. 'Free trade' became a secular religion, which,

Nugent's panorama of London and Westminster from Millbank, 1819. This work by a little-known artist is quite different in style and spirit from the elegant architectural views of the 18th century. Here houses, workshops, prisons, palaces and river-craft are all crowded together, under a threatening, smokey sky, to create an almost Blake-like image that seems a prophecy of the dark Victorian metropolis that was then taking shape.
British Museum, Dept of Prints and Drawings.

it was believed, could cure all social ills. But the truth was that this pursuit of wealth depended on the exploitation by the few of huge numbers of others: workers, who, for much of the nineteenth century, were excluded from its benefits. The primacy of commerce was the creed of Thomas Gradgrind, so mercilessly attacked by Dickens in *Hard Times*, while the philosophy derived from the works of Thomas Malthus argued that poverty and hunger were inevitable features of modern society, and could not be alleviated.

The great problem for Victorian London was to reconcile these two facts - unprecedented opportunities for the pursuit of wealth, and a seething, swelling population living in various degrees of poverty. If they could not be reconciled, what were the prospects for social stability, and equally important, what became of the ideal of a Christian society? Movements of social protest in England began with rationalism and radicalism during the 1790s, and progressed to full-blooded socialism or anarchism in 1890s. No less a figure than Karl Marx had analysed these challenges, and had concluded that reconciliation between them was impossible, and that revolution was historically inevitable, and it was from his observation of life in London that he reached this conviction. 'The moment the workers resolve to be bought and sold no longer,' his friend Engels warned grimly, 'at that moment the whole political economy of today is at an end.'

So how was society to ward off this danger? There were two principal lines of defence: private philanthropy, and centrally directed social reform, and the aim of both was to humanise the city, to bring some measure of

order and justice to the maelstrom, and to reconcile its citizens. But there was also room for unplanned, accidental social changes to defuse these tensions and, in London, probably the greatest of these changes was the advent of the railways.

This new pattern of life in London and these new conflicts did not become obvious before the 1840s. They therefore belong firmly in that smoky, angst-ridden complex of streets which we think of as Victorian London. By contrast, the opening decades of the nineteenth century had been hailed as an 'Age of Improvement', and with some justification. Churches, roads, bridges, canals, docks, all were newly built (many using iron and steel for the first time in structural engineering) or improved in the years between 1800 and 1830, while the face of central London was subject to probably the greatest single planned transformation it had ever seen - the Regent's Park-Regent Street-Waterloo Place scheme, masterminded jointly by the Prince Regent and John Nash. The terraces around Regent's Park had a grandeur never before seen in London's domestic architecture - they were like palaces conjured up on the edge of London. The death of the Prince in 1830 (by then King George IV) put an end to this scheme before it was fully realised: it was to have included the great public open space which later became Trafalgar Square, with a wide new road linking it with the British Museum.

This was not the only unrealised vision of a new London, for further new bridges, grand avenues, parks, palaces and embankments were planned by architects such as Soane, Wyatt, Holland and Dance. Enthusiastic amateurs also entered into the spirit of the Age

Above: Cumberland Terrace, Regent's Park, from a panorama showing the entire circuit of the park by Richard Morris, 1831. The buildings surrounding the park were Nash's masterpiece, on which he worked from 1814–28. Prevented from building grand individual houses within the park, Nash turned his genius to the design of sweeping neoclassical terraces of a kind never seen before in London.
B.L. Maps 14.a.29.

of Improvement, most famously Frederick Trench, who in 1824 published a revolutionary plan for a grand new Italianate quayside along the Thames, from Westminster to Blackfriars, lined with classical terraces. It would have shifted the focus of London's traffic from the Strand area down towards the riverside, and, visually irresistible as it was, it brought howls of protest from all those who had trading interests anywhere in the west-central district. Given the controversy and disruption which attended the building of Regent Street, it seems clear that plans like Trench's were always impossible, socially and financially. But they and the beauty of Nash's work inspired the most elegant new residential quarter in London - Belgravia, the final phase of the Grosvenor Estate development. It is an interesting question how far this vogue for architectural display, for beautifying London, arose from a sense of national pride in the post-Napoleonic period, and from a desire to match Napoleon's Parisian monuments. It was as though London needed concrete symbols of a renewed sense of national identity.

Although unrealised and almost utopian-looking, the plans of these years did prepare the way for the new era of public architecture, which saw the building of the National Gallery and the completion of Trafalgar Square, the British Museum, the General Post Office and, of course, the new Parliament building. The last was forced onto the government by the fire of 1834, but it seems likely that it would have happened anyway, given London's mood for urban renewal, and given the spread of the government machine through the imposing edifices that were rising in Whitehall. All these London buildings during the first thirty years of the century had been in the neoclassical style, but Barry's design for the new Parliament was pure Gothic, evidence of the dramatic shift in taste that swept through the capital and the nation. The strange thing

is that the same men who had been building in the classical style now switched to embrace the Gothic, which was now felt to be more earnest, religious and English. The combination of Gothic architecture, gaslight and smoke created the essential Victorian townscape.

But while the architects of the 1820s, 30s and 40s were remodelling the face of London, another revolution was at work changing the very foundations of the city's social life. From its origins in the north of England, railway mania hit London in the 1830s, with the first line being built from London Bridge to Greenwich on the four-mile viaduct which still stands. The journey time was slashed from one hour to ten minutes, and that figure illustrates the impact which the new mode of transport would exert on the pattern of people's lives. It dispersed population, it made distant villages part of London, and soon it created new suburbs. The building of lines which radiated out from the city centre in all directions was immensely destructive of property: thousands of houses were demolished in their path, with no compulsion in the early decades to resettle their inhabitants. This was untrammelled development, as a dozen separate, private companies scrambled for lines and profits. The long-term effects of the railways on London's layout and population emerged slowly. At first, in the 1850s, it was the existing inner villages which were developed: Battersea, Wandsworth and Lewisham in the south, Acton, Holloway, Leyton and Stratford in the north. But in time whole new outer settlements with their endless grids of tranquil streets were called into existence, where before there had been only fields and lanes: Hayes, Ruislip, Finchley, Edmonton, Romford, Beckenham, Morden. What is more, all these places were linked; they were now part of a new ring of nascent communities around London, called suburbia, all made possible only by the railways. So successful were the

Right: 'Improvement' was the great buzz-word in town planning in the Regency period: churches, roads, bridges, docks – all the places where the public gathered, and especially where they did business, should be redesigned on rational lines. All these schemes were private initiatives, but they prepared the way for the public works of the later Victorian era. This scheme for Charing Cross and the Strand dates from 1827.
B.L. Maps Crace XVII/35.

METROPOLIS IMPROVEMENTS

PLAN *of the proposed* CHARING CROSS & STRAND *Improvements*.

PLAN *of the proposed* NEW STREET *from* NEW LONDON BRIDGE *to the* BANK.

railways in dispersing the population, that people began to ask where London would stop. The Commons Preservation Society was formed in the 1860s, just in time to save Epping Forest, Hampstead Heath, Wimbledon Common and many other green spaces from the developer. Nevertheless, by 1900, while politicians, philanthropists, socialists and philosophers had agonised over the problem of London and its teeming population, the railways had spontaneously and miraculously come up with a large part of the answer.

And it was not before time, for the second half of the century had seen a deepening sense of crisis in London, and an awakening social conscience eager for change, for the poverty, disease and crime visible in the streets were felt to be a reproach to a Christian society. The first and most direct response was private philanthropy, led by figures such

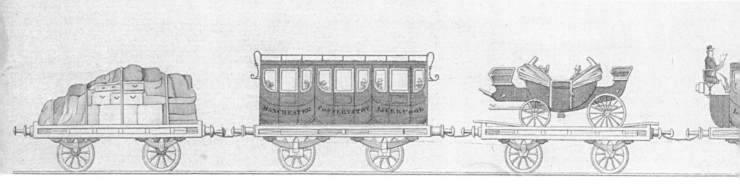

as Lord Shaftesbury, Angela Burdett-Coutts and Thomas Barnardo, who worked for decades, often investing their private fortunes, to improve working conditions, housing, health provision and education. There was also an intellectual response. Benjamin Disraeli had

coined the phrase 'the two nations' to describe the great social divide, and some of the pre-eminent minds of the age joined the debate on what Carlyle called the 'condition of England' problem. Dickens evoked in his fiction the darkness and deprivation which London cast over its poor, while others reported directly on 'the bitter cry of outcast London'. John Ruskin, Thomas Carlyle and William Morris all dreamed of the medieval social ideal, before trade and money became

the new religion. Religious leaders were made to face the uncomfortable fact that, while they had built a network of missions to the heathen in distant lands, there was a 'darkest England' of vice and irreligion on their own doorstep in the very heart of the capital.

Christian charity was one spur, social fear was another, but perhaps the key practical issue was public sanitation, for this brought Londoners, rich and poor alike, face to face with filth and disease. From 1831 onwards, cholera broke out in London, a direct result of the squalid conditions in which many of its people lived. The Thames was an open sewer, yet it was also still the principal source of water for the capital, and over the next twenty years, the 'great stink' rising from the river was sometimes so bad that Parliament would suspend its business – this happened as late as the summer of 1858. Health hazards on this scale were not something that private philanthropy could tackle; science, reform, planning and investment would all be needed – in a nutshell, metropolitan government. This had already been recognised in a limited sense by the formation of the Metropolitan Police in 1829, but in 1850 *The Times* calculated that the administration of the metropolis was still being carried out by no fewer than 300 separate bodies, responsible for roads, water supply, sewers, lighting, open spaces, hospitals, and so on. There was almost complete consensus that this was no way to run the greatest capital city in the world. In 1855 the decisive step was taken of forming the Metropolitan Board of Works, the first body with social responsibility for directing and reshaping the infrastructure of London. A transitional body, to be replaced in 1889 by the London County Council, the MBW began the work of modernising London, in both political and engineering terms. It built new roads, laid out parks and cemeteries, cleared slums and sourced new water supplies. Guided by the social reformer Edwin Chadwick and the engineer Joseph Bazalgette, its greatest achievement was to build a huge new system of sewers which did not enter the Thames until

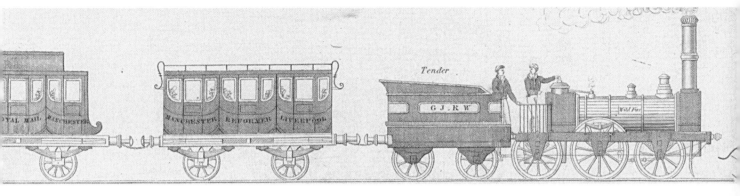

far downstream of the city, at Beckton. Above part of the main sewer in the centre of London rose the magnificent Victoria Embankment, holding back the Thames, easing the traffic congestion, and providing a superb walkway from which to view the now purified

by building schools, to sow the seeds of a better future. But the truth was that the LCC was outdated even when it formed, for London was already greater than the LCC's boundaries, and would grow even bigger.

Nevertheless, the government of London was

Above: the railways which transformed urban life. B.L. Maps Crace XIX/57.

Opposite and right: Gustave Doré bequeathed us the archetypal images of Victorian London, the docks, the slums, the markets and the prisons, where gaunt figures dragged out their lives in a world of permanent shadow. B.L. wfi/1856.

river. The Embankment is one of those London features which feels timeless, as though it must always have existed, yet before 1870 the Thames still lapped at innumerable stairs, wharfs and pilings, and there was no direct riverside road between Westminster and Blackfriars.

The London County Council would enter still more directly into people's lives, tackling the problems of housing by demolishing slums and building its own new homes, and

beginning to mature in a way fitting for a great imperial capital, a role confirmed by the greatest public party London had ever seen - the Great Exhibition of 1851. London had always had a vitally important relationship to the rest of England as its economic motor, but this event celebrated its relationship to the rest of the world, above all, its place as the heart of the empire. The exhibition was in Hyde Park, between Royal Westminster and Royal Kensington, but the power which it

Bird's-Eye View of London and Westminster by Wyllie and Brewer, 1884, taken from a balloon some 1500 feet above Westminster. In some ways complementing the earlier Nugent panorama, the much higher viewpoint here, and the magnificent new Parliament building in the foreground, give this picture a nobility and a breath-taking realism. The Guildhall Library, City of London.

really celebrated lay to the east, in the City. The City too had undergone dramatic social change: it had built new streets to ease the traffic flow, and new railway stations; it had lost much of its resident population to the suburbs, and drastically increased its commercial premises. It was, at this time, still a physical centre of trade, with warehouses and vaults full of tea, ivory, silk, fur, tobacco, bullion, cutlery, leather and a hundred other things. But more important still, it had built up its greatest asset: professional expertise in finance, insurance, services, and deal-making. Backed by the Bank of England, with lines of supply and information throughout the empire, the City was a clearing-house not only for goods, but also for expertise in money, in banking, in insurance, in freight and in investment. It brought together buyers and sellers, borrowers and lenders, entrepreneurs and aristocrats, those with wealth and those wishing to acquire it.

The City, with its banks, offices and railway stations, as well as its Wren churches and its few remaining old merchants' houses, epitomised the forces of commercialism that were now dominating London, dominating its architecture, its social life and its psychology. But it also demonstrated that wealth generated in the City could be used in the cause of progress and social justice. By the end of the century, everything in London had become bigger, more organised, more planned and more professionalised. And it had worked: there had been no revolution; Engels's grim prophecy had failed; London had somehow, and in a tentative way, been civilised; the health plague had been averted and the poverty plague lightened; the principles of a Christian society had been reaffirmed, partly through private charity and partly through political action; and the railways had dispersed the teeming millions. Somehow social reform, money and technology had come together to reconcile London's disparate populations, to achieve a measure of consensus. The great mansions of the West End still existed, the banquets, the carriages in Hyde Park, the theatres, the gentlemen's clubs in Pall Mall, the court presentations, and the House of Lords. But a great lesson had been learned, and, as one member of that august body remarked, when acquiescing in the need to impose death duties on the rich, 'We are all socialists now.'

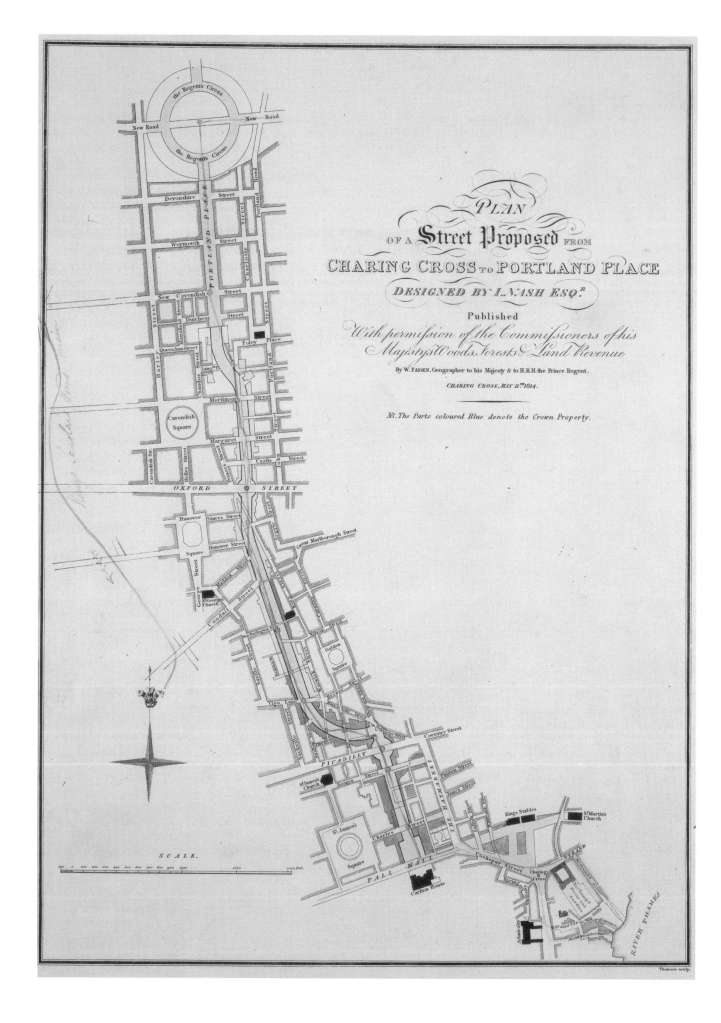

PLAN OF A Street Proposed FROM CHARING CROSS TO PORTLAND PLACE

DESIGNED BY J. NASH ESQ.R

Published With permission of the Commissioners of his Majesty's Woods, Forests & Land Revenue

By W. FADEN, Geographer to his Majesty & to H.R.H. the Prince Regent.

CHARING CROSS, MAY 11TH 1814.

N.B. The Parts coloured Blue denote the Crown Property.

the Regents Circus
the Regents Circus
New Road
New Road
Devonshire Street
PORTLAND PLACE
Portland Road
Weymouth Street
Charlotte Street
New Cavendish Street
Mansfield Street
Dutchess Street
Harley Street
Queen Ann Street
Foley Place
Chandos Street
Lang.th St.
Mortimer Street
Portland Street
CAVENDISH SQUARE
Cavendish Str.
Holles Street
Margaret Street
Princes Street
Castle Street
John Street
OXFORD STREET
Hanover Square
Princes Street
Hanover Street
Argyle Street
Great Marlborough Street
Conduit Street
Maddox Street
George Street
St George's Church
Burlington St.
GOLDEN Square
Savile Row
Coventry Street
PICADILLY
Vigo Lane
Panton Street
THE HAYMARKET
James Street
St James's Church
Jermyn Street
Kings Stables
St Martin's Church
St James's Square
Charles Street
Cockspur Street
STRAND
PALL MALL
Carlton House
Charing Cross
Admiralty
RIVER THAMES

SCALE.

Thomson sculp.

Regency London

London was a city that had never been planned or even replanned. The individual genius of Wren had created great buildings, and the forces of social change had given birth to the West End. But unlike Rome or Paris or Lisbon or St Petersburg, no single ruler or architect had ever stamped his vision upon London. Probably the nearest that London ever came to a grand design arose from the chance association of a spendthrift egoist - the Prince Regent - and an ageing property developer - John Nash. Between them in the early nineteenth century, they sketched out a magnificent new vision of central London, never completed and now partly destroyed, which was unmatched before or since. They epitomised, on the largest possible scale, the vogue for 'Improvement' which occupied the attention of so many landowners, architects, engineers and businessmen of the late Georgian years.

Nash was almost fifty years old before he even met his royal patron, and it is said that the encounter came about when he married one of the prince's former mistresses. Their friendship coincided with the prince's new role as regent, and also with the reversion to

invisible to the others, and set in magnificently landscaped grounds; one of the villas was to be a pleasure pavilion for the prince. This aristocratic garden city was to be linked with the prince's palace of Carlton House, a mile and a half away, by a spacious new avenue - Regent's Street. Perhaps fortunately for posterity, the villas were vetoed by the Crown Commissioners, but the idea of a new park found favour, and Nash quickly turned his designing genius to the park's periphery. Here, a series of classical terraces arose to create a richly various façade of almost theatrical grandeur such as London had never seen before: Cumberland Terrace, Chester Terrace, Sussex Place, Park Crescent - all different from each other but all complementary. The many columns of the classical façades were of cast iron concealed with stucco; indeed Nash was said by his critics to sculpt houses rather than build them.

Regent's Street was intended, from the first, to display shops at ground level, with dwellings above. Its unique feature was to be the colonnade outside the shops, covering the pavements in a way quite new in London. Nash made clear his own ideas about the

Opposite: Nash's plan for Regent Street, 1814. This was to be the heart of the metropolitan improvements which Nash and his royal patron envisaged: a wide elegant street, part residential, part commercial, linking the new Royal Park with the Regent's home, Carlton House. B.L. Maps Crace XII/17.

Right: Cumberland Terrace, perhaps the grandest of the buildings flanking the park. B.L. Maps 563.c.7.

the Crown of a large tract of land in Marylebone, just beyond the West End, formerly leased for farming and now ripe for development. Nash had been occupied in designing neoclassical country houses in partnership with the landscaper, Humphrey Repton. Instead of simply choosing to extend the square grid of streets, Nash's plan was to create a 'Regent's Park' of fifty exquisite villas, each

character of the street and its function in the social map of London. 'It would provide,' he wrote, 'a boundary and complete separation between the streets and squares occupied by the nobility and gentry, and the narrow streets and meaner houses occupied by mechanics and the trading part of the community ... Those who have nothing to do but walk about and amuse themselves, may do so every day

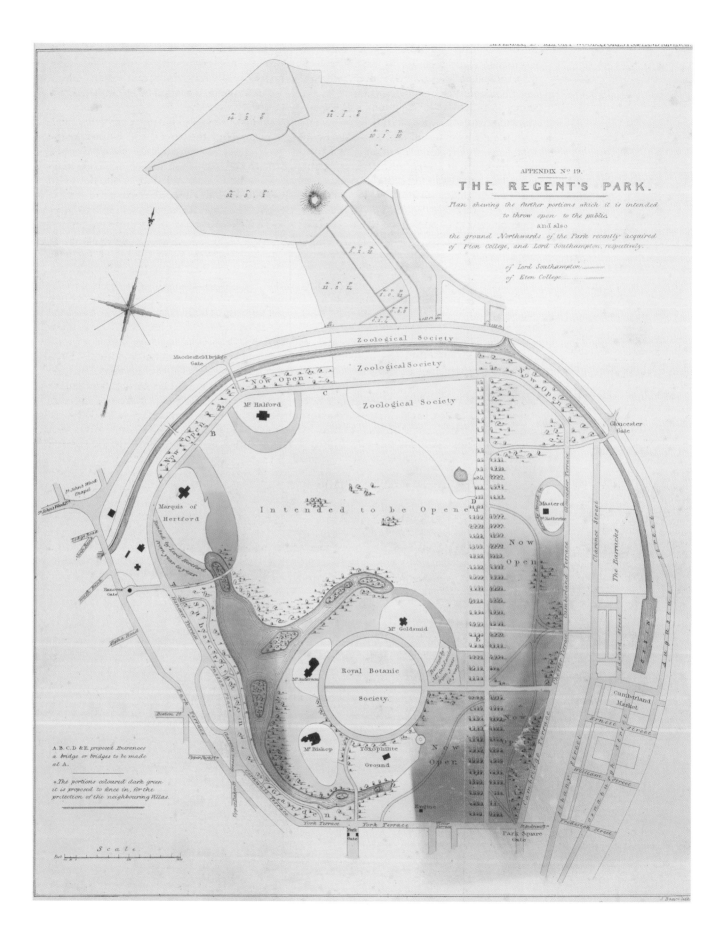

APPENDIX Nº 19.

THE REGENT'S PARK.

Plan shewing the further portions which it is intended
to throw open to the public.
and also
the ground Northwards of the Park recently acquired
of Eton College, and Lord Southampton, respectively.

of Lord Southampton ....
of Eton College ....

Zoological Society

Zoological Society

Now Open

Mr Halford

Zoological Society

Gloucester Gate

Macclesfield bridge Gate

B

C

D

Master of S.ᵗ Katherine

Now Open

St John's Wood Chapel

St John's Wood

Marquis of Hertford

Intended to be Opened

Fenced by Lord Hertford from year to year

Now Open

Clarence Street

The Barracks

Hanover Gate

Alpha Road

Mr Anderson

Mr Goldsmid

E

Leased by Mr Goldsmid for a year, from year to year.

Cumberland Market

Boston St

Upper Ren.ᵗ

Royal Botanic

Society.

Mr Bishop

Toxophilite Ground

Now Open

Now Open

Ernest Street

William Street

Albany Street

Engine

York Terrace

York Terrace

York Gate

Park Square Gate

A. B. C. D & E. *proposed Entrances*
a bridge or bridges to be made
at A.

The portions coloured dark green
it is proposed to fence in, for the
protection of the neighbouring Villas.

Scale.
Feet

J. Bear del.

in the week, instead of being frequently confined many days together to their houses by rain; the balustrades over the colonnades will form balconies to the lodging-rooms over the shops, from which the occupiers can see and converse with those passing in the carriages underneath, which will add to the gaiety of the scene.' These unique colonnades had to be demolished in 1848, for they proved to be, after the shops had closed, a magnet for certain 'ladies of the night'. The design of the street was to include two circuses, at the intersections with Piccadilly and Oxford Street, and its most pleasing visual feature was the westward curve from Piccadilly, known as the Quadrant. The street could not drive directly north from Carlton House without demolishing Golden Square and its surroundings, so it followed the line of what was then Swallow Street.

The building of the street over some six years between 1817 and 1823 was the most radical, extensive and disruptive change so far seen to London's topography. Hundreds of old houses were demolished, businesses were moved, and the conflicts with residents were innumerable. The absolute refusal of Sir James Langham to sell part of his property is responsible for the kink at Langham Place, which Nash took brilliant advantage of by placing there the circular portico of the Church of All Souls, forming a focal point. The combination of a Greek peristyle with a church spire was at first ridiculed by many, but appropriately this is where a portrait bust of Nash was placed, looking south down his new street. Lower Regent Street was always quite different from the rest - residential and institutional; this was where Nash himself took one of the new houses, and where the façade of the Athenaeum, although designed by Decimus Burton, is pure Nash in style.

Rather ironically, having completed both the park and the street, the climax to the grand design was completely changed in the late 1820s, when the prince determined to move to Buckingham Palace and to demolish Carlton House. Therefore, instead of ending at a royal palace, the new street ended simply in a flight of steps, leading down into St James's Park. The building of the Duke of York's column in 1835 placed an effective focal point at this empty spot. The final collaboration between Nash and his royal patron, the renovation of Buckingham Palace, ended with the death of the king and the dismissal of Nash for extravagance. Despite this inglorious end, it is fitting that the most lasting achievement of the prince's reign is without doubt the work of his favourite architect, and the grace and daring which it brought to the face of central London. Nash's influence was central in the wave of neoclassical building in London, before the vogue for Gothic took over. The British Museum entrance was a huger, sterner version of Cumberland Terrace, and it was Nash who proposed a second new street to link the Museum with Charing Cross, which was never built. Nash's use of stucco prepared the way for Cubitt's Belgravia, while the neoclassical style reached into the age of steam when it greeted passengers at Euston Station, the first of London's great termini, built in 1837.

Opposite: the Regent's Park newly landscaped by Nash. The whole Nash project began when this land reverted to the Crown in 1811, having been long-lease farmland for a century and a half. Nash's original plan for luxury villas in the park was vetoed.
B.L. Maps Crace XIV/33.

Below: Waterloo Place, the southern end of Regent Street, as it was to appear from Carlton House. George IV changed the whole plan by re-building Buckingham Palace and demolishing Carlton House.
B.L. Maps K.Top. 22.26.1.

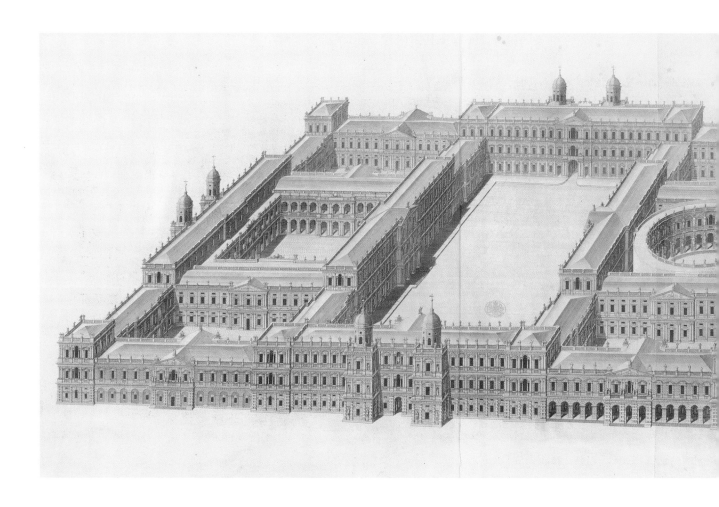

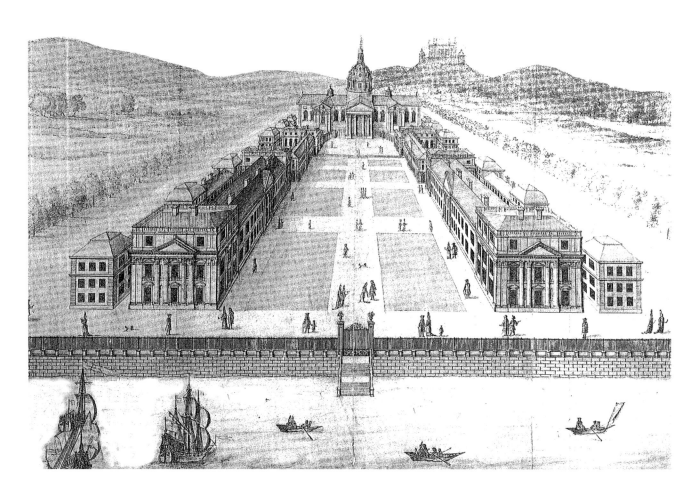

Unbuilt London

Wren's post-Fire plan for the new city is the most famous and dramatic vision of a London that was never built, but there were many others. So many streets, bridges, squares, public buildings and private palaces which now seem so essentially a part of London's heritage could easily have looked completely different had their architects and patrons had different ideas or, in some cases, more money. It is worth remembering that Wren, England's

have imagined that a destructive fire had once again presented him with an magnificent architectural opportunity, and he revived the Inigo Jones concept of a grand palace reaching westwards from the river into St James's Park. But William and Mary had lost interest in Whitehall, preferring to live at Kensington Palace and Hampton Court. Dreams of new royal palaces did not vanish at the Glorious Revolution, however, for James Stuart,

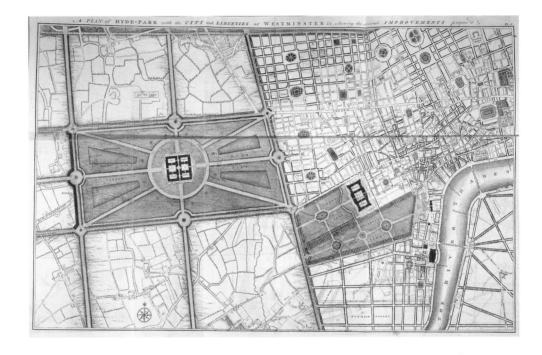

Above: Inigo Jones's plan for a vast new Whitehall Palace for Charles I; we are looking at the north wing, which would have faced Trafalgar Square. B.L. K.Top. 26.5.BB.

Left: Wren's first plan for Greenwich hospital, rejected by Queen Mary because it would have destroyed her view of the river from the Queen's House. Private collection.

Right: John Gwynn's 1766 plan for a new royal palace bang in the centre of Hyde Park. B.L. Maps 191.1.19.

supreme architect and the presiding genius of post-Fire London, suffered the rejection of some of his grandest schemes. His first plan for Greenwich Hospital included a central chapel that was tall, broad and capped with a large dome. This would have completely blocked the view down to the river from the Queen's House to the south, and it was summarily dismissed by Queen Mary, forcing Wren to come up with the new design of the double-winged building which we now see.

But Wren was not the first royal architect who failed to see his plans realised. When Charles I asked Inigo Jones to redesign Whitehall Palace in the 1630s, he was rewarded with a gigantic multi-winged vision of halls, colonnades and courtyards in a vast rectangle, far greater than EL Escorial, built for Philip II of Spain. Jones's plan would have covered some ten acres of land, planted squarely across Whitehall, and St James's Park would have become its back garden. The Civil War killed this scheme, and the Banqueting House was the only section completed. When Whitehall Palace was burned down in 1698, Wren must

the Old Pretender, apparently whiled away his exile in Italy with schemes for new palaces in St James's Park, which he hoped one day to inhabit. A notable feature of his plan was to be a deep lake fed from the Thames, so that the monarch could sail directly from his palace to the continent; perhaps he liked the idea of an instant escape-route if things went badly.

The development of the royal parks and palaces in the eighteenth century was rather piecemeal and haphazard, and this age of order and elegance produced many critics who regretted that London was not subject to a more systematic designing genius. One of the many who published his ideas on this subject was John Gwynn, a theorist rather than a practising architect, although he designed Oxford's Magdalen Bridge. In 1766 Gwynn proposed new grids of elegant right-angled streets for Westminster and the City, and quays along both banks of the Thames. But most radical of all, he advocated the demolition of Kensington and Buckingham Palaces, to be replaced by two new royal residences,

Top: George Dance's 1800 plan for a magnificent new double London Bridge terminating in Italianate piazzas. Guildhall Library, City of London.

Above: an unsuccessful plan for the British Museum by Cornelius Johnston in the French rococo style; imagine this in the middle of Bloomsbury. B.L. K.Top. 22.17.a.

Opposite: Spurrier and Phipps's plan for a great Bath-inspired circus in St John's Wood, 1794. B.L. Maps Crace XIV/37.

one on the north side of Green Park, and the other much grander one plumb in the centre of Hyde Park. To be built on a raised terrace, at the centre of radiating avenues, this English Versailles would enjoy an uninterrupted view down to the river – what Gwynn called 'the finest scene in the universe'. Presumably Gwynn hoped for royal patronage for this scheme, but none was forthcoming. This was certainly not the end of the Palace-in-the-Park idea, for the Regency years and then the accession of George IV prompted more heady plans to tempt the extravagant monarch. Between 1820 and 1824, John Soane revised and

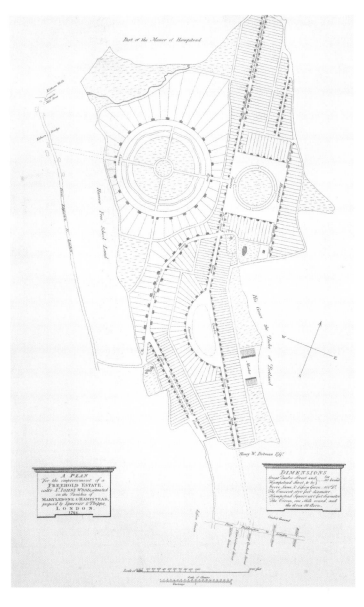

polished his dream of a vast neo-Roman pile in Green Park: three massive wings around a grand central courtyard, entered by a triumphal

arch rather similar to the one later designed by Burton and built on Constitution Hill. Soane's design would have been wildly expensive, and it lost out to Nash's plan for a rebuilt Buckingham Palace. Soane also conceived one of several plans for new bridges, which should be far more than functional river-crossings. His design for a triumphal bridge at Lambeth was almost 100 feet across, with a central dome and colonnaded parapets, and it would have formed a magnificent distant feature in the view from his palace. New bridges over the Thames were favourite projects among architects in the Age of Improvement, none more spectacular than Charles Dance's double London Bridge plan of 1800; the attendant rebuilding on the riverside would have made the Thames area and the Southwark bank resemble Rome.

However, it was not only grand and royal buildings which formed the substance of such plans. The growth of the West End also inspired many designs for residential developments that would have been elegant and imaginative, and which would certainly now form a valued part of London's heritage – if they had ever been built. In 1794, the auctioneers Spurrier and Phipps produced a scheme to build on land in St John's Wood, bordering the Portland Estate. The variety contained in this tentative plan was outstanding, for this was no simple grid of streets, but a new square, a crescent and a magnificent grand circus, obviously inspired by the one in Bath. The architectural unit of this plan was the semi-detached town-house, with long rear gardens, and, in the circus, facing a central landscaped green. This may have been the first time that the idea of the semi-detached house appeared in England. The circus never materialised (except in the name Circus Road), but the large semis did, and are still to be seen gracing the streets of St John's Wood.

It was in the nineteenth century, as the battle of architectural styles and of social ideals really gathered pace, that many more radical and visionary schemes were conceived. National monuments, national cemeteries, opera houses, grand boulevards, triumphal arches, government buildings and riverside walks all figured in the dreams for a London that was never built. Not only architects but also enthusiastic amateurs entered the fray, the most famous being Colonel Frederick Trench, who designed a vast Thames-side terrace extending from Scotland Yard to Blackfriars, which would have utterly transformed the whole riverside and anticipated the building of the Victoria Embankment – if it had ever materialised.

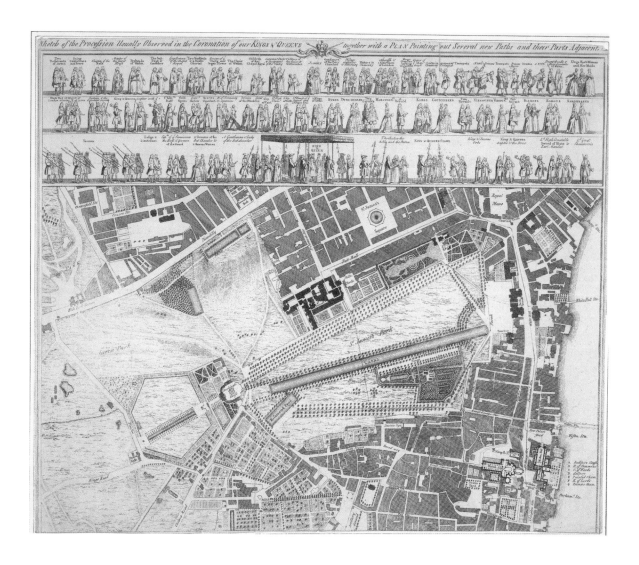

Sketch of the Procession Usually Observed in the Coronation of our KINGS & QUEENS together with a PLAN Pointing out Several new Paths and their Parts Adjacent.

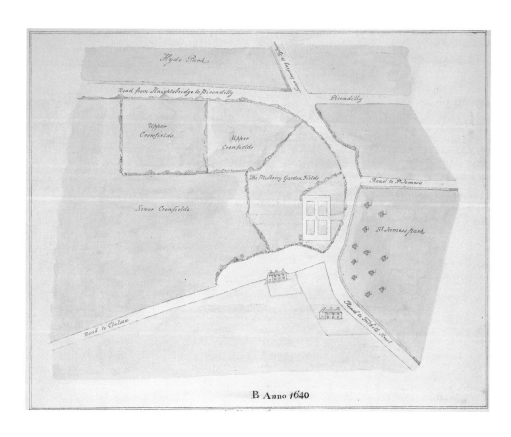

B Anno 1640

Buckingham Palace

Around the year 1615, James I sponsored a plan to introduce the production of silk into England, and for this purpose he created an enclosed garden on royal land west of St James's Park, which was planted with thousands of mulberry trees, on whose leaves the silk-worms feed. 'The Mulberry Garden', as it was long known, was the first identification of the site on which Buckingham Palace would be built. Decades after the experiment had failed, the land was leased by John Sheffield, Duke of Buckingham, and here between 1702 and 1705 he had a fine house built, which a contemporary described as 'One of the great beauties of London, both by reason of its situation and its building ... at the west end of St James's Park, fronting the Mall and the great walk, and behind it is a fine garden from whence, as well as from the apartments, you have a most delicious prospect.' This was the house which was bought by George III in 1762 for £28,000, intended to be a private family home. Here the king built up the rich collection of books which was given to the British Museum after his death; here he entertained Dr Johnson in the library; and here he descended into madness.

When George IV came to the throne in 1820, it was the splendour of its location which determined him to transform Buckingham House into a palace. This meant abandoning Carlton House, on which he had lavished huge sums of money for thirty years, perhaps attempting to make it his own Versailles. Nevertheless, it was demolished, although some of its features such as doors and fireplaces were conveyed to Buckingham House. The government of Lord Liverpool reluctantly agreed to an expenditure of £200,000 on the new palace, and to the king's nomination of John Nash as the architect. Thus began a saga of extravagance, conflict and repeated replanning, which would last almost thirty years and cost, in the end, more than £700,000. The king's death in 1830 left Nash in the role of scapegoat for the whole sorry affair, and this controversy spelt the end of his career. Many years later Buckingham House was finally completed by another architect, Edward Blore, who added the east front facing the Mall, for the original design had been for a three-sided structure with an open courtyard to the east; the Marble Arch was designed to be a grand entrance to this courtyard. Neither George IV nor his brother William IV ever lived in the palace. When the work was completed in the late 1840s, it was Queen Victoria who settled there and gave it its identity - as the headquarters for what would become the House of Windsor.

Between the years 1600 and 1800, England's royals had occupied a bewildering number of London palaces: Whitehall, St James's, Kensington, Hampton Court, Greenwich, Carlton House - all these in turn were burnt down, disliked, outgrown, or became places to escape from, because of family conflict. Yet the royals remained anchored in London: they never emulated their continental cousins and moved permanently to Versailles-like dream-palaces. With the passage of time, the isolated site of the Mulberry Garden finds itself now at the heart of London and the focus of non-stop public attention.

Opposite, top: Buckingham Palace as the apex of royal and ceremonial London: a plan decorated with the order of precedence at coronations, published for that of George III in 1761. B.L. Maps Crace XI/39a.

Opposite, bottom: the original site of Buckingham Palace in 1640 when it was merely a mulberry garden. B.L. Maps Crace X/31.

Right: Buckingham House as it was was when George III bought it in 1762. B.L. Maps K.Top. XXVI.3.a.

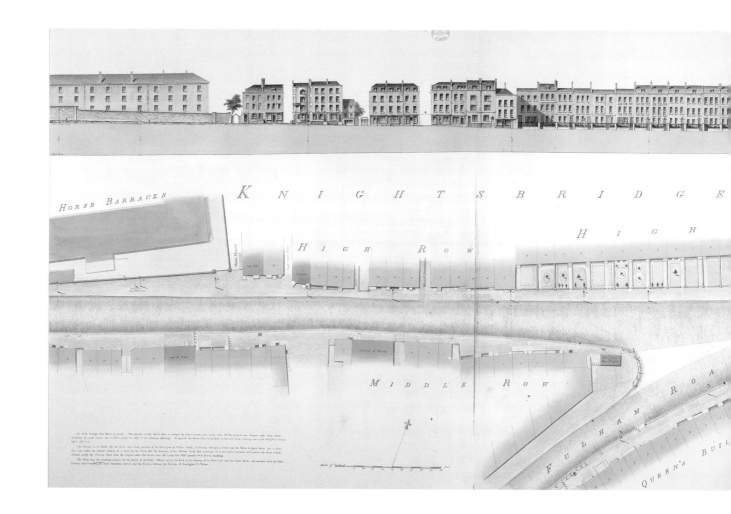

Top and above: part of the extraordinarily detailed plans of Knightsbridge and Kensington made in 1819 by James Salwey for the Kensington Turnpike Trust. Each section of the plan was complemented by frontal elevations of the buildings. B.L. Add. MS 31325/3.

Kensington Turnpike

Road-making had been a forgotten art in London for centuries, during which almost all travel had been on foot or horseback. The advent of wheeled carriages in the seventeenth century revealed how awful the roads in and around the capital had become – mired in deep mud in winter, rutted and uneven in summer. The favoured solution was to license private investors – the turnpike trusts – to rebuild roads and to charge tolls for their use. These trusts had to be authorised by Acts of Parliament and the earliest on record was in 1663; by 1750 the number of such trusts was more than 1,000. Half a dozen important turnpike roads stood at the entrance to London: the Elephant and Castle, Mile End, Islington, Tottenham Court Road, Tyburn, Hyde Park Corner and so on. With charges of a shilling for each carriage and four or five pence for a horseman, the turnpikes became extremely lucrative, and when they were sold they could change hands for thousands of pounds. They were also notoriously corrupt, with the tolls often going into the pockets of the owners and the gate-keepers, rather than on improving the roads. The turnpikes themselves were rowdy places, the scenes of almost daily quarrels and assaults, and the gate-keepers had to be a pretty tough breed. Nevertheless, those around London were very important in improving access to and from the surrounding countryside, both for private travellers and for the transport of goods. They were also influential in encouraging the development of suburban villages, such as Kensington.

further such building. The seal was set on Kensington's desirable status by the decision of King William and Queen Mary to buy Nottingham House in 1689, and convert it into Kensington Palace. Kensington Square was built at the same time to accommodate courtiers. The availability of many large houses and Kensington's reputation for healthy air made the district a centre for private schools and academies, a tradition which still continues. By the end of the eighteenth century, Kensington High Street was lined with houses interspersed with shops, as far west as Edwardes Square. The central area always remained highly desirable, attracting as many artists and writers as Chelsea. It was in John Stuart Mill's house in Kensington Square that a housemaid lit the fire with the manuscript of Carlyle's *French Revolution*, and Vaughan Williams came there to study music at the house of Charles Parry. Melbury Road off the High Street was long known as an artist's colony, with Holman Hunt, Lord Leighton, G.F. Watts and many others among its residents.

The estates north of Holland Park were developed from the 1840s onwards, and they replaced some notorious slums, known, for obvious reasons, as the Piggeries and the Potteries. The centre of Ladbroke Grove around Lansdowne Terrace was, and still remains, very elegant in plan, but many surrounding streets to the north and east struggled to maintain their original character. South Kensington was transformed in the aftermath of the Great Exhibition by the development of Museumland, the largest ensemble of public

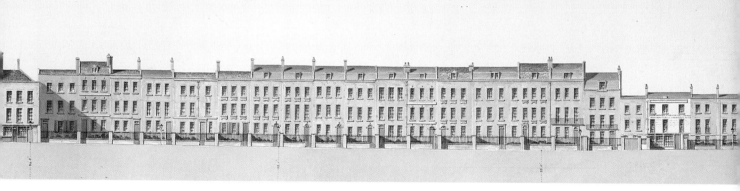

The property of the de Vere family - Earls of Oxford, whose home is recalled in the name Earl's Court - Kensington was always protected from London's encroachment by the presence of the royal parks. In the seventeenth century it was already the home to several aristocratic mansions, such as Holland House and Campden House, and these attracted

buildings ever seen in London. The great shops of the High Street and the Brompton Road added a new focus to this most desirable of inner suburbs, already favoured with parks, museums and some of the most attractive streets in London.

The Kensington turnpike, along with the others in London, was abolished in the 1860s.

MAP
of part of the
RIVER THAMES.
Shewing a general Idea of the Improvements
proposed in the Channel, as far as this Map reaches;
with Three different Modes of making
WET DOCKS,
by cutting off Branches of the River, and
making a NEW CHANNEL, as proposed
By W.ʳ REVELEY.

submitted to Parliament in 1796 and declared
novel, grand and captivating
but Rejected.

Right: the most radical of all the dock plans: Reveley's 1796 proposal to straighten the river and use the resulting creeks as docks. Private collection.

Below: looking west across the West India Docks shortly after their construction in 1802. B.L. K.Top. 21.31.6.

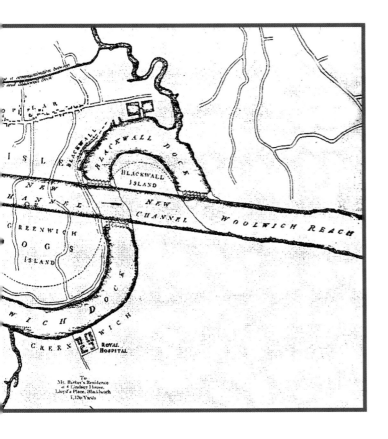

London's Docks

In the years 1800 to 1830, far removed from the grand architectural designs of Nash's royal London, the map of the city was being redrawn by very different forces. London's docks were a visible sign of the industrial and commercial revolutions which were shaping the nineteenth-century world. The Thames had long been the highway through which raw materials and luxury goods had arrived in London from the rest of Britain, from Europe and the wider world. Coal, timber, grain, hay, sugar, tea, tobacco, hides, wines, and a thousand other cargoes filled the ships which crowded into the river. In 1727, Defoe claimed that two thousand ships, large and small, were to be seen every day on the Thames, between Deptford and London Bridge - so many that the river itself was virtually invisible. Most of these would anchor in the Pool, the deep water down river of the bridge, where their cargoes would be taken off by lighters to the quays. This system was plagued by delays, the river was gridlocked much of the time, and the opportunities for theft were gigantic - pilfering from ships was probably the greatest single occupation of the riverside population. In 1796, a Parliamentary commission reported on the appalling congestion on London's river and, as a result, a number of ambitious plans were put forward for new docks to be excavated where ships could moor, and free up the river itself.

The new docks were built piecemeal by private companies over the next thirty years. The first was the West India Docks, opened in 1802, cutting across the narrow neck of the Isle of Dogs, with import and export quays, both entered through basins where the ships would await the opening of the entry locks. There was also an unrealised plan to dig a great cut through Limehouse and Wapping which would link these docks directly to the Pool. The West India Docks were highly successful, for ships could unload and leave in a couple of days, instead of being confined to the Pool for weeks, while their goods were stored in vast, secure warehouses. To protect the docks from theft, they were surrounded by fortress-like walls thirty feet high, and patrolled by their own guards.

Other docks followed. The London Docks in Wapping, opened in 1805, boasted vast underground wine vaults. The East India Docks, in 1806, were on the old Blackwall site and were entirely in the hands of the East India Company; here the great sailing ships, and the China tea clippers such as the *Cutty Sark* would dock. The East and West India merchant companies, between them, built a broad new road - the Commercial Road - linking these docks with the City. The only

docks south of the Thames were the Surrey Docks, opened in 1807, which were built around the old Howland Dock and specialised in imports of timber. St Katherine's Dock, opened in 1828, was the nearest to the City, lying almost in the shadow of the Tower, and it concluded the first phase of London's dock building. After the middle of the nineteenth century, the Royal Victoria (1855), the Millwall (1868) and the Royal Albert (1880) would follow. The Royal group, lying furthest east, were designed on a grand scale, to receive the largest ocean-going vessels, and the Royal Victoria was the first dock to be served by rail. Millwall Dock occupied a large area in the centre of the Isle of Dogs, south of the West India Dock. The last of the Royal group, the King George V Dock, was begun in 1912, but delayed by the Great War and not opened until 1921.

Most of these docks were sited on virgin land, rough pasture or marsh; the exception being St Katherine's, for which some three thousand mean houses were demolished and the occupants made homeless with no compensation. The architecture of the docks and warehouses had a monumental scale and quality: they were functional counterparts of the classical or Gothic edifices arising in the City and the West End. Just as the banks, the museums, and the mansions of the rich housed the wealth and plunder of the empire, so the warehouses of the docklands were crammed full of raw materials and artefacts drawn from around the world. The docks transformed the map of London, and they reinforced the historic character of the East End as the place of labour, employing tens of thousands of working men, and stimulating the siting of industries along the riverside which depended on raw materials, such as rubber, chemicals and sugar, and which demanded huge supplies of coal and later of oil. The docks also called into being the mean terraced streets of Bermondsey, Poplar, Millwall, Canning Town, East Ham and Woolwich, where the dockers lived, as well as the pubs, the shops and markets and the sports fields where they spent their money and their leisure. For well over a century these docks would be central to the wealth of the nation and to the life of the East End, until they were made obsolete by technological and social change.

The emerging dock system from Cruchley's map of 1829, published 1847. The Surrey Docks are being planned, but not yet the Millwall. The Royals are many years in the future. B.L. Maps Crace VII/253.

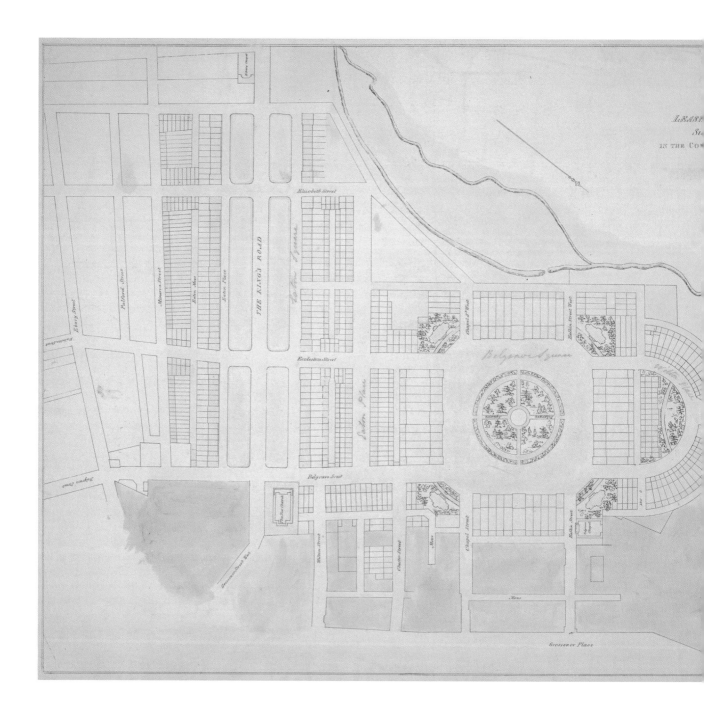

Above: Belgrave Square, final phase of the development of the Grosvenor lands, whose western boundary was the Westbourne stream, still clearly visible here; south-west is at the top of the map.
B.L. Maps Crace X/25.

Right: Basevi's eastern terrace.
B.L. Maps 563.c.7.

Opposite: Thomas Cubitt, house-builder extraordinary to 19th-century London.
London, National Portrait Gallery.

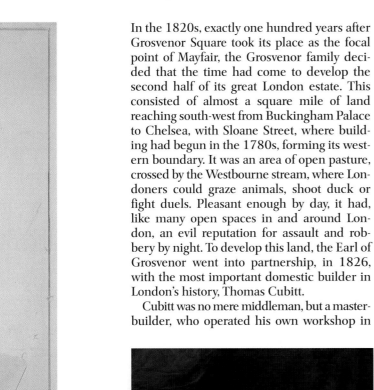

Belgravia

In the 1820s, exactly one hundred years after Grosvenor Square took its place as the focal point of Mayfair, the Grosvenor family decided that the time had come to develop the second half of its great London estate. This consisted of almost a square mile of land reaching south-west from Buckingham Palace to Chelsea, with Sloane Street, where building had begun in the 1780s, forming its western boundary. It was an area of open pasture, crossed by the Westbourne stream, where Londoners could graze animals, shoot duck or fight duels. Pleasant enough by day, it had, like many open spaces in and around London, an evil reputation for assault and robbery by night. To develop this land, the Earl of Grosvenor went into partnership, in 1826, with the most important domestic builder in London's history, Thomas Cubitt.

Cubitt was no mere middleman, but a master-builder, who operated his own workshop in

Gray's Inn Road, where almost 1,000 men were employed in preparing all the materials for his new houses: stonework, metalwork, woodwork, doors, windows, garden and street furniture, pipes and sewers. Cubitt could almost be said to have mass-produced houses, almost a century before Henry Ford mass-produced cars. He had already built houses in Stoke Newington and Highbury, and was an important figure in developing the Bedford estate in Bloomsbury. He was not an architect, but an imaginative entrepreneur who understood the forces that were at work in London's social development, and he was prepared to gamble on his instincts. Sometimes he lost, as he did

in Bloomsbury, which stubbornly refused to attract fashionable residents. 'Everybody is running away to the west,' he lamented, 'and though my houses may be classed with the best, yet I cannot get rid of them.' But where he lost in Bloomsbury, he gained handsomely in Belgravia.

He commissioned the architect George Basevi (designer of Cambridge's Fitzwilliam Museum) to create a series of Nash-inspired terraces, four storeys high, pedimented, faced with white stucco, their doorways graced with bold Grecian columns and their high windows crowned with ornate mouldings. Between 1826 and 1840, Belgrave Square was laid out as the centrepiece of the development and named after one of the Grosvenors' estates in Leicestershire, while the huge rectangle of Eaton Square was completed soon afterwards. In the early days, bars restricted traffic access and kept intruders out. Pimlico, a stone's throw further south, was also Cubitt's work, but was deliberately less grand in scale and aimed at a different clientele. The land was slightly damp and marshy, and was raised and reinforced with thousands of tons of spoil from the excavation of St Katherine's Dock, carried up-river in barges.

Belgravia was a social and financial success from the first, while the fashion for white Italianate stucco spread through Kensington, Bayswater, Paddington and Notting Hill. It became the trademark façade for the embassies and professional institutions which later came to occupy these houses.

The building of Belgravia completed the West End. Other districts further west and north would become fashionable in their own way, but Mayfair, St James's and Belgravia retained their elite status. From the architectural point of view, Belgravia was not without its detractors. Stereotyped, vulgar, wedding-cake - these were some of the criticisms levelled at the Belgrave style. Perhaps its appeal was that it was both opulent and banal at the same time. It signalled the arrival of the West End house as an instant status-symbol available to anyone prepared to pay for it. Cubitt created the houses, but London created their residents - an endless stream of bankers, industrialists, ship-owners, colonial investors and entrepreneurs, whose numbers seemed always to expand to fill all the available houses which Cubitt could build. The city's growth had acquired a momentum that had apparently become unstoppable. When he died in 1855, Cubitt was a millionaire, and he had placed his own special mark upon the face of London, perhaps in a humbler way than Nash, but just as unmistakably.

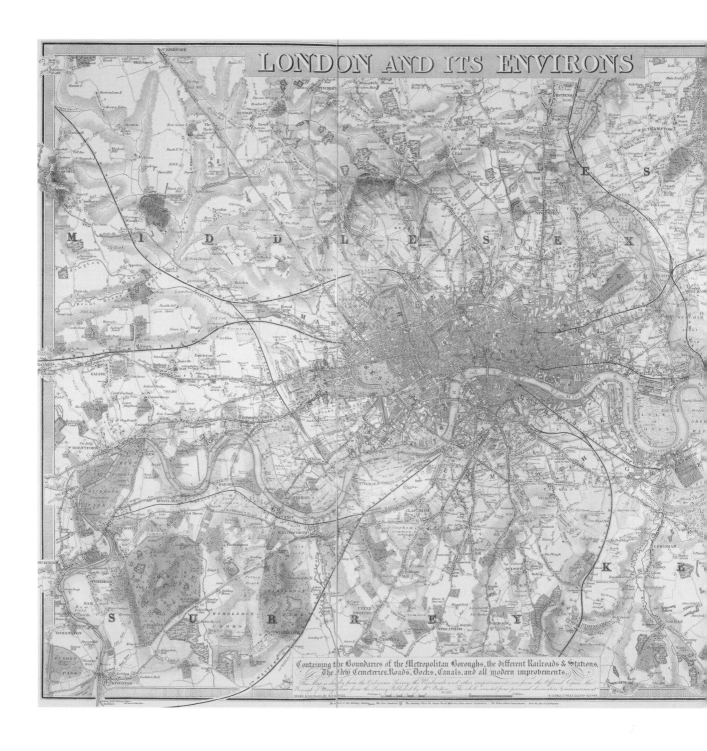

LONDON AND ITS ENVIRONS

Containing the Boundaries of the Metropolitan Boroughs, the different Railroads & Stations,
The New Cemeteries, Roads, Docks, Canals, and all modern improvements.

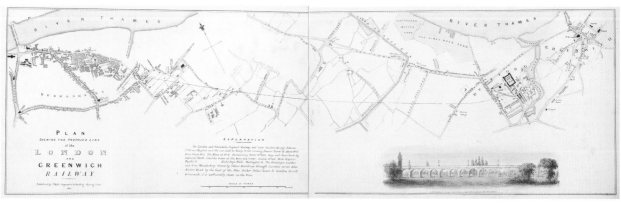

PLAN
SHEWING THE PROPOSED LINE
of the
LONDON
AND
GREENWICH
RAILWAY

The Railway Age

Thirty years after the first docks were built, a second transport revolution began which changed both the map of London and its social life forever. Pioneered first in the north of England, the railways hit London in the mid-1830s, with the first line running from London Bridge to Greenwich, and built upon a viaduct raised above the rooftops. It reduced the travelling time from an hour to ten minutes, and before long it was attracting some 5,000 passengers a day. The first great inter-city terminus, Euston Station, was opened in 1838, linking London to Birmingham. Waterloo, the terminus for Southampton, followed ten years later. For two decades railway mania gripped London, as dozens of separate companies with privately subscribed capital furiously scored their black lines across the map of the city to the north, east, south and west, desperate to embrace the railway age and the dizzying profits which it promised, but little realising the long-term impact of their schemes. The City itself and the West End resisted the railway invasion, and this, combined with the fact that separate companies operated the various lines, produced the ring of mainline termini around central London. These were not linked in any way, and created a huge increase in road traffic between them, much to the delight of the cab trade. Other cities in Europe would choose instead the *Hauptbahnhof* idea, with inner-city rail or tram lines to disperse passengers from the point of arrival. The main termini all generated their ring of hotels, some grand but many squalid. These great stations with their imposing architecture became, for Londoners, gateways to the rest of England; as E.M. Forster later wrote, Cornwall and the West Country seemed to be latent in Paddington, the Fenlands and East Anglia in Liverpool Street, Scotland in Euston, and the South Coast in Waterloo.

These initial years of railway development were unrestrained by any rules. The companies had to have their route-plans approved by Parliament, and thereafter they had the power to pull down anything in their paths, without compensation and without relocating householders. Thousands of people were evicted from their homes, and forced into still more overcrowded tenements. Just two miles of line built in 1866, between Finsbury and Kingsland, required the destruction of almost one thousand homes. Contemporaries were not blind to this destruction of London's fabric, and many disapproved. In 1845, *Punch* pub-

lished a satirical plan for a 'Grand Railway from England to China', with its terminus on the site of the demolished St Paul's Cathedral. In areas where many lines converged, such as Clapham, Willesden or St Pancras, huge acreages disappeared under junctions and marshalling yards. Viaducts and tunnels were built to cross steep contour lines, bridges to cross roads and rivers. Never had such a swift and visible change been imposed on the face of London. It was destructive, alarming and exciting all at once, an unmistakable icon in the religion of progress. 'We who lived before the railways,' wrote Thackeray in the mid 1840s, 'and survive out of the ancient world, are like Father Noah and his family out of the Ark.' Nor was this destruction of bricks and mortar only: fatal accidents occurred from the outset, to both builders and passengers, so that *Punch* again commented, 'A railway is long but life is short, and generally the longer the railway, the shorter your life.'

But if the railways brought change and destruction to London, they also brought a new form of life, later to be called suburbia. Initially, the railways were conceived as relatively long-distance transport, linking London with Birmingham, Southampton, Bristol, Edinburgh and so on. The early planners seem not to have anticipated local passenger traffic, so that in 1850 on the Birmingham line, the first stop was at Harrow, eleven miles from Euston. Only in the 1860s did the railway companies awaken to the fact that intermediate stations could be built on the same lines, and served by local trains. The growth of City finance, of industry and the docks had created thousands of new jobs, while the destruction of houses during the building of the railways had actually moved potential workers away. This problem was addressed by the 1864 Cheap Trains Act, requiring the railways to offer cheap working-men's fares in and out of central London. This second phase of railway history gave rise to an unprecedented growth of suburbs, both the meaner working-class districts like Leyton, Tottenham and Willesden, with their endless brick terraces, and later the wealthier garden suburbs like Barnet, Bromley and Harrow, none of which could have flourished without their rail links to central London. The vast man-made lakes of docklands had transformed the map of London, but the thin black lines of the railways had a still more profound and all-pervasive influence on its social life.

Above: Davis's map of London, 1832, witness to a transport revolution, with the main lines snaking into the capital from all directions. Except at London Bridge, they halt at the edge of the central area, at the points where the great terminal stations will soon be built.
B.L. Maps Crace VII/248.

Left: London's first railway, from London Bridge to Greenwich, carried on the viaduct which still stands.
B.L. Maps Crace XIX/56.

PLAN
OF THE
PARISH OF PADDINGTON.
IN
THE COUNTY OF
MIDDLESEX.

SURVEYED BY
GEORGE OAKLEY LUCAS
1842.

Paddington: A Canal, a Railway, a Miniature Venice and a Teddy Bear

The district north of Hyde Park - originally known as Tyburnia - formed an estate in the possession of the Bishops of London. Purely agricultural land until 1800, it then became part of the extended West End, as the streets between Connaught Square and Cleveland Square were laid out. The shifting of the raucous and brutal place of execution from Tyburn to Newgate, in 1783, may have provided the spur for this spate of new building. The new district soon acquired one unique feature when it became the terminus for the great new canal which linked London with Birmingham.

Immediately before the advent of the railway age, there came a few decades in which the transport of the future seemed to be the canal. By 1805, one of the most impressive of

all the long-distance waterways, the 100-mile Grand Junction Canal, had been completed and terminated at Paddington. To continue on directly to the Thames, digging through the West End would have been socially impossible and commercially pointless. Instead, it was decided to excavate a great arc to the east, taking in London's commercial districts, and entering the Thames at Limehouse. Ten years' work followed, involving the cut itself, tunnels, locks and innumerable bridges, until the Regent's Canal was finally completed in 1820. Two decades of full use and prosperity lay ahead, before this canal, like all the others in England, was overtaken by the railway revolution and it became literally and metaphorically a backwater. It was worth no one's while to fill in the canal again, so it survived to carry generations of pleasure traffic.

The original Great Western Station at Paddington was built in 1838, but was replaced by Brunel's great new edifice in 1854.

An accidental legacy of the canal was one of London's unexpected beauty spots. Both Byron and Browning compared the waterway beside Warwick Crescent to a little Venice, and the name has stuck. Only a few yards away, however, in Paddington Basin, it was certainly no beauty spot, as tons of London's rubbish were brought to the canal each day for loading into barges to be dumped in the Kent and Essex marshes. However, Little Venice itself, just to the north, attracted many artists and writers, like a miniature Chelsea, and Compton Mackenzie placed the denouement of his great novel of Edwardian London, *Sinister Street*, in a fantastic imaginary mansion islanded in the lake.

Paddington itself was always difficult to classify. Elegant and desirable mansions overlooked the park, and it has always been attractive to horse-riders, yet a few streets away the houses were subdivided and colonised first by the canal men and then by railway workers. Waves of immigrants - French, Jewish, Greek, Arab and West Indian - have made the area highly cosmopolitan. By the 1950s, it had become a byword for slum properties, rack-renting and vice, made all the more scandalous because most of the land was owned ultimately by the Church Commissioners. Sliced through by the canal, the railways and the Edgware Road, it was not exactly the West End, and it lacked any clear focus, except perhaps Whiteley's great department store, the mecca of West End shoppers for fifty years or more. At its height, Whiteleys employed 6,000 staff, and styled itself 'the Universal Provider', offering to supply anything from a pin to an elephant. William Whiteley himself was shot dead in his office in 1907 by a man claiming to be his illegitimate son. Social change in the Paddington district caused the closure of the store in 1981. Perhaps all the district's older inhabitants - the Bishops of London, Byron, Browning, Compton Mackenzie, William Whiteley and Peter Rachman - would have been astonished to know that its name would acquire a completely new meaning for generations of children, thanks to a bear named Paddington.

Opposite: the parish of Paddington, developed in the 1820s on lands belonging to the Bishop of London. B.L. Maps Crace XIV/2.

Above: Little Venice, unique London beauty-spot on the Grand Junction Canal. Private collection.

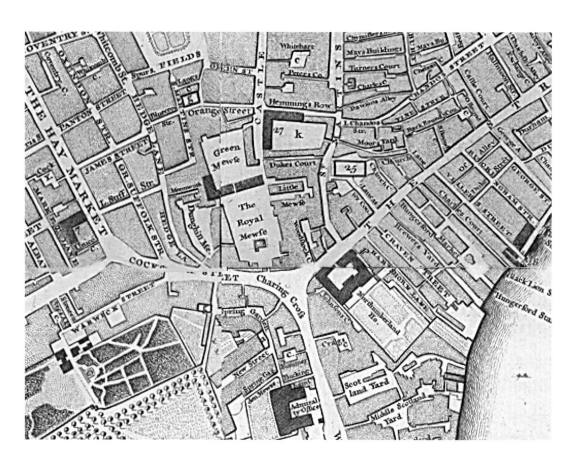

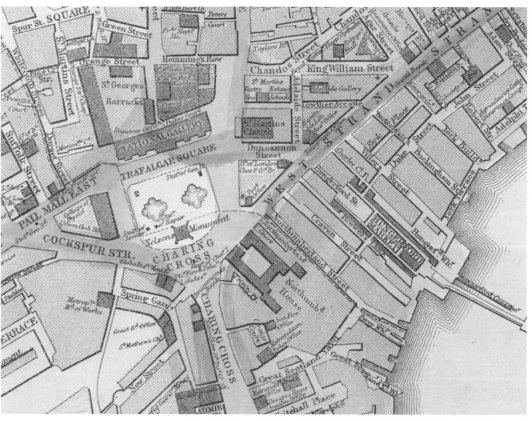

Trafalgar Square

Trafalgar Square was the first deliberately planned public space in London. It evolved in stages between 1830 and 1860, and was London's first attempt at a grand historical monument, commemorating military victory and embodying national pride. It was to some extent an answer to Paris's Etoile and Arc de Triomphe, and Sir Robert Peel described it patriotically as 'the finest site in Europe'. A square of this kind formed part of Nash's original vision for central London: it was to be the focal point between Whitehall, Pall Mall, the Strand and a new road north to the British Museum, although this was never built. Nash's fall from grace, in 1831, meant that he was involved only in the early planning. The square was essentially a grand enlargement of Charing Cross, itself a modest open space which had nevertheless served London for centuries as a place of public meetings, proclamations, pillory and execution. It was proverbial that anyone wanting to know what was happening in London or the world at large had only to go to Charing Cross to be told. The northern side had been occupied since the late Middle Ages by the King's Mews, which had functioned variously as a stable, a barrack, a menagerie and a public record office. In front of the mews, facing the equestrian statue of Charles I, various taverns, shops and tenements had encroached, while still leaving a large open space behind them which would become Trafalgar Square. In the 1630s, Charles I had discussed with Inigo Jones his wish for a grandiose new Whitehall Palace, which would have covered northern Whitehall as far as Charing Cross. Had this royal palace been built, it is doubtful that Trafalgar Square would have emerged in its front garden.

The demolition of the mews and the adjacent buildings was an essential first step, and this coincided happily with the project to build a national art gallery. The origins of the national art collection lay in the government's decision, in 1824, to buy for the nation the paintings collected by John Julius Angerstein, which included fine works by Rembrandt, Rubens and Claude Lorrain. These were housed in Angerstein's mansion in Pall Mall until a new gallery could be built. The architect

William Wilkins secured the commission, and by 1832 work had begun on his classical building, sited on the north of the square exactly where the mews had been. Meanwhile, a second architect, Sir Charles Barry, was levelling and replanning the whole site. Its characteristic feature, which has always contributed to its great sense of spaciousness, was its distinct slope from north to south. To accentuate this slope, Barry constructed a great terrace on which the National Gallery should stand, from which flights of stone steps descended to the square itself. The gallery was completed in 1838, the same year in which the commission for the Nelson monument, the centrepiece to the whole site, was awarded to William Railton. The 150-foot granite column, with its bronze bas-reliefs and crowning statue, was not completed until 1859, while the Landseer lions at its base became a public joke, as year after passed by and they failed to appear. Only in 1867 did the lions put the finishing touch to the square conceived by Nash forty years earlier.

Yet there were still major changes to come on the square's periphery. The opening of a new road to the riverside - Northumberland Avenue - required the demolition of Northumberland House, a vast Jacobean pile, the last of the great noblemen's houses which had once stretched along the Strand between Westminster and Blackfriars. By the mid nineteenth century it was an anachronism, surrounded by shops and hotels, and its owner, the Duke of Northumberland, preferred his fine Adam mansion at Syon House. In 1874 Northumberland House was pulled down, not without some protests about the destruction of London's past. The final act in the creation of Trafalgar Square as we know it came only in 1910, when Admiralty Arch was built as a grand gateway to the Mall. It is hard now to imagine London without Trafalgar Square: Nelson's column, complemented by Lutyens's twin fountains, seen against the background of the National Gallery, has become London's most familiar landmark. But perhaps the London before political demonstrations, New Year's Eve revellers and tourists had no need of such a place.

Opposite, top: old Charing Cross with the Royal Mews, from the Rocque map of 1745 (see pp. 62–63); notice the very large gardens of Northumberland House. B.L. Maps Crace III/107.

Opposite, bottom: the completed site on Weller's map of 1865, but Northumberland House still stands, and there is no road through to the Mall. B.L. Maps Crace VII/271.

Above: the views of 1855 show, (*top*), the approach to the Strand with Northumberland House on the right, and, (*bottom*), St Martin-in-the-Fields and the equestrian statue of George IV. B.L. 10350.g.6. (*top*) B.L. 648 c.16 (*bottom*).

Bloomsbury

Of all the aristocratic estates that were built on to be transformed into residential London, one became famous as a place not of wealth or fashion but of learning. Bloomsbury was part of Georgian London in appearance, but in spirit it was never the West End, becoming instead home to lawyers, doctors, writers and intellectuals, and to the many learned institutions which they formed. After the building of Bloomsbury Square in the 1660s, there was no further development for fully one hundred years when Bedford Square and Gower Street were built, and it was this lapse of time which saw the establishment of the West End, leaving Bloomsbury behind and cut off from the current of fashion. Russell Square, Tavistock, Brunswick, and Mecklenburgh followed Bedford Square, between 1780 and 1810. James Burton and Thomas Cubitt were the builders, commissioned by the fifth Duke of Bedford reputedly to pay for his ambitious rebuilding schemes at his country estate of Woburn. But the tenants who moved in were not the aristocrats and the exquisites, but professional and business people. In *Vanity Fair*, Thackeray placed the unfortunate Sedleys and the odious Osbornes there, while in *Emma* Isabella Knightley talks the place up rather self-consciously: 'Our part of London is so very superior to most others! You must not confound us with London in general, my dear sir. The neigh-

institutions, the Foundling Hospital, opened in 1745, the brain-child of the philanthropist Thomas Coram, who had been appalled at the number of children cast out to live or die on the streets of London. Well supported by the rich and famous, the hospital contained works of art by Hogarth and others, and Handel conducted performances of *Messiah* here.

The institution which really determined the character of Bloomsbury was, of course, the British Museum, created around the antiquities and manuscripts acquired from a number of scholars in the 1750s. The site chosen to house these collections was Montague House in Great Russell Street, and the whole project was financed by a public lottery which raised £300,000. The museum was opened to the public in 1759, but under conditions so forbidding that they succeeded admirably in keeping people away. Over the next sixty years magnificent bequests of books and manuscripts, including the Royal Library, and antiquities from Greece, Egypt, China and India filled Montague House to overflowing, and a new building became imperative. This was the great quadrangle designed by Robert Smirke and built between 1823 and 1847, with its massive Grecian portico. Had it been commissioned twenty years later, we would undoubtedly now have a British Museum in the Gothic style. The

bourhood of Brunswick Square is so very different from all the rest. We are so very airy!' By 1820, the map of Bloomsbury was completed northwards as far as the New Road. The Bedford family always remained concerned to uphold the tone of Bloomsbury, frowning on shops and taverns, and gating the entrances to the square. Just to the east lay the oldest of the district's many distinctive

central courtyard was filled by the construction of the domed reading room in the 1850s, to house what was the national library in all but name. A vivid portrait of the shabby, down-at-heel geniuses and hack writers who haunted the reading room can be found in George Gissing's *New Grub Street*.

Long before Smirke's new museum was completed, Bloomsbury had become home to

Above: the British Museum, twenty years in the building, the culmination of neoclassical architecture in London; a few years later and it would undoubtedly have been a Gothic building, as tastes shifted dramatically.
Guildhall Library, City of London.

Right: Charles Holden's original plan for the University of London head-quarters, 1932. Work on this massive structure was halted by the war, and only the southern section with the great tower was completed.
B.L. P.P. 7611.

yet another institution which reinforced its intellectual character. Unlike every other European capital, London had no university, a matter of shame for generations. In the early nineteenth century – the era of reform, utilitarianism and free-thinking – the moment had obviously arrived to found one, which would be free of the church influences which dominated Oxford and Cambridge. In the face of huge disapproval, University College was conceived by Bentham, Mill, Brougham and other radicals, and opened in 'godless Gower Street' in 1826. William Wilkins's elegant Greek façade, crowned by its dome, was a trial-run for his design for the National Gallery. Science, history, philosophy and languages were all taught here upon modern lines, long before such subjects were studied in Oxbridge, and the college became the embryo of London's university. The presence of the museum, more especially perhaps its library, and the university decided Bloomsbury's future. Subsidiary schools and learned institutes, houses for staff and students, the severe Georgian architecture, all gave it the feel of a campus before its time, especially when, in the 1930s, the university extended its grip with Senate House, which, massive though it is, is mercifully smaller than originally planned. When a group of Cambridge intellectuals seeking to cultivate the inner life migrated to London, Bloomsbury was their natural destination. The Woolfs, the Bells, Keynes, Russell, Forster, Strachey and the rest dallied, gossiped and intrigued together at numerous addresses between Bedford Square and Mecklenburgh Square, and set their seal on Bloomsbury's unique image. From the late nineteenth century, too, publishers had moved in here, and T.S. Eliot clocked in to work at Faber's in Russell Square every day for forty years. Bloomsbury has never been chic or showy or hedonistic, in fact it is rather austere and impersonal, but it has always been interesting, with a sense of spaciousness that is both physical and intellectual.

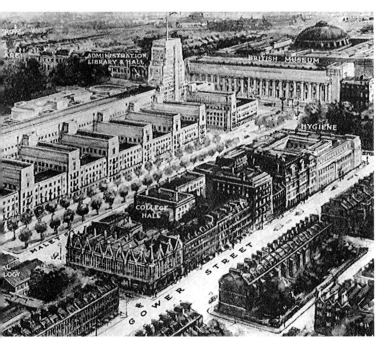

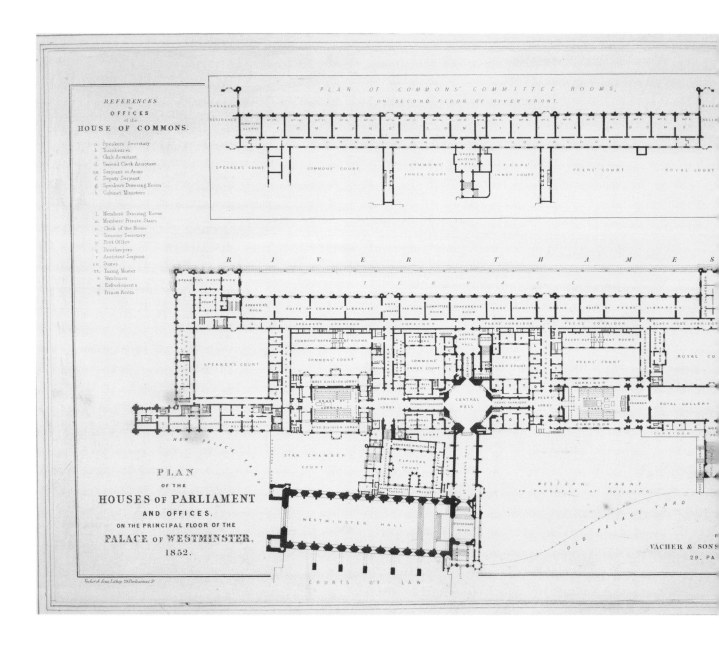

REFERENCES
to
OFFICES
of the
HOUSE OF COMMONS.

a. Speaker's Secretary
b. Trainbearer
c. Clerk Assistant
d. Second Clerk Assistant
ee. Serjeant at Arms
f. Deputy Serjeant
g. Speaker's Dressing Room
h. Cabinet Ministers

l. Members' Dressing Room
m. Members' Private Stairs
n. Clerk of the House
o. Treasury Secretary
p. Post Office
q. Doorkeepers
r. Assistant Serjeant
ss. Stores
tt. Taxing Master
v. Watchmen
w. Refreshments
z. Prison Room

PLAN OF COMMONS' COMMITTEE ROOMS,
ON SECOND FLOOR OF RIVER FRONT.

PLAN
OF THE
HOUSES OF PARLIAMENT
AND OFFICES,
ON THE PRINCIPAL FLOOR OF THE
PALACE OF WESTMINSTER,
1852.

VACHER & SONS
29, PA

Above: Barry's plan of the new Houses of Parliament, 1852. B.L. Maps Crace XI/55.

Left: the completed structure, which marked the definitive transition to Gothic as the obligatory style for Victorian public buildings. B.L. 10350.g.6.

Opposite: the Albert Memorial, the apogee of 19th-century Gothic art. B.L. f 725.94* 401*.

Gothic London

When the old Palace of Westminster went up in flames on the night of 16 October 1834, the task of building a new Parliament offered striking proof of the dramatic change in architectural taste that was sweeping England. It was at once agreed that the new building must not simply perpetuate the classical fashions that had dominated Georgian London, but must reach back to an older, more authentic style, rooted in English history: it must, therefore, be Elizabethan or, better still, Gothic. Just one year after the fire, the design submitted by Sir Charles Barry was accepted, and the result was the first, triumphant expression of what would become Victorian London's great architectural legacy – the Gothic style.

The fire itself was the most sensational in the capital since that of 1666, which destroyed much of the City. It is said to have begun when some government officials decided to burn a huge quantity of ancient exchequer tally sticks. These had been accumulating for centuries in the vaults, and were tinder-dry; they were heaped recklessly into a furnace situated directly underneath the House of Lords. The resulting blaze soon engulfed the whole building, was watched throughout the night by an enthusiastic crowd, and was painted by Turner from a boat in the river.

Barry's mentor in the theory and practice of architecture was Augustus Welby Pugin, who saw Gothic art as spiritually and morally superior to the classical, pagan models:

There is no need of visiting the distant shores of Greece and Egypt to make discoveries in art. England alone abounds in hidden and unknown antiquities of surpassing interest. What madness then, while neglecting our own religious and national types of architecture and art, to worship at the revived shrines of ancient corruption, and profane the temple of a crucified redeemer by the architecture and emblems of heathen gods.

The exterior style of Barry's new Parliament was a superb version of perpendicular Gothic, with turrets, oriel windows, stonework tracery and carved figures. The interior was a sumptuous suite of carved oak, hammer-beam roofs, memorial statues, and walls painted with scenes from English history or legend. The great bell-tower at the north of the building – containing the bell nicknamed Big Ben – further strengthened the cathedral-like appearance of the structure. With the final completion of this building in 1860, central to the life of the nation, the Gothic style was triumphant in London, and other great examples followed. Gilbert Scott's St Pancras in 1872, G.E. Street's Law Courts in 1882, Waterhouse's Prudential Building in 1872, his Natural History Museum in 1881, and Horace Jones's Tower Bridge in 1894, the last a medieval structure concealing the most advanced hydraulic machinery of its time. On a smaller scale, there was the jewelled splendour of William Butterfield's church of All Saints, Margaret Street, and perhaps the ultimate expression of Gothic imagination, the Albert Memorial by Gilbert Scott, completed in 1876. This takes the form of a gigantic medieval reliquary, framed of iron but overlaid with marble and mosaics, enshrining not the relics of a saint but the memory of a blameless prince.

So why was Gothic so exactly right for Victorian England? The Albert Memorial answers this question as clearly as possible: it was the religious connotations of the style. Any building must be better if it resembled a medieval church, even it were really a parliament, an office block, a museum or a courthouse. The style would, it was felt, somehow inspire its users with devotion to work, to law, to science or to government, for all these things were under God's direction. Thus, the Gothic style fulfilled the nineteenth-century desire to unite social, aesthetic and religious ideals.

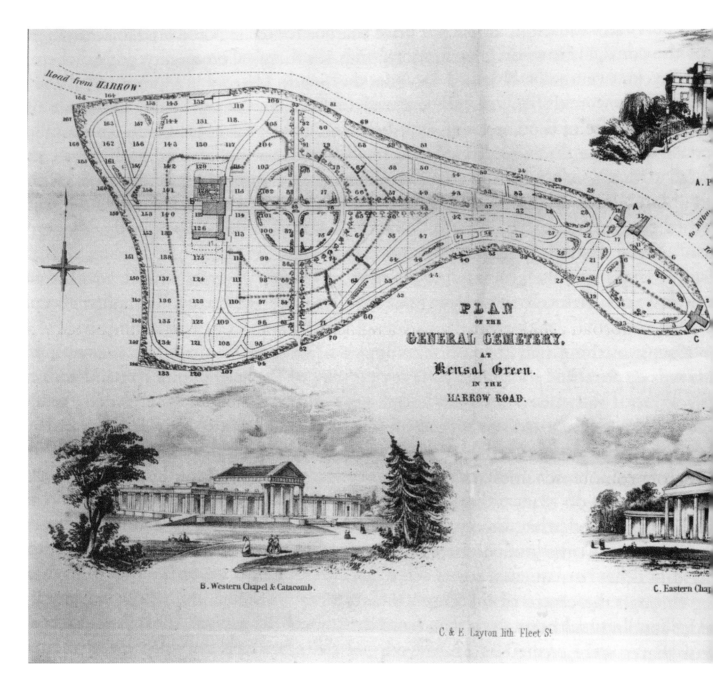

PLAN
OF THE
GENERAL CEMETERY.
AT
Kensal Green.
IN THE
HARROW ROAD.

B. Western Chapel & Catacomb.

C. Eastern Chap

C. & E. Layton lith Fleet St

Above: Plan of Kensal Green, the first of the great private cemeteries of Victorian London.
British Museum, Dept of Prints and Drawings.

Opposite: an exquisite watercolour view of the cemetery by Thomas Allom soon after its opening, making it look like the Elysian Fields. Museum of London.

Victorian Cemeteries

London's explosive growth in the early nineteenth century put pressure not only on the living but also on the dead: the city's graveyards began to overflow. Old coffins were dug up and pushed aside to make room for new, and they in turn were prey to grave-robbers and body-snatchers. By the 1820s, serious concerns about the health risks emanating from old graveyards led to demands for new cemeteries outside the city limits. They should be tastefully designed and professionally managed, and the obvious course was to permit burial to be provided as a commercial service. Parliament agreed and the first operating company, the General Cemetery Company, was formed in 1830. It at once acquired a fifty-acre site beside the Harrow Road, where Kensal Green Cemetery was laid out and consecrated by the Bishop of London in

1843, by which time the company's original share price had more than doubled. Kensal Green seemed to hold a special attraction for literary and showbiz figures. Tom Hood, Sydney Smith, Thackeray, Wilkie Collins and Charles Kemble all elected to be buried here. But so too did soldiers, politicians, inventors and explorers, including Sir Robert McClure, the first man to traverse the North-West Passage, on whose tomb are carved the chilling words 'Thus we launch into this formidable frozen sea'. With its superbly sculptured tombs and graceful tree-lined walks, the place seemed an imposing Anglican ante-room to the next world. G.K. Chesterton sensed this when he penned his famous line 'Before we go to Paradise by way of Kensal Green'. The really interesting thing about this select and expensive graveyard was that it extended class

1833. An Anglican chapel, in the classical style, was approached along wide gravel paths after passing through an imposing gateway. Beneath this chapel and in colonnades along the perimeter wall, extensive catacombs were built, while large individual plots or ornate tombs were for sale in the open ground. Even death failed to unite the Christian churches, however, for a special area was reserved for Dissenters, while a separate Catholic cemetery was laid out to the west.

The venture was an immediate success and Kensal Green became at once the fashionable place to be buried. The final seal of approval came with the burial of the Duke of Sussex in

and social division from London's streets and houses into the realm of death itself. It offered grandeur in death which only the rich could afford, just as only the rich could afford the grandeur of Mayfair or Belgravia.

Other commercial cemeteries followed, based on the Kensal Green model, among them Abney Park, Brompton, Nunhead, West Norwood Manor Park and Willesden Lane, originally called Paddington. In plan, this last was shaped strikingly like a coffin or tombstone, whether by accident or design is impossible to say. Ultimately the most famous of all the Victorian cemeteries was Highgate, which was consecrated in 1839. It scored

Left and opposite: the funerary art of Highgate Cemetery, made all the more melancholy and expressive by being half concealed in the undergrowth. Private collection.

Below: Highgate Cemetery, from the Stanford Map of 1861. B.L. Maps 3480 (260).

over Kensal Green with its exotic mix of sculptural styles - Egyptian and Byzantine, as well as the more familiar classical and Gothic - and through the views which it afforded across London. It quickly became not only a desirable place to be entombed, but also a tourist attraction, meriting a star in Baedeker's London guide. Its centrepiece was the 'Circle of Lebanon', a circle of catacombs built around a magnificent cedar tree which was already old in 1839 and which long dominated the scene. 'In such a place,' wrote one contemporary, 'the aspect of death is softened.' In the realms of the dead, Highgate Cemetery became the best possible address, and within Highgate the Circle of Lebanon was the most sought-after of all - a simple burial plot here costing around two hundred guineas. Sir Julius Beer paid eight hundred for his plot, and a further £5,000 for his massive mausoleum. Galsworthy captured the atmosphere of the place when he wrote in *The Forsyte Saga*: 'From that high, sacred field, where thousands of the upper middle classes lay in their last sleep, the eyes of the Forsytes travelled across the flocks of the graves; there spreading in the distance lay London, with no sun over it, a hundred thousand houses and spires ...' In more sinister circumstances Highgate was the scene of the most famous exhumation of the Victorian era, when Rossetti opened the tomb of his dead wife, Elizabeth Siddal, to retrieve the poems which he had buried with her seven years before; and it was surely Highgate which Bram Stoker had in mind in *Dracula* when he described the entombment and resurrection of Lucy Westenra.

The era of the grand private London cemeteries was necessarily finite: they became full and so their managements ran out of money. In any case, people demanded the right to be buried decently without paying high prices, and the running of burial grounds passed into the hands of public authorities. The Victorian cemeteries became neglected, overgrown and melancholy, and in the process they became infinitely more poignant as reminders of human mortality. The most famous inhabitant of Highgate - Karl Marx - remained quite untypical with his modern, clinically tended tomb. Because they flourished for just fifty years, Kensal Green and Highgate function as a Who's Who of eminent Victorians, many of whom were kept out of Westminster Abbey for social or intellectual reasons: George Eliot, Herbert Spencer, Christina Rossetti, both the Brunels, Faraday, and Mrs Henry Wood, not to mention Fred Lillywhite the bowler, Tom Sayers the prize-fighter and Emil Blondin, the legendary tightrope walker.

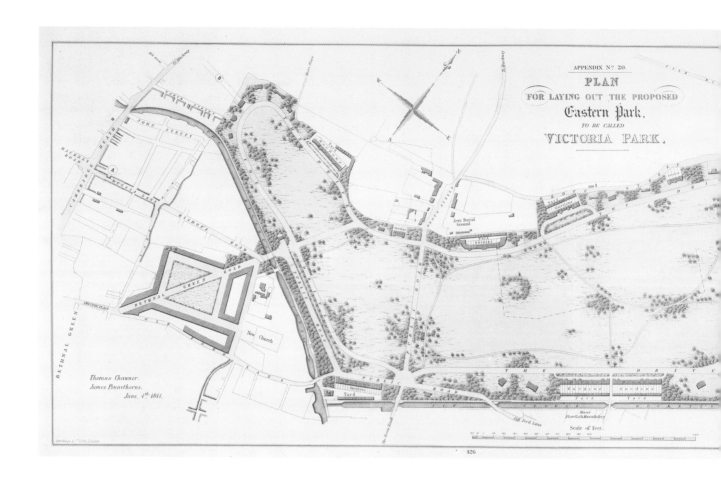

Victorian Parks

One of the most visible of Victorian legacies throughout London's suburbs is the park. Inhabitants of central and western London had for centuries enjoyed the Royal Parks, but the poorer districts to the east and the newer suburbs had no such luxury, and Victorian social reformers realised that it was imperative to offer the poor some healthy alternative to the taverns that dotted every street corner. They believed that their debased existence could be readily enriched by green grass, fresh air and running water. The ancient fields and greens on the borders of the City – Moorfields, Lamb's Conduit, Finsbury, Stepney, St George's – all these were disappearing fast under bricks and mortar. If sites for recreation were to be provided, new land must be released.

The first fruit of this idea was Victoria Park in Hackney, conceived and planned in 1841 and opened in 1848. Almost 300 acres of land reaching north and east from Bethnal Green almost to the River Lea was bought by the government from the Crown, and the landscaper James Pennethorne was commissioned to lay out the new park. To shrubberies, flower beds, fountains and promenades were added a boating lake, cricket-pitch and refreshment pavilion – all the familiar ingredients of the traditional park. In the summer, as many as 30,000 people a day thronged the park, and terraces of respectable middle-class houses were built around its edges. Perhaps its originators may not have envisaged its use as a place of public meetings and demonstrations. A great Chartist crowd gathered there soon after the park was opened, and various secular preachers soon established a kind of Speaker's Corner there, so that in the 1880s the park could be described as 'an arena for every kind of religious, political or social discussion'. Dockers' mass-meetings were almost always held in Victoria Park.

The park experiment was an outstanding success, and others soon followed. In 1858 Pennethorne was chosen again to be designer of Battersea Park, transforming 200 acres of scrubland haunted by gypsies and tramps into a working-class arcadia of cricket pitches, bandstands and boating lakes. In the 1890s, Battersea became especially known as the centre of the new cycling craze, when the safety bicycle replaced the penny farthing, permitting women to ride. Initially banned from the Royal Parks, cyclists would gather in their hundreds in Battersea to practise their new skills.

Victorian London's new governing body, the Metropolitan Board of Works, was established in 1855, unfortunately too late to secure more than a few remaining open spaces in the inner area – Finsbury Park and Southwark Park were among them. But the outer areas were more fortunate, and every suburban borough exercised its public duty by laying out extensive parks, most of them combining sports fields and flower gardens. Wandsworth, East Ham, Ilford, Tottenham, Walthamstow, Ealing – all these borough councils dotted the map of London with green. The park, along with the library, the museum and the public baths, became part of the civilising machinery of Victorian government.

Opposite, top: Victoria Park, first and largest of London's new public parks for the masses, an oasis for generations of east Londoners. B.L. Maps Crace XIX/43.

Opposite, bottom: Battersea Park from the Stanford Map of 1861, by the same designer as Victoria Park, James Pennethorne. B.L. Maps 3480(260).

Left: Battersea became in the 1890s the recognised centre for the new cycling craze.
B.L. 103550.dd.6.

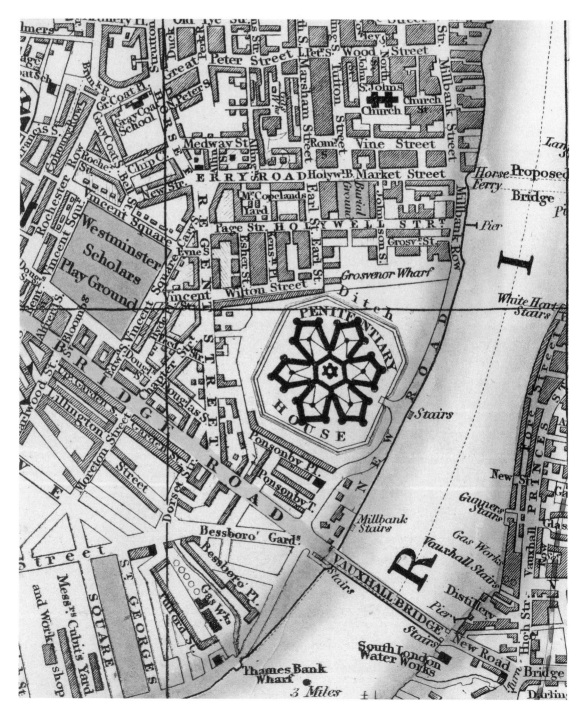

Millbank: From Prison to Art Gallery

On any map of Victorian London, one of the most eye-catching features was a vast six-pointed star to be found near the river between Westminster and Chelsea. This was the Millbank Penitentiary, opened in 1821, a prison conceived by the reformer, Jeremy Bentham, on entirely new and rational lines to replace the squalid and corrupt prisons of the eighteenth century. Architecturally it was designed as a 'panopticon', which meant that the prison galleries were built around a central watchtower, from which the supervisors could see into every corner of the institution at every moment. The prisoners were confined in separate cells, and in another radical innovation, they were made to do therapeutic work, such as making shoes or mail sacks. All this was part of the Benthamite programme of social and institutional reform which influenced so much of nineteenth-century thinking.

However, in spite of the high ideals that inspired it, the early years of the Millbank Penitentiary were disastrous, as cholera from the polluted, marshy ground on which it was built killed dozens of inmates. The building was emptied, fumigated, and its conditions improved, then for fifty years it stood in its vast, gloomy isolation, discouraging the appearance of any neighbouring buildings on Millbank. It was soon judged to be a failed experiment; it was closed in 1890 and demolished a few years later.

The site was soon covered by the new art gallery, built to house the collection of British art assembled by the sugar magnate, Sir Henry Tate. To this collection were added the paintings of Turner, previously kept in the National Gallery, while in the 1920s the collections of modern European art given by Sir Joseph Duveen and Sir Hugh Lane required new galleries. The spacious classical interiors of the Duveen galleries made the Tate the most enjoyable of London's art galleries, where Blake and Turner were displayed alongside Gauguin, Matisse and Rodin. It would be difficult to imagine a site playing host to two more contrasted institutions. The Penitentiary is long forgotten, and no memories of it haunt the site, although Millbank east of the Tate has once again become a succession of blank and massive walls, behind which business executives and bureaucrats are more or less willingly confined.

Opposite, top: few pictures of the prison survive: in this one we see just two of the six great wings, while a goods wagon from Gloucester and Cirencester trundles by. B.L. 563.c.7.

Opposite, bottom: the unmistakable shape of the Millbank Penitentiary seen on the Cruchley map of 1829. B.L. Maps Crace VII/253.

Above: the Tate Gallery opened in 1897 exactly where the prison had stood, in the assertive neo-Palladian building by Sidney R.J. Smith. B.L. 10349.r.9.

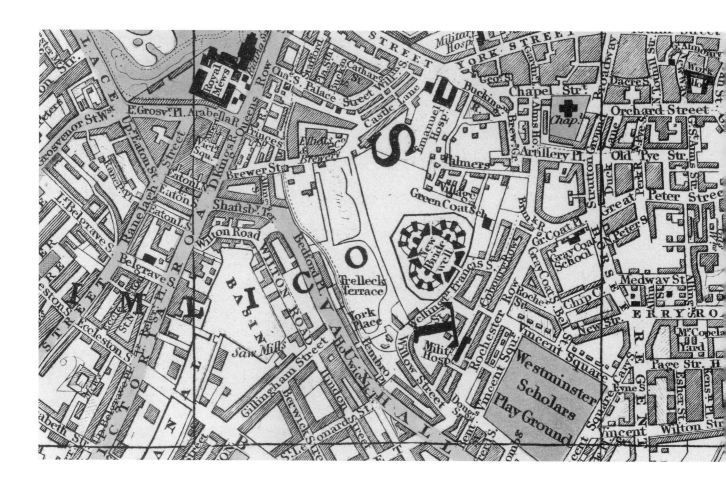

Above: the maze of streets in Westminster and Pimlico through which the new Victoria Street was driven in the 1840s, from Cruchley's map of 1829. B.L. Maps Crace VII/253.

Opposite: Victoria Street in the 1860s, lined with hotels and the earliest apartment blocks in London. Private collection.

New Roads

Where it had not been transformed by Nash or Cubitt, London in the 1840s was the London of Charles Dickens - a web of narrow crowded streets, crammed all day with horse-drawn traffic, and overshadowed by ramshackle buildings. Some of the worst of these

so on. It was the first stage in the modern metropolitan government of the city, and it became the forerunner of the London County Council, formed in 1888. One of its major preoccupations was to modernise London's archaic road network.

slums - known graphically as Rookeries - were in the shadow of Westminster Abbey and in St Giles. They were nests of poverty, disease and crime, and to the early Victorians there occurred the happy thought that if they could simply be demolished, their inhabitants would be dispersed to the four winds, and at the same time broad new roads could be created through which the traffic could flow freely. Between 1840 and 1900, half a dozen such schemes changed the map of central London. Many of the programmes were directed by the Metropolitan Board of Works, the new body set up in 1855 to improve London's infrastructure. This was an historic innovation, for the board was the first planning authority which recognised that greater London was now one huge city. It centralised powers which had previously been held by scores of parish vestries and commissioners for streets, sewers, lighting, open spaces and

Work on Victoria Street, conceived as a link between Westminster and Belgravia/Chelsea, had begun in the 1840s, before the MBW was born. It was twenty years in the making, so that it became, quite fortuitously, the approach road to Victoria Station when it was opened in 1861. Many slum dwellings were demolished to make way for this new thoroughfare, but so too was Palmer's Village, a group of eighteenth-century almshouses west of Artillery Row. By the 1880s the new street was lined with hotels and blocks of mansion flats, the first of their kind in London. By far the best-known building on the street was the Army and Navy Store, formed originally to supply members of the forces, but opened to the general public in 1918; for more than half a century their massive catalogue was the shopper's bible for everything from mousetraps to grand pianos.

A new road to link Charing Cross with

Top: before the Victoria Embankment was built, numerous lanes and streets descended from the Strand to the water's edge, and there was no continuous riverside walk. B.L. Maps Crace VII/271.

Above: the construction of the Albert Embankment, reclaiming a long strip of muddy shoreline from the river. B.L. 010348.q.8.

Right: the typical 'rookeries' which were demolished as new roads were driven through central London; the worst of these slums were in St Giles and Westminster. B.L. 010348.q.8.

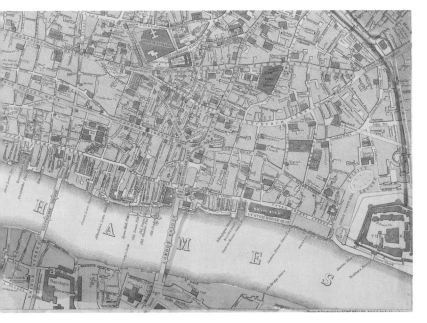

Large areas of mud were reclaimed from the river, permitting the creation of new gardens at the Temple, Charing Cross and Cheyne Walk. Beneath these new roads ran underground rail lines and sewers. The sweep of the river seen from the Victoria Embankment is now so familiar that it is hard to imagine a time when only a succession of narrow lanes sloped down from the Strand, ending in stairs lapped by the river.

Two other ambitious projects were not the work of the MBW but of the City: Farringdon Road followed the now-submerged Fleet River from Clerkenwell to the verge of Blackfriars Bridge. Laid out in 1845-6, it destroyed the notorious Saffron Hill and Chick Lane rookeries (site of Fagin's den in *Oliver Twist*). It was bridged by the Holborn viaduct, linking Holborn to the City, a magnificent Victorian Gothic iron structure embellished with bronze statues complemented by Italianate houses at each corner. Exactly contemporary was the cutting of the long, diagonal Queen Victoria Street from the Bank of England to the river, the most significant new road to be built in the City since the Great Fire.

The last of the great reshaping roads of Victorian London was the Kingsway-Aldwych project, not finally completed until 1905. Its aim was to relieve congestion in the narrow and and ancient routes between the Strand and Holborn. At 100 feet wide, Kingsway resembled a Parisian boulevard, while the crescent-shaped Aldwych was unique to London. Among the small streets sacrificed to this scheme was the curious Holywell Street, centre of the Victorian trade in pornographic books. The Kingsway-Aldwych project was the last of these new roads, conceived as attempts to cut through London's traffic jams and slum enclaves.

Bloomsbury had long been meditated, indeed it had been part of Nash's grand design, but Charing Cross Road did not become a reality until the 1880s. The design did not end as Nash had envisaged at the British Museum; instead it simply widened existing streets as far north as St Giles Circus. At the same time, the opportunity was taken to drive a new street - Shaftesbury Avenue - east from Piccadilly to meet Charing Cross Road at Cambridge Circus. Both streets cut through Dickensian slums without rehousing their inhabitants, and both quickly acquired their own special character. Shaftesbury Avenue became home to half a dozen theatres, all for some inexplicable reason on the north side of the street, while Charing Cross Road was colonised by the booksellers who have made it famous.

In engineering terms, the MBW's greatest road-building challenge was the building of the Thames embankments west of the City - the Victoria, Albert and Chelsea Embankments. They were the work of the chief engineer, Sir Joseph Bazalgette, who was also responsible for modernising London's sewer system. Begun in 1868 and completed in 1874, the embankments transformed those sections of the riverside, creating broad new roads and walkways, embellished with their superb granite parapets and ornate iron lamps.

The price in money and chaos during the building period was enormous, and no further such schemes were undertaken for fifty years, during which traffic jams and slums remained just as much a part of London life as they had ever been. As a result of these schemes, London was faced with two sharp lessons, although whether they were learned is another matter. First, traffic will always grow to fill whatever roads are made for it; and second, demolished slums have a habit of reappearing somewhere else. Could it be that *people* are responsible for both problems?

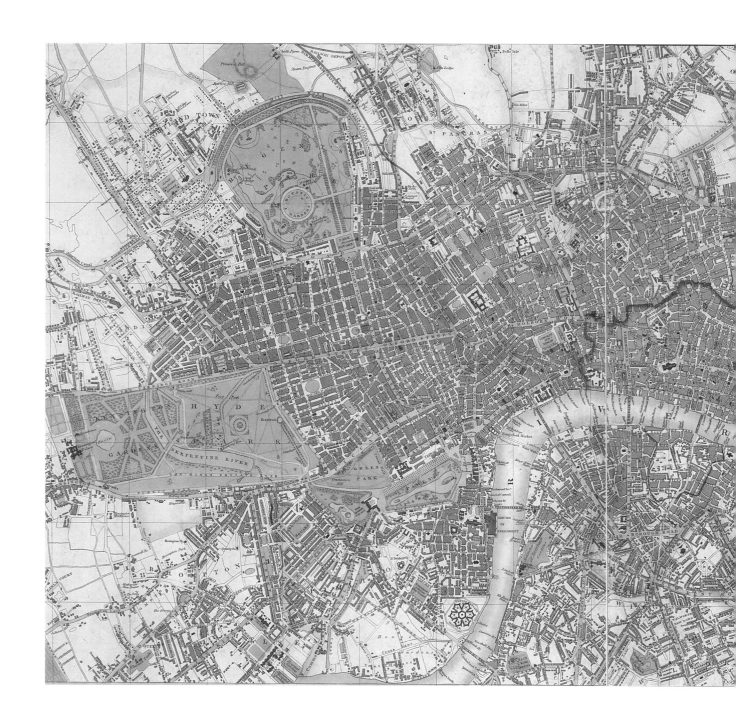

Dickens's London

If Hogarth was the presiding genius of eighteenth-century London, then the nineteenth century indisputably belongs to Dickens. Dickens was not a Londoner by birth, and his novels contain excursions into Kent, Norfolk and even America, but the essential setting on which his imagination worked was always London. The association works on various levels. First, there is the fun of spotting the locations which he used: the Adelphi Hotel, where Pickwick ate and drank; the City Road, where Micawber lived; Clare Market, where the Trents kept the Old Curiosity Shop; Saffron Hill, where Fagin had his thieves' den; Jacob's Island, where Bill Sykes met his end; Hanging Sword Alley, where Jerry Cruncher lodged; the Fleet Prison, where Mr Pickwick was confined; Doctors' Commons, where David Copperfield studied the law, and many more. The fact that most of these places have been swept away or changed beyond recognition does not spoil the fun – in fact it adds to the fascination of trying to recreate them in our imagination as they once were. Second, there is the resonance that comes from our knowledge of Dickens's own life. We know that his father was held for debt in the Marshalsea Prison; that his mother tried to run a small school in Gower Street, as also did Mrs Micawber; that he worked as a boy in a blacking factory in Hungerford Market; that he was employed by a legal firm in Gray's Inn; that he dined at Rule's in Maiden Lane; that he acted in a theatre in Dean Street; that he lived in Doughty Street and at various other addresses, and so on.

These topographical details, however, are very far from being the whole story. London in Dickens's work is a gigantic labyrinth where people drift inexplicably around with no sense of purpose. Who rules the city? Not Parliament, which is scarcely ever mentioned; not a king or queen, and certainly not the Church. If there is an answer lying just beneath the surface of these novels, it is money which rules everywhere – money that is cultivated and guarded by the vast grinding machinery of the law. Law courts, lawyers' offices and prisons fill every book, counterbalancing the Pickwickian good-humour; indeed, these are the twin meanings of the word Dickensian. On the one hand it means a benign, slightly zany humour, and on the other a dark, fusty, hopeless scrabbling in a bewildering maze.

Above left: Cross's map of 1844 – Dickens's London.
B.L. Maps Crace VII/254.

Left: Doré's grim, atmospheric engravings are the visual counterpart to Dickens's vision of London.
B.L. wfi/1856.

Dickens's London

Money lies behind nearly all his plots: the Chuzzlewit money, the Harmon money, the Dombey money, the Jarndyce money, the Trent-Quilp money, the Magwitch money – all these fortunes loom in the background and prove a poison to those who pursue them. The younger protagonists have to learn to see beyond money to a more authentic set of values. In the extreme cases like Scrooge and Gradgrind, the pursuit of money has utterly corrupted their lives. Certain money-lenders and blackmailers like Quilp, Wegg and Gride are presented as disgusting physical monsters, while the few aristocrats who appear are decadent and reptilian, like Sir Mulberry Hawk and Lord Verisoft. All these people are trapped in a hell of their own making, which is perhaps how Dickens saw London. Only those who use their money beneficently, like Mr Brownlow, the Cheerybles or the reformed Scrooge, can escape this hell.

This is essentially a child's vision of the world, full of angels and monsters, and it sprang from Dickens's own miserable childhood in London. On the one side are the masters who keep the machine going – the men of business, the bankers, the lawyers and the prison-officers; while on the other side are the victims – the clerks, the small shopkeepers, the debtors, the skivvies, the river-scavengers and the street urchins, struggling to rise above their misfortunes. Fog, dirt and mystery pervade London and surround their lives. Who are their unknown parents? Where are their lost children? Who has stolen their inheritance? Where has their money come from? Who knows the truth about them? How will they escape from these shadows and emerge into the daylight? These are the plots which fill the novels, and the streets of London are the perfect setting for them. In this respect Dickens can be seen as the first great novelist of the city, in a way that Jane Austen, for all her concern with money, obviously was not. Thackeray, too, was a novelist of London, but for Thackeray the city was a vast stage, all was show and theatrical pretence. Dickens responded to the more brutal commercial forces of the nineteenth-century city, and exposed its darker aspects.

Opposite, far left: the master storyteller, who brought his books to life in a series of melodramatic public readings. B.L. Dex. 316.

Top: the river played a strong part in many of the novels. B.L. 1035.g.6.

Opposite and left: Cruikshank was Dickens's first illustrator, and he captured both the humour and the squalor of the lives of Dickens's characters. B.L. G18068.

George Cruikshank

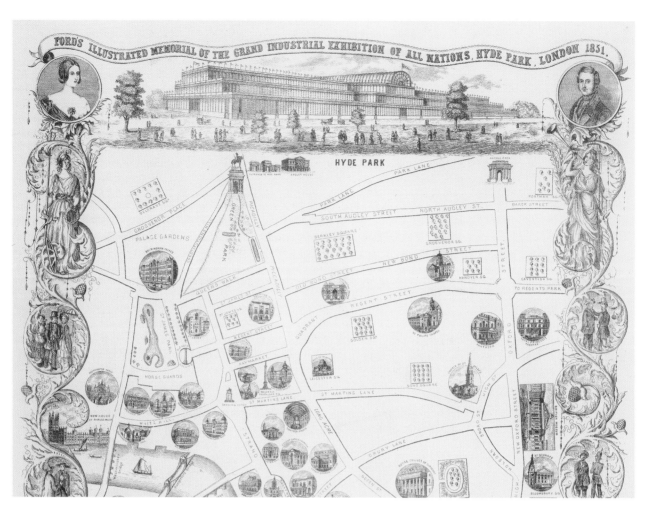

FORD'S ILLUSTRATED MEMORIAL OF THE GRAND INDUSTRIAL EXHIBITION OF ALL NATIONS, HYDE PARK, LONDON 1851.

HYDE PARK

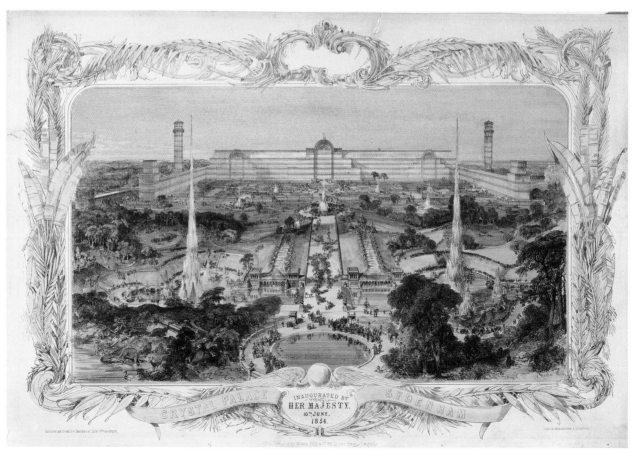

CRYSTAL PALACE   INAUGURATED BY HER MAJESTY, 10TH JUNE, 1854.   SYDENHAM

The Great Exhibition and its Legacy

The laying-out of Trafalgar Square, the building of new roads such as Victoria Street and Kingsway, the creation of public parks like Victoria and Battersea - all these were evidence of something new in London's history. So was the awareness that London needed and benefited from direction, planning and collective action. In a word, the city was acquiring a modern consciousness of itself, of its complexity and of the fact that growth and change were everywhere. This consciousness was marked by the greatest public celebration of the Victorian era, the Great Exhibition of 1851. It was designed with two aims: to bring the world to London and to demonstrate London's centrality in the modern world. The planning committee included the greats of Victorian England: Wellington, Peel, Gladstone, Cobden, Cubitt, Barry and Prince Albert himself. Idealistic they may have been, but there was nothing other-worldly about

their idealism, for the exhibition was a showcase of human ingenuity and material progress. It brought together the scientific and artistic achievements of scores of nations, both their traditional crafts and their technological marvels. But, undoubtedly, the greatest exhibit of all was the hall in which these things were proudly displayed, the legendary 'Crystal Palace', the gigantic temple of iron and glass erected in Hyde Park. Visited by six million people in five months, the exhibition was seen by contemporaries - and by historians since - as epitomising much of the Victorian outlook on the world.

When it closed in the autumn, the exhibition left a clear legacy behind, a desire for a permanent site to be devoted to the display and the study of technology and the applied arts which were evidently reshaping the nineteenth-century world. The Royal Commission that had steered the project through acquired almost 100 acres in South Kensington where, in the course of the next fifty years, there appeared the Victoria and Albert Museum, the Science Museum, the Natural History Museum, the Geological Museum, and the Imperial Institute, as well as the Royal Albert Hall and the Royal College of Music. The resulting 'Albertopolis' transformed this corner of London into a permanent Museumland, where generations of children have marvelled at dinosaur bones, electrical machines, mechanical volcanoes and replicas of ancient Rome. The museums were like secular cathedrals, devoted to the deification of human knowledge and skill. The presence of so many huge museums so close together has had an astringent effect on the surrounding streets: one seems to walk for miles without seeing a shop, a pub, a café or any of the familiar clutter of London's streets.

The Crystal Palace itself was dismantled and re-erected in 1854 in Sydenham, where it became the focus of virtually a new suburb. With its interior filled by orchestras, exhibition rooms, fountains and restaurants, it became a latter-day Vauxhall Gardens, insulated from the weather and with a slightly more elevated ethos. It outlived the Great Exhibition itself by eighty years, and had it survived it would now have been revered as one of the supreme gifts of the Victorian age, but sadly it was destroyed by fire in 1936.

The Crystal Palace inspired a rival building in north London, Alexandra Palace, which opened in 1873 and promptly burned to the ground sixteen days later; so confident were its owners, however, that it was immediately rebuilt, to become the home to a very mixed bag of events: musical concerts, indoor and outdoor sports, flower-, horse- and dog-shows, circuses, fireworks, evangelical gatherings and political rallies. Taken over by the government in the Great War, it was later acquired by the BBC, and it was from here in 1936 that Britain's first television programme was broadcast - perhaps a fitting culmination to the Victorian zest for science and showmanship which had inspired the original exhibition of 1851.

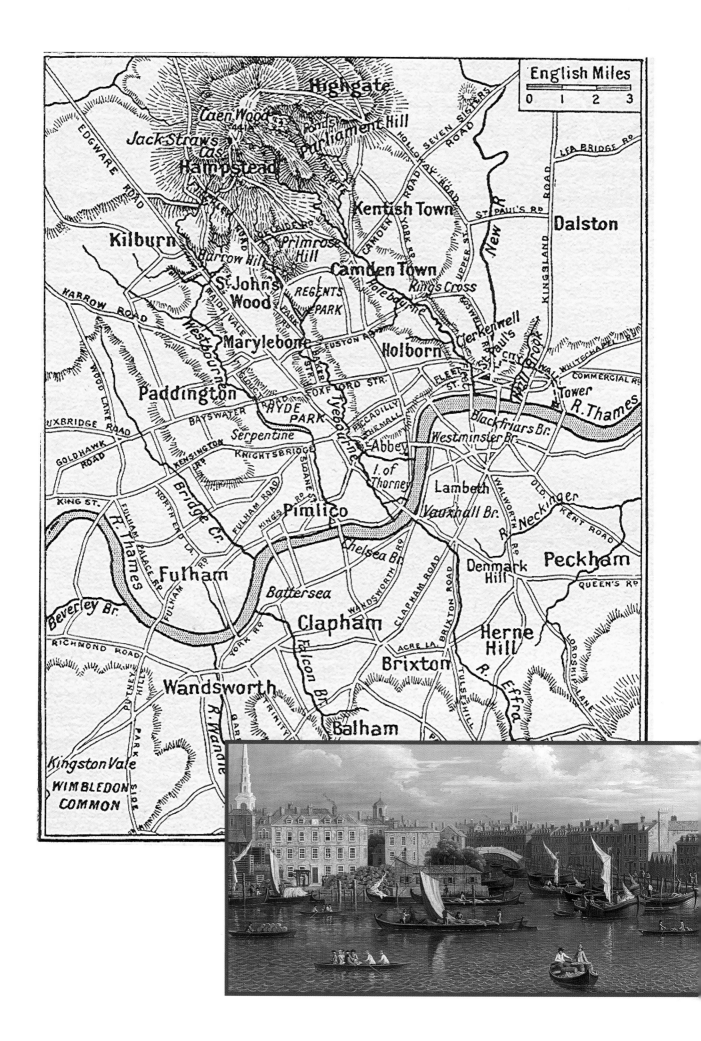

London's Vanished Rivers

Central London is not a city of hills; compared with places like Edinburgh, Salzburg or Lisbon, the streets are all pretty level. Nevertheless, the walker or cyclist will often notice the ground rising or falling in a way that is obviously not man-made. These undulations are a reminder of the contoured landscape buried for centuries under the stone streets, and especially of the low hills of sand or gravel that sit on top of the London clay. These hills to the north, and the chalk outcrops to the south, were the source of numerous springs and brooks which once found their way to the Thames, for surprising though it may seem, London was once intersected by half a dozen considerable streams. They have long since been imprisoned beneath the pavements and the houses, but they have left their traces in a number of ways: in the miniature valleys which once led down to their banks, in the winding streets which followed their course, and in the street names which commemorate them. The fundamental reason why they have vanished is always the same: they were used as sewers and rubbish-tips, and had to be enclosed to cover up their offensive filth. This was also the reason why they soon ceased to be used as a water supply. In the City itself, the Walbrook, the very centre of the Roman settlement, was covered as early as the fifteenth century, while the others survived for two or three centuries more, until the detritus of urban life poisoned them.

The northern streams – the Westbourne, the Tybourne and the Holbourne - have imprinted their names much more strongly on the map of London than the southern ones. All three rise on the slopes of Hampstead Heath and meander by various routes to the Thames. The Westbourne crossed the Edgware Road at Kilburn and flowed south to Paddington, where it entered the property of a certain Baynard, becoming known locally as Baynard's Water, and later contracted to Bayswater. Just west of Lancaster Gate tube station is a distinct dip in the road, marking the point where the stream crossed into the royal park. Here it formed the pool which was landscaped in the eighteenth century into the Serpentine. It then crossed the sites of Eaton Square and Pimlico Road, to join the Thames close to Chelsea Bridge. The Serpentine is one visible legacy of the Westbourne, and the other is one of London's curiosities: a massive pipe slicing through Sloane Street tube station which carries the captive river over the railway line and its passengers.

A little to the east, the Tybourne ran through what was to become Regent's Park, picking up a tributary stream to form the Y-shaped pool. Amid the regular grid of streets between Euston Road and Oxford Street, Marylebone Lane curves like a village street because it follows the winding of the old river. When Marshall and Snelgrove's store in Oxford Street was being built in the 1870s, the excavators found themselves digging down into the stream and uncovering the remains of an ancient bridge. Brook Street and Conduit Street recall its presence before it crossed Green Park, passed very close to Buckingham Palace, divided around the gravel island on which Westminster Abbey was built, before finding the Thames near Vauxhall Bridge. The Tybourne gave its name to the whole district north of Hyde Park, and especially to the place of public execution.

The Holbourne rose in Highgate Ponds, and followed the course of Highgate Road down through Camden Town to King's Cross. Just to the south, it then entered the most pronounced valley in central London, where its name changed to the Fleet. Here it was, until the seventeenth century, a navigable river; indeed part of Wren's post-Fire plan was to widen and embank it, so as to bring river craft up as far as Clerkenwell to supply City markets. By the mid-eighteenth century, however, it had become the foulest open sewer in London, and was covered over bit by bit to create Farringdon Street.

The southern streams which flow down from the Kentish chalk are less familiar, even though two of them are still above ground. The Wandle is still very much in evidence: from its source in Carshalton to the Thames at Wandsworth, it drops just 100 feet in ten miles. The Effra, which flows from Norwood to Lambeth, is shorter and is lost beneath the ground, as is the Neckinger, which curves from St George's Fields to St Saviour's Dock; its odd-sounding name is said to derive from the hangman's noose on the gibbet there. The longest of the southern streams is the Ravensbourne, which covers some fourteen miles from its source in Farnborough in Kent to Greenwich, where it is more familiarly known as Deptford Creek. South London was less urbanised before the age of Victorian sewer-building, hence these southern streams did not suffer the same fate as the northern ones, and they have a less picturesque history.

Green London Preserved

Where would London end? In absolute terms no one knew, but there were a handful of green open spaces on the edge of the metropolis where the advancing tide of bricks and mortar was deliberately halted. Epping Forest and Hampstead Heath in the north, Blackheath, Wandsworth and Wimbledon in the south: as these open spaces were threatened with building and suburbanisation, Londoners woke up to what was happening and cried 'enough'. The places in question were ancient commons and from the 1850s onwards the lords of these manors were beginning the process of enclosing and disafforesting them, ending the ancient forest laws which included people's right to take fuel, as the first step towards their future development. Resistance to this process sprang up simultaneously in Hampstead and Epping.

In the case of Epping, the old forest uses of hunting and timber-cutting had fallen out of use, and its future lay either in development or recreation. The principal lord of the manor was Lord Mornington, a dissolute spendthrift eager to profit from his possession, who had been encroaching on the forest for years. In the 1860s, a labouring family named Willingale insisted on their ancient rights to take firewood from the newly enclosed areas, and as a result the father and two sons were imprisoned for malicious trespass. One of the

sons died in prison, and it emerged that one of the magistrates who had condemned him had been gifted a part of the enclosed land by Lord Mornington. There was fury and indignation throughout the district and in the country at large. By this date, scarcely 6,000 acres of a once huge forest remained, and the case gained great public attention. The result was the birth of the Commons Preservation Society, which included figures such as John Stuart Mill, Octavia Hill, Lord Eversley and others, many of whom would later be instrumental in forming the National Trust, both organisations dedicated to preserving the countryside and historic buildings. The conservationists engaged the enclosers in legal proceedings which dragged on for ten years, during which time the forest continued to shrink alarmingly. Judgement was finally given in 1874, and not only were the spoliators of the forest ordered to stop their activities, but also, all the enclosures of recent years were pronounced illegal; the enclosers were condemned as virtual thieves, and ordered to pay high legal costs. As a result, the forest was taken into the care of the Corporation of London, and in May 1882 Queen Victoria travelled to High Beech to hear the Lord Mayor dedicate the forest to public use in perpetuity.

In Hampstead, the lord of the manor, Sir Thomas Maryon Wilson, had begun legal

Opposite: the southern portion of Epping Forest, which might all perhaps have been lost to suburbia. B.L. 10351.f.60.

Above: in 1882 Queen Victoria dedicated the Forest in perpetuity to the people of London.
Guildhall Library, City of London

[165]

WIMBLEDON COMMON.

PROPOSED IMPROVEMENTS.

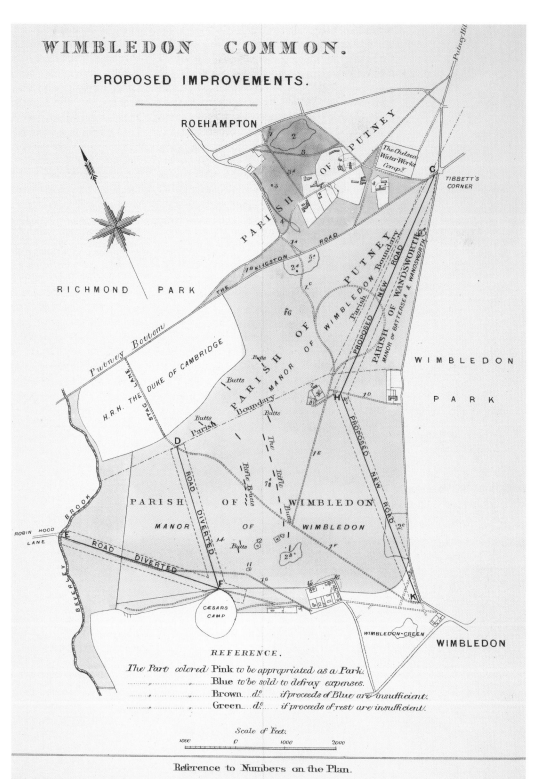

REFERENCE.

The Part colored Pink to be appropriated as a Park.
.... Blue to be sold to defray expenses.
.... Brown d.º .... if proceeds of Blue are insufficient.
.... Green d.º .... if proceeds of rest are insufficient.

Scale of Feet.

1000 — 0 — 1000 — 2000

Reference to Numbers on the Plan.

N.ᵘˢ 1, 1.ᴬ 1.ᴮ 1.ᶜ 1.ᴰ 1.ᴱ 1.ᶠ 1.ᴳ	Roads.
2, 2.ᴬ 2.ᴮ 2.ᶜ	Gravel Pits
3, 3.ᴬ	Footpaths
4, 4.ᴬ	Ponds & Streams
5,	Conduit
5.ᴬ	Cottage

N.º 6	Iron House
7, 7.ᴬ	National Rifle Assoc.ᵗⁿ Stores.
8,	The Windmill, Enclosure, Cottages and Sheds.
9,	The Common Keeper's House.
10,	The Clock Tower

11, 12, 13,	Cottages and Enclosures
14,	The Well
15,	Croft's Enclosure, Sheds and Saw Pit.
16,	Part of Common used for deposit of Timber.

Charles Lee,
Surveyor,
20, Golden Square,
Dec.ʳ 1864.

moves to enclose the Heath as early as 1856. These were vigorously opposed, but he nevertheless began building there. To save the Heath, the Metropolitan Board of Works opened negotiations with him to buy it, and the rapacious baronet valued his land at £5,000 an acre, since it was now potential building land. This would have netted him well over £1 million. The battle was brought to an end by his death in 1869, and his more civilised brother accepted £45,000 for extinguishing his manorial rights, and the Heath became public property. Parliament Hill Fields was added in 1888 to prevent its development, otherwise the view from the Heath would have looked down over a sea of rooftops. The Heath was left largely in its natural condition, and it still forms 'the most convincing illusion ever created of real country brought to the heart of a vast city'.

The legal and personal conflicts in these cases were often complex and acrimonious. In Wimbledon, the lord of the manor, Earl Spencer, considered that he was being fair and generous when he proposed to sell one third of the common for development, in order to pay for the care of the remainder. He claimed to be the legal owner of the land, but to be powerless to maintain it properly. Many London commons were indeed run-down at this time, with fairs, illegal camping, undergrowth being stripped for fuel, and rubbish being dumped on them. Spencer's case was that enclosure as a park was the only answer. This proposal was strongly rejected by the local residents, who could not agree that common rights were an anachronism, and who refused to accept that a third of the common must be sacrificed. As in Hampstead and Epping, legal action became essential to save the land for public use. In Plumstead, the lord of the manor was Queen's College, Oxford, and their agents infuriated local residents when they enclosed half of the common and Bostall Wood between 1860 and 1865. The fences were torn down, and again the courts ruled against the spoliators. Nearby Blackheath, however, was acquired amicably by the Metropolitan Board of Works from the Earl of Dartmouth, who took a more democratic view of things. The legal status of these commons was indeed extremely obscure, and involved the most difficult judgements about fundamental property rights, yet in all these cases the 'right' decision was always made – a fact for which Londoners must be eternally grateful.

Opposite: the rejected 'improvements' to Wimbledon Common, 1864, by which the owner proposed to develop part of it, in order to improve the rest.
B.L. Add. MS 78155, v.2.

Right and far right: sylvan peace on London's doorstep in Epping Forest.
B.L. 10351.f.60.

Cuckoo Pits.

High Beach.

Map 1.	Maps 2—5.	Boundaries.	Description.
c.	outside map—north.	E. Holloway Road. N. Midland Railway. W. Brecknock Road. S. Tufnell Park Road.	Group of streets near the Board school, contain many poor and some doubtful characters, but district has improved from what it was. The other inhabitants vary from good class mechanics, clerks, and travellers, to the professional and well-to-do classes.
54. a.	outside map—north.	HORNSEY ROAD, UPPER HOLLOWAY E. Stroud Green Road. N. Midland Railway. W. Hornsey Road. S. Seven Sisters' Road.	Very large block, considerably deteriorated, the better class residents moving towards the outer suburbs, and their places filled by a poorer class from inner districts. Many clerks and others in light occupations, railway men, labourers, street sellers, &c.
b.	outside map—north.	E. Hornsey Road. N. Midland Railway. W. Holloway Road. S. Seven Sister's Road.	A mixed population, mainly artisans, clerks, and ordinary labourers. There is a small percentage below this, mostly casual labourers only occupying one room, and a rather larger one above, chiefly shopkeepers and professional men. District is rapidly going down.
55. a.	outside map—north.	UPPER HOLLOWAY E. Mount Pleasant and Villas. N. Hornsey Lane. W. Highgate Hill, Holloway Road. S. Midland Railway.	Some of the streets contain a very mixed population. Much building going on, and the operatives, some very rough in character, live in the neighbourhood. Women work at the numerous laundries round about. Many well-to-do streets.
b.	outside map—north.	E. Holloway Road, Highgate Hill. W. Dartmouth Park Hill. S. Midland Railway.	Generally eight and ten-roomed houses, many filled with a well-to-do class. Others contain many good mechanics, policemen, &c., while the remainder are very mixed, containing some very poor and rough characters, with many quiet, respectable folk.
			TOTAL Finsbury School Board Division .
56. a.	J—4.	BETHNAL GREEN (WEST) E. Across from Selby Street to Hare Street, Abbey Street. N. Bethnal Green Road, Church St. W. Shoreditch. S. Fleur-de-Lis Street, Great Eastern Railway, Brick Lane, across Brewery, south of Weaver Street.	Houses are large, many being erected for weavers, of whom but a few remain. Many engaged in furniture trades and bird breeding ; quite a fair on Sunday mornings in some streets. Many Polish Jews. Amount of poverty and ignorance very great.
b.	J—4.	E. Tyssen Street, Turk Street. N. Old Castle Street. W. Shoreditch. S. Church Street.	This block has been scheduled for demolition by the London County Council. Many cabinet makers, French polishers, carvers, and chair makers, also hawkers and labourers. Several bad characters. Much poverty and dirt, many families only occupying one room. Houses often very old and dilapidated.
c.	J—4.	E. Hart's Lane, Barnet Grove. N. Barnet Street, Virginia Row. W. Turk Street, Tyssen Street. S. Bethnal Green Road.	Good many workshops in this block, mostly engaged in the furniture trade, and employing many cabinet makers, &c. The smaller houses seem decent, but many of the larger ones, let out in tenements, are in a very bad state of repair.

Mapping Wealth and Poverty

As there is a darkest Africa, is there not also a darkest England? May we not discover within a stone's throw of our cathedrals and palaces similar horrors to those which Stanley has found existing in the great equatorial forest?

These are the words of Charles Booth, Victorian social analyst and reformer, and author of one of the most intriguing London maps ever published. Booth's map had nothing new to say about London's layout or geography, but instead it presented a thought-provoking analysis of its people and their way of life. Booth's work was part of the great discovery of the urban poor, published in numerous moving or lurid reports late in the nineteenth century. Much of this writing had a religious inspiration, and called for a home mission to match that of the unfortunate savages overseas. The poverty, vice, crime and disease which existed in the heart of London were seen as a reproach to a civilised Christian nation.

The Booth map - sometimes known in shorthand as the 'Wealth and Poverty Map' - was actually a series of maps published with his great work *Life and Labour of the People in London*, which appeared in several parts between 1889 and 1903. Booth came from a successful ship-owning family, and he used his wealth to finance his original social research. His work was less sensationalised and evangelical than that of his contemporaries, offering instead a precise classification of London's wealth and class structure. His work was based on thousands of interviews and door-to-door enquiries, from which he and his team tried to establish how the people of the capital actually lived. From their answers, Booth built up a picture of seven social groups, four of them above the poverty line and three below it:

G: Upper class and upper-middle class, wealthy.
F: Middle class, well-to-do.
E: Fairly comfortable, good ordinary earnings.
D: Small regular earnings.
C: Intermittent earnings, poor but not in chronic want.
B: Casual earnings, very poor, chronic want.
A: Lowest class, vicious and criminal.

These bands were colour-coded on his map, not merely street by street, but block by block. When he came to enumerate his findings, Booth found that almost ten per cent of all Londoners - some 350,000 out of 4 million - lived in extreme poverty. They were ill-fed, ill-clothed, without work, permanently in want and permanently drawn towards crime. Just above these were those classes whose lives were, in Booth's words, 'an unending struggle, and lack comfort, but I do not know that they lack happiness'. Above this line were those in regular work, not struggling with poverty, shading up into the middle classes. Booth's scheme is overtly based on regular work as the key to worldly comfort and social position. No doubt he was right in this, but he cannot have knocked on many doors in Mayfair, or he would have been faced with the puzzle of a group who had never worked in their lives, but who were awash with money; he might even have found one or two criminals among them.

In geographical terms, the great lesson of Booth's map is how intermingled the social classes still were in London in the 1890s. Obviously the West End squares were resolutely upper class, but elsewhere all the colour shades from the red-gold of the upper classes to the black of the criminals seem to be scattered across the map with no very clear pattern. From Bedford Square to Drury Lane is about 400 yards, and Booth's map shows it descending from red to black in that short space. Likewise, in Westminster, Booth shows splashes of black and dark blue just a couple of hundred yards from the Abbey and the seat of government. Side streets around Lincoln's Inn and the Temple - the law's heartland - are dense with the dark shades of poverty and crime. Nash's idea that Regent Street should mark a visible boundary between the West End and London's inferior districts is amply confirmed on this map: in a few blocks we pass from the red-gold of Cavendish and Hanover Squares to the dark blue of Soho. Bloomsbury at this date does extremely well, not yet infested with intellectuals and publishers, while the very worst areas seem to be not in the East End but south of the river from Lambeth to Bermondsey.

If we accept that Booth's researchers were accurate, then it seems evident that the darkest London which he had spoken of did, indeed, exist in the heart of Victorian London. The builders of the West End squares had achieved their aim in creating enclaves for the elite, but once outside their bounds it was difficult to avoid the swarming poor, except perhaps by heading for the distant suburbs.

The Shock of the New

If the Victorian era presented challenges to the people and rulers of London, the twentieth century was a time of outright assaults on the city, physical and social, coming from within and without. The continued expansion of the boundaries of London has been matched by transformation and destruction in the centre. As the twentieth century approached its close, the legacy of this destruction was a nest of problems that were apparently intractable. One of the most troubling aspects of this legacy is that, after centuries in which the powers shaping London were informal, private and elitist, the age of democratic planning should fail its people so disastrously.

This searing experience of destruction came with the Second World War and its aftermath: the early years of the twentieth century had been far less threatening. There

were then two forces at work in London: the centrifugal flight from the centre to the suburbs for ordinary living, and the centripetal pull to the centre for work and entertainment. The commercialisation of the West End and of the whole central area was under way late in the Victorian era, but it leapt forward dramatically in the 1920s and 30s. Companies large and small, and many institutions and societies, felt it desirable to set up offices in the heart of London, with the result that whole streets and squares were lost to residential use. St James's Square, Grosvenor, Berkeley, Hanover, Cavendish, Bedford, Russell – how many people now live here, or in the streets of Bloomsbury, Holborn, Covent Garden and Clerkenwell? At first, existing houses were converted into offices, but increasingly they were demolished to make way for purpose-built commercial premises. Work

was becoming professionalised: it was a serious business, requiring its own designed environment, while companies demanded a building that reflected their status.

Then there was the still more overt form of commercialisation – the flood of shops, restaurants, clubs, hotels, theatres, cinemas and dance halls which turned the West End into a playground, one made possible by the availability of electricity to power lights, lifts, telephones, escalators, and the illuminated adverts outside. Even the aristocrats gave up their mansions, allowing their sites in Piccadilly and Park Lane to be redeveloped as hotels or blocks of flats – Devonshire House, Grosvenor, Dorchester, Chesterfield, Londonderry, Norfolk and many others. These two forms of commercialisation combined to produce the London of the Monopoly board, the game launched in 1935, where money reigned supreme and redevelopment was the aim. The diversity of building types now reflected the diversity of social life: in the eighteenth century, every building in London was a house, with the exception of churches, and a handful of prisons and theatres. Now there were offices, private or governmental, banks, shops,

restaurants, institutes, clubs, pubs, museums, libraries, courts, stations, cinemas, markets, each with its own style and its own identity.

Thanks to the tube system, the West End became to some extent democratised, for anyone could go out after work to a restaurant or a theatre, and get back to the suburbs before midnight. The tube was the second phase of the railway revolution, criss-crossing London north of the river with a quick, flexible transport network which penetrated the central core where no railways existed, and linking the centre with the suburbs. The tube map with its neat, interlocking lines gives the impression of rational, central planning, but in fact it, too, was entirely the product of private finance, some of it American, and ad hoc development over a sixty-year period, before it was taken under public control in 1933 with the founding of the London Passenger Transport Board – in effect the first nationalised industry in Britain.

London was, by then, becoming well used to the consolidation of powers and functions, for in 1889 the London County Council had been formed as the successor to the Metropolitan Board of Works. With 150 elected councillors and cohorts of bureaucrats, the LCC was responsible for roads and buildings, drainage and sewers, the fire service and housing. Major additions to these powers came in 1904, when all London schools were placed under its control, and again in 1929, when the running of London's hospitals and poor relief was also transferred to it. It undertook major building projects, including tunnels under the Thames and bridges over it, the Kingsway–Aldwych development, and much later the Royal Festival Hall. In addition, a second tier of London local government had been created in 1899 with the twenty-eight Metropolitan Boroughs within the LCC area, from Woolwich in the east to Hammersmith in the west, and from Lewisham in the south to Hampstead in the north, which were to administer local services such as libraries, swimming pools and parks, although they, too, could undertake road works and build houses. This new era of intensive local government was the fruition of the long nineteenth-century progress towards central administration and planning for London; even though the LCC was not controlled in its early years by the Labour Party, it undoubtedly represented the triumph of municipal socialism in a general sense. The City, of course, always remained quite outside all these new institutions, jealously guarding its ancient privileges of self-government.

The LCC intervened most directly in people's lives in the field of housing, clearing slums

Above: the London County Council, established in 1889 was the first, historic recognition of London's identity beyond the City and Westminster; ten years later the Metropolitan Boroughs were created. B.L. Maps 53.f.2.

Opposite: the explosion of the suburbs, made possible by the transport revolution: houses (top), factories (*centre*), and, (*bottom*), commuters flow over London Bridge. Simmons Aerofilms.

and building its own new estates of model flats and houses. At the turn of the century, the first new estates were built at Millbank, behind the Tate Gallery, and in Shoreditch, and they took the form of five-storey blocks of flats. Even before the Great War, however, the Garden City style had influenced the LCC architects' department, and cottage-style houses became the order of the day, pioneered on the Old Oak Estate in Acton and in Tooting. This style reached its culmination in the building of Dagenham between 1928 and 1932, which was also the first deliberate attempt to shift population out of London. With 100,000 people, Dagenham became probably the largest planned community in the world, yet the LCC had no power to offer these people employment, for it was planned as a dispersal suburb, with a lifeline to central London via the District Line. Dagenham might have proved a gigantic disaster, had not Ford decided to build its great car factory there in 1931.

By 1939, a quarter of a million people were tenants of the LCC estates across London, yet this figure was dwarfed by the millions who had found their own solution to the city's housing problems by moving to the mushrooming suburbs. Some of these suburbs were monotonous rows of near-identical terraces for the upper echelons of the working classes, in places like West Ham, Leyton, Lewisham, Wandsworth or Willesden, while others were distinctly leafier, with detached or semi-detached villas for the middle classes in Barnet, Woodford, Bromley, Petts Wood, Raynes Park, Worcester Park, Harrow and all of Metroland beyond. But in both these types of suburb, home ownership was available on easy terms, and this effected a revolution in social and economic life. The promise of 'homes fit for heroes' after the Great War had been, at best, only partly fulfilled, but people had voted with their feet and gone off to buy their own. The rows of bay-windowed terraces and the mock-Tudor villas were much scorned by architects and critics at the time of their building in the 1920s and 30s, but in comparison with what came later, they came to look solid and desirable, offering privacy

and tranquillity away from the maelstrom of working London. The early phases of suburban expansion, from the 1860s to the 1930s, were dependent entirely on public transport, and only later did the private car come to play a major role.

This new era of home ownership between the wars stimulated a new form of manufacturing and consumerism, which probably saved London from the depression which engulfed much of the rest of Britain. On the edges of the city, especially in the west along the A4 and A40, a new type of American-style factory sprang up, making cars, electrical goods, pharmaceuticals and toiletries, processed food and drinks, and household goods, many of them plastic. In districts like Wembley, Park Royal, Brentford and Hounslow, these light industries employed hundreds of thousands of people, while in between the factories there sprang up the 'parade' of shops, often with a cinema, or perhaps a library or swimming pool close by. As with the commercialisation of the West End, electric power was the key to this type of factory, and Wembley had a special place in this new development, for it was at the British Empire Exhibition of 1924 that American-style electric funfair rides were first seen in London; when the exhibition was over, the site became partly an industrial estate and partly what we would now call a leisure complex. This was a very different urban environment from that of the East End, with its traditional dirty, heavy industries, and different again from the depressed industrial towns of northern England, and the mainspring for all this activity was the suburban housing boom. In fact, London was so successful in the interwar years and grew so fast that two planning responses emerged: the designation of the Green Belt to set a deliberate limit to the engulfing of the countryside, and the planned dispersal of population outside the LCC area.

The other great planning challenge that was rapidly building up was traffic. The dispersal of population to the suburbs, the growth of new light industries across a huge area, and the mass production of cheap vehicles all created a rising tide of traffic, both lorries and private cars. The Ministry of Transport was formed to deal with the new challenges, driving licences were introduced, traffic lights, roundabouts, by-passes, and all the paraphernalia of the car age. The streets of central London were gridlocked for much of the day, and there was as yet no restriction on vehicle parking. By the late 1930s, it was becoming obvious that London was choking with traffic, and the first of a series of master-plans was commissioned to cut through the problem. The

Bressey Report of 1938 proposed sweeping changes: new roads through the city, and orbital roads around, with new viaducts, tunnels and Thames bridges. The plan involved huge cost and huge destruction of property to make way for these roads, but it promised a confident solution to the problems. At this stage, and for many years afterwards, it was evident that no one foresaw the relentless growth in traffic, such that any new road would be quickly filled, and the jams would merely be moved from one place to another. Forestalled by the war, some elements of this plan reappeared in the Abercrombie plans of 1943 and 1944, commissioned by the government and partly adopted by the LCC.

The Second World War was a watershed in London's modern history, a turning point even greater than the Great Fire had been. The physical destruction wrought by the Blitz was the spur to a new era of planned development, not only in the east where the bombing had been so catastrophic, but also throughout the whole metropolis. The Blitz was an unprecedented outside assault on the capital, although prefigured during the Great War when Zeppelin raids killed some 800 people. By comparison, the air campaign of 1940–1 was an inferno, claiming 22,000 lives in eight

months, reducing thousands of acres to rubble, and destroying or severely damaging landmark buildings such as the Guildhall and Westminster Hall. The second phase of the battle for London, the V-bomb attacks of 1944–5, were said by those who lived through them to be even worse, in their devastating power and their suddenness. They inspired a fear that the conventional bombing never did, and people left London in their thousands to escape them. Ultimately, none of this appalling civilian suffering had the slightest effect on the outcome of the war, but it undoubtedly reinforced the determination that when the war was over not merely a better city but a better society must arise. In this, London was a microcosm of Britain as a whole, the Britain that embraced the welfare state as the culmination of all the social ideas and experiments of the previous hundred years.

Post-war London now seems a place of austerity and greyness, like the black-and-white films of the period, the newsreels and the photographs of those years. Images published in *Picture Post* show the hut-like prefabs that housed thousands of those made homeless by the Blitz – ragged children racing their old bikes around bomb-sites, people worshipping in the roofless shells of churches, and women

Opposite: devastation and survival in 1941; St Paul's narrowly escaped.
Private collection.

Right: the city of towers which took shape in the 1970s, almost before we noticed it.
Simmons Aerofilms.

queuing for the food which was still rationed six years after the war had ended. Two events captured on those newsreels lifted London's spirits: the Olympic Games of 1948, staged in the face of considerable criticism that the money should be spent on house building, but which quickly captured the public imagination, especially through the running of the 'flying housewife', Fanny Blankers-Koen, who won four gold medals. Three years later, the Festival of Britain was an official attempt to say goodbye to the years of austerity, celebrating the new age of science and art which, it was hoped, was dawning over London and which would soon come to be known as the new Elizabethan age.

However, when the rebuilding began it all went wrong, in a story which has several threads and which proved traumatic for London. The first tactic of the post-war planners was to move people out of the grey, half-ruined city to the half-dozen new towns that were built in a ring around London – Crawley, Stevenage, Harlow and so on. Density planning was the great watchword. But this was only a beginning, for by 1950 London's planners and architects had drunk deep at the springs of modernism: functionalism was the new religion and Le Corbusier its high priest.

Intellectual games played on drawing boards led to the rebuilding of the shattered East End in a form that was alien and dehumanised. At the same time, the City, eager to restore its structure and functions, abandoned its centuries-old restriction on building height and embraced the new architectural styles. The massive wartime destruction and the consequent rebuilding started a boom time for property developers, as thousands of companies large and small re-established themselves or relocated, and this process spread throughout central London. Thus, in a strange way, public municipal planning and the private market for commercial property were pulling in the same direction – towards a city of concrete towers, some for living and some for working, but all cold, featureless and depressing, with a deadening effect on the spaces around them. This process lasted for thirty years, and the result was the generation of tower-clones which invaded all London's skyline. At the same time, the city was being redesigned to make way for the car. Streets were widened and made into dual carriageways, flyovers and underpasses were built, crossroads became massive roundabouts, and multistorey car parks rose into the air. Each new scheme was claimed to solve a particular traffic

[175]

The urban landscape of the 1960s: old and new housing side by side in Walthamstow. Simmons Aerofilms.

problem, but still the roads were choked and the air filled with noise and exhaust smoke. Years were to pass before it was finally acknowledged that traffic would grow to fill the available road space, and that the only rational strategy was to keep traffic out of the city. The dehumanising of the urban environment encouraged a further exodus of population from the centre to the suburbs, or out of London altogether, leaving the growing social problems of those left behind in the inner city.

Strangely, however, this process of degradation in the urban environment was not widely noticed or condemned at the time and, in fact, it was accompanied by a renaissance in London's image as a place of dynamism and style - the swinging London of the 1960s. To a large extent, this was based on the burgeoning youth culture of music and fashion, which was hyped to the skies by the media. Perhaps there was a psychological link between the so-called 'urban renewal' and swinging London - the link of rebellion, iconoclasm, and breaking with the past. The destructive costs of this process would only emerge with time. One immediate result, however, was a phenomenal growth in foreign tourism in London, which would soon become one of the capital's major industries.

An awakening and a reaction began in the late 1970s, flowering into the movement for conservation. Great planning battles were fought over the future of Piccadilly Circus and Covent Garden, over the proposed inner London motorway, and the third London airport. The faults of the new architecture were becoming evident, both aesthetic and social, while planners were realising that the city did not consist of buildings alone, but of the spaces and the lives between them. Such was the disillusionment with what had happened, and the controversy over new schemes, that major development decisions became almost impossible, and planning itself was discredited. It was for this reason that one special area of London - the Docklands - had to be given special development status as the only possible way out of the paralysis which had followed the dereliction of the area after the docks had all closed in the 1970s. Throughout this entire period, political conflict and uncertainty fatally weakened London's government. The LCC was replaced in 1965 by the much larger Greater London Council and thirty-five London boroughs. London's admin-

istration was full of divided responsibilities and tensions: between the centre and the boroughs, between the outer boroughs and the inner ones, between local and national government, between socialist planners and privatisers. The abolition of the GLC in 1986 left London without a metropolitan government, just as it had always been, from the time when its growth outside the City walls began in the Tudor era, through until it stood as the sprawling capital of the empire in the Victorian age.

The architectural profession now claims to have learned the lessons of the post-war disasters. Imaginative new projects and welcome renovations abound, now in a variety of postmodern styles. The city centre is booming, for the electronic revolution - which ought, in theory, to have had a destructive effect on commercial life in the City - has not diminished by one iota the desire of top companies for a central London address. The new London Authority has, at last, begun the attempt to heal London's cancerous traffic problems. The Olympic Games of 2012 are being hailed as the divine event which may regenerate the entire eastern reaches of the city. But in the spaces between these new-flowering oases, a great deal of desert still reigns. London is no more easy, or agreeable or pleasant than it ever was. It is impossible to govern, and impossible to leave ungoverned. The history of London offers two or three lessons which may sound like truisms, but in an age reeling from the shock of the new, truisms can be valuable. First, change has always been unpredictable, and attempts to plan and direct social life have a habit of being overtaken by events: life is always one jump ahead. Second, London is a commercial enterprise, a place to make money, and to display it stylishly; this fact has guided its growth and been built into its bricks and mortar for centuries. Private enterprise and ambition might be controlled, but is there any evidence that democratic planning produces anything better? Third, almost nothing is forever: houses and churches, palaces and prisons, the lovely and the unlovely, they can all come down, while London still continues on its way. All these truisms add up to the central fact that London will never reach a plateau of stability and order, never become a utopia, because it is nothing more nor less than a mirror of ourselves. As with our own lives, we never quite give it up as hopeless, but neither should we cherish the illusion that it can be perfect.

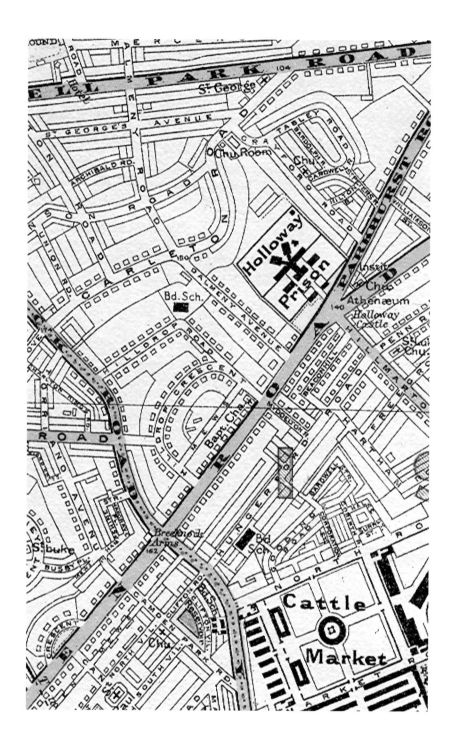

Unfashionable Suburbs

Between 1850 and 1900 the two salient facts in London's story were the population explosion and the transport revolution. In two generations the head-count of Londoners leapt from two million to six million, while buses, railways and the underground completely changed the rhythm of people's lives. You no longer lived a few steps from your place of work, but could criss-cross the capital at will. The offspring of these twin revolutions was suburbia – the horizontal sprawl of housing which felt interminable if you walked through it, but which the trains clattered through in half an hour or so. Suburbia dispersed the exploding population, and the railways made suburbia possible. In every direction, north, east, south and west, as fast as the builders could work, the new tenants moved in. Miles and miles of new streets and new houses appeared, each someone's personal domain, but all very nearly identical, whose inhabitants migrated every morning to work in the old, historical London, then returned each evening to their private dormitory. The great characteristic of urban life became incessant movement in time and space, movement between different modes of life: day and night, work and leisure, public and private, weekday and weekend, office and home, city and suburb.

In reality, the suburbs were far from featureless. Those on the northern or southern heights, for example, were built precisely because their setting was attractive – places like Hornsey, Highbury, Denmark Hill and Wimbledon. There were really several gradations of suburb. The spacious, leafy, semi-rural enclaves whose names often ended in Hill or Green or Park were resolutely middle class, and at least five or six miles from the City. Before these were reached, there was an inner ring of mixed-class suburbs, which obliterated the older villages, especially those north and east of the City, in Middlesex and Essex: Islington, Holloway, Tottenham, Hackney, Stratford, Leyton and Walthamstow. From these places clerks could reach the City and labourers could reach their warehouses and workshops by the cheap early-morning trains. The Great Northern Line from King's Cross and the Great Eastern from Liverpool Street effectively created all these northern suburbs, from Camden Town to Enfield, from Hackney to Ilford. People in their thousands exchanged the overcrowded warrens of Stepney and Shoreditch for the terraced streets of East Ham or Tottenham, and the same pattern was repeated as south London was built over from Brixton to Croydon, and west London from Paddington to Harrow.

As early as 1720, Defoe had written that the road from the City almost as far as Enfield

appeared to be one continuous street, lined with cottages and taverns. Yet, until the coming of the railway more than a century later, the hinterground was still entirely rural – farms, woods, heaths, ponds and green lanes. The new era of suburban transport was marked symbolically in 1864 when the old tolls and turnpikes in and out of London were abolished, for they belonged to the vanished age of horses and coaches. By 1900 the green lanes had long disappeared beneath the endless ranks of houses, punctuated by shops, pubs and two fortress-like prisons. A few Holloway streets remained staid and respectable, the sort made famous as Pooter-land in *The Diary of a Nobody*, but this was also the land of music halls, gaslight, prostitutes and murder. The Crippen case in Hilldrop Crescent was the most sensational crime of the age, involving jealousy, poisoning, a dismembered body in the cellar and an attempted escape by ship to America; it sank deep into the nation's folk-memory. Other murderers of suburban north London included Frederick Seddon and George Joseph Smith, who killed to gain inheritance or insurance money, and Mary Pearcy, the blood-stained pram murderer. All these cases sprang from 'malice domestic', and seemed to symbolise the hidden lives that were lived behind the respectable façades.

Where Holloway bordered Tottenham lay the Seven Sisters Road, subject of a whole mythology among Edwardian Londoners. Its cheap lodging-houses were home to thieves, fences, prostitutes, drunkards and gamblers. One side street at its western end, Campbell Road, colloquially known as 'The Bunk', was legendary as the worst street in London, inhabited by an underclass living at war with society. Suburbia may have been like a frontier, constantly expanding to give people the chance to escape urban pressures, but obviously a whole class was being left behind, and these inner mixed-class suburbs could easily degenerate into hopeless slums. It is hard to imagine that Housman wrote *A Shropshire Lad* while he was a lonely clerk living a stone's throw from the Seven Sisters Road.

These northern suburbs were almost entirely residential, but directly east of the City the industrial suburbs had developed just as fast. Whitechapel and Stepney had long been the home of trades unwelcome in the City itself, and this was intensified by industrialisation, especially around the River Lea in Stratford and Poplar. New legislation in the 1850s prohibited more and more trades and industries in the metropolis itself, so they moved east. Gunpowder, oil, rubber, spirits, chemicals, soaps, varnish, dyes, matches, creosote, animal carcases – these just some of the goods processed or

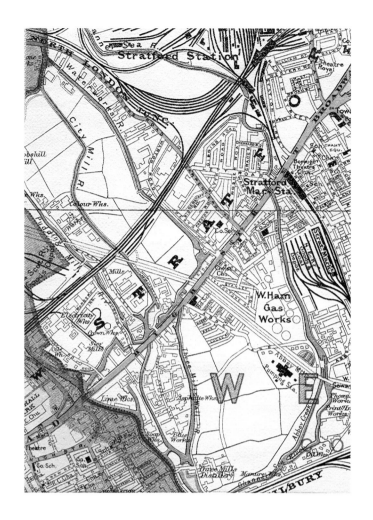

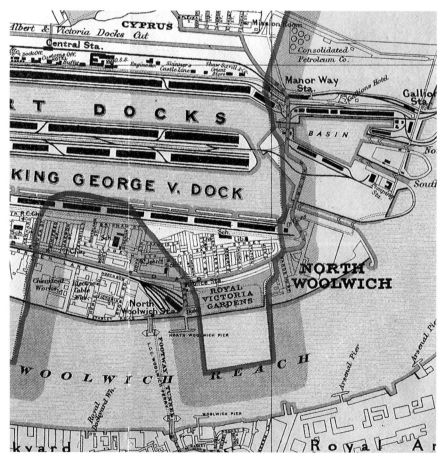

shipped in and out of Stratford. It became a huge rail junction and the site of a railway engineering works. Stratford's connections with the docks and the river by water, rail and road passed through West Ham, Plaistow, Canning Town and Silvertown, while at Beckton stood the gigantic coal-gas works. The houses built for those who worked in these industries were smaller and more cramped than those of the northern suburbs, and resembled a London version of the terraced cottages of northern miners or mill-workers; indeed, contemporaries compared these parts of London to some northern Coketown. 'Half a century ago,' wrote one observer in 1912, 'West Ham was a straggling village of some five or six thousand inhabitants on the east bank of the Lea, and might have remained so but for the Act of 1854, which placed many restrictions on the manufactures existing within the metropolis. Their owners naturally sought a retreat where nobody could interfere with them, and they found at West Ham the liberty to make smells and generally pollute the atmosphere, cheap land and proximity to water carriage. So West Ham increased rapidly, and became one of the busiest and dirtiest places in the kingdom.'

The oddest of these grimy, working-class suburbs was surely North Woolwich, a community called into existence purely by the railway and the riverside industries. Built on a strip of ancient marshland just up-river of Gallion's Reach, it eventually became completely islanded between the river and the Royal Docks. A penny ferry crossed from the south bank to a point where, in 1847, a rail line from Stratford was laid; this was to provide cheap access for workers from south of the river to the docks and factories of the East End. There were still no houses in North Woolwich when a syndicate of investors laid out the Pavilion Garden, accessible by rail or by steamer from London, where there was music, dancing, balloon ascents and fireworks. During the 1850s and 60s this garden (now a small park) was visited by thousands, but it lost its appeal when electrical and chemical industries were set up nearby, and Tate and Lyle built its great sugar refinery. Rows of terraced houses were run up for the workers, and schools for their families. The opening of the Royal Albert Dock to the north reinforced the isolation of this tiny suburb, for its exit road was closed at the lock-bridge for several hours each day. The people of North Woolwich looked across the river for supplies and entertainment, and they must surely have been the only group of Londoners who had to use a ferry to reach civilisation, while generations of their children spent much of their time riding back and forth on the paddle-steamers across the river. The King George V dock was added in 1921, and for fifty years the huge liners which berthed there would loom over the streets, until the death of the docks in the 1970s. Unlike Chelsea, Hampstead or Greenwich, North Woolwich is a place unknown to history or to the guidebooks, but its story was unique, and it surely merits at least one star as London's most unfashionable suburb ever.

Opposite, top: map and photograph of Stratford, London's nearest equivalent to the heavy industrial towns of the north of England.
B.L. Maps 3480(357), photo Simmons Aerofilms.

Opposite, bottom: map and photograph of North Woolwich, a tiny community islanded between docks and river.
B.L. Maps 3480(357), photo Simmons Aerofilms.

Left: typical scene on the river Lea at Stratford.
Private collection.

1

2

3

6

4

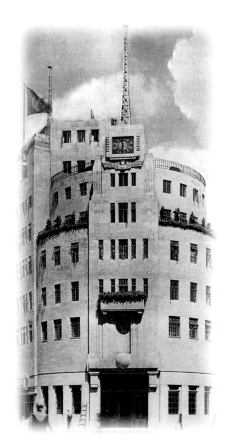

7

5

8

Architecture: Edwardian and Modernist

The early years of the twentieth century continued the confident, exuberant style of public buildings that had marked the Victorian years. A form of Edwardian baroque became the dominant mood. It was seen in royal London with the completion of the Mall, entered through the glories of Admiralty Arch, in the Victoria Memorial, and culminated in the remodelled Buckingham Palace. The splendour of baroque erupted all over the capital: in the Old Bailey, with its Wren-inspired dome, in the riotous façade of the Port of London Authority headquarters in Trinity Square, in the new County Hall on the south bank, and in the City in the superb Institute of Chartered Accountants. Outside central London, it was employed on numerous suburban town halls, libraries and museums. In a slightly sparer form, more like the French Beaux-Arts model, it was also the accepted badge of style for high-class commercial building: the new Regent Street, the Ritz, the Piccadilly Hotel and the RAC club. Selfridges was built along more classical lines, but very freely interpreted. Pure classical public buildings were very rare in this period, the King Edward VII Galleries at the north end of the British Museum being the sole example.

Even after the Great War, the stately imperial style remained architectural orthodoxy, appearing in the 1920s and 30s in the rebuilding of the Bank of England, in all the major bank headquarters in the City, and in imperial offices such as India House and South Africa House. It was also employed in commercial buildings such as Bush House, Unilever House, and Britannic House. The appeal of this style was obviously its massiveness, its muscular display of wealth and power, and its reference to the architectural glories of the past. It was intended to be both reassuring and inspiring. These buildings added enormously to the character of London; they have a timeless quality that makes them feel older than they really are.

Architectural modernism was emerging during these years in Europe and America, but it struggled to find much of a footing in London. The first truly modern buildings in London were in the art deco style, the steel and black glass of the *Daily Express* offices in Fleet Street, Simpson's in Piccadilly and the Peter Jones store in Sloane Street. Then there were the factories of west London – Hoover, Gillette and Firestone. Out-and-out square modernist blocks were seen only in a few private flats in north London, the work of European exiles. In the public arena there was a group of transitional buildings, such as Broadcasting House and Senate House, which were massive, but shorn of baroque exuberance. This style interested commercial clients, too, and Shell-Mex House in the Strand was the first American-style office block in London. Modern functionalism was seen at its starkest in the Battersea Power Station, an industrial monument of a kind never seen before in central London. These structures represented the shape of things to come, and in the post-war rebuilding of the capital, London's architects would avidly embrace modernism, often with disastrous results.

Opposite and right: public monuments and map of central London:

1. Unilever Building

2. Admiralty Arch

3. Institute of Chartered Accountants

4. Old Bailey interior

5. PLA Building

6. Daily Express Building

7. Broadcasting House

8. Shell-Mex House.

Private collection.

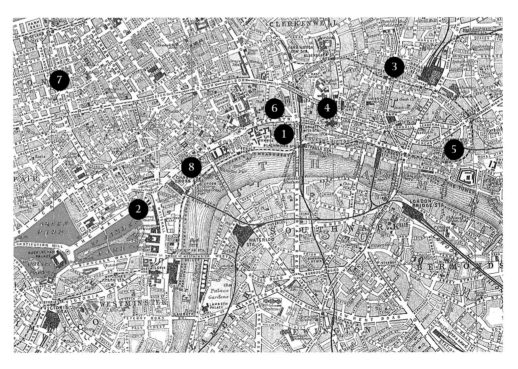

UNDERGROUND ELECTRIC RAILWAYS OF L...

HAMMERSMITH, PICCADILLY, KINGS CROSS, FINSBURY PARK
(G.N., PICCADILLY & BROMPTON RAILWAY.)

Hammersmith.
Barons Court.
Earls Court.
Gloucester Road.
South Kensington
Brompton Road.
Knightsbridge.
Hyde Park Corner.
Down Street.
Dover Street.
Piccadilly Circus.
Leicester Square.
Covent Garden.
Holborn.
Russell Square.
Kings Cross.
York Road.
Caledonian Road.
Holloway Road.
Gillespie Road.
Finsbury Park.

BAKER STREET AND WATERLOO RAILWAY.

Elephant & Castle.
Westminster
 Bridge Road.
Waterloo.
Embankment—
 Charing Cross.
Trafalgar Square.
Piccadilly Circus.
Oxford Circus.
Regent's Park.
Baker Street.

CHARING CROSS, EUSTON & HAMPSTEAD RAILWAY.
(Open June, 1907.)

Charing Cross.
Leicester Square.
Oxford Street.
Tottenham
 Court Road.
Euston Road.
Euston.
Camden Town.
Chalk Farm.
Belsize Park.
Hampstead.
Golders Green.

Castle Road.
Kentish Town.
Tufnell Park.
Highgate.

The Underground

Above: the early maps of the Underground showed the geographical layout of the lines, which the later, more famous Beck map does not. B.L. Maps 3485(170).

Opposite, left and right: the earliest underground trains of the 1860s, and the characteristic art nouveau style Edwardian stations. B.L. wfi/1856. (*left*). Private collection. (*right*).

One of the most ingenious and celebrated maps ever designed was Henry Beck's 1932 map of the London Underground system. Its geometric lines, artificial spaces and softened angles serve brilliantly to hide the reality of the contorted network of rail lines which run beneath the streets. Moreover, the map undoubtedly gives the impression that the Underground was the outcome of a conscious, unified, intelligent design – which it certainly was not. London's Underground was in fact built up piecemeal over half a century by competing private companies, with no central control or design, and often using foreign investment.

The story of London's Underground opens in the 1860s, as part of the railway mania of the age. The costs of purchasing property and compensating owners when building railways were very high, until it was realised that this could be avoided by burying the lines. This could be achieved by digging a deep trench, usually along a road, laying the track, then re-covering the entire excavation – the so-called 'cut and cover' technique. It was first pioneered in the 1860s by the Metropolitan Railway to carry passengers arriving at Paddington on to the City. It was an immediate success, the only technical problem being ventilation, for this was still the age of steam. This problem led to the idea of cable-car trains, drawn on wires from a stationary engine, but this proved to be fraught with difficulty. The District Railway from South Kensington to Westminster followed in 1868, extending to Mansion House by 1871. By 1884, the District and Metropolitan Railways had linked to form an inner circle – the later Circle Line. In many places these trains ran clear of their tunnels, allowing the smoke to escape into the spaces between the buildings; in one of the Sherlock Holmes stories, the key to the mystery is that a dead body was dropped from a house onto the roof of a train at such an opening.

Two crucial technical developments led to the next generation of underground lines. First, there was the tunnelling shield, which permitted deep-level tunnels to be dug and consolidated in one operation. Second, there was electric power, which solved the ventilation problem. Both were first used in constructing the City and South London Railway between the Bank and Stockwell, which opened in 1890. This was the original section of what later became the Northern Line. The triumph of these two innovations came in the Central London Railway – later the Central Line – opened in 1900 by the Prince of Wales.

This was London's first real tube line, extremely fast and comfortable, following the busiest of all overground traffic routes from Shepherd's Bush to Bank via Bayswater Road, Oxford Street and Holborn. It was accessed by electric lifts, another essential ingredient of the system until the advent of the escalator in the 1920s.

These electric lines were hugely successful with the travelling public, but they demanded enormous capital investment. In the years after 1900, the development of the system was driven forward by the American magnate, Charles Tyson Yerkes, who first bought the District Line, then laid the foundations of the Bakerloo, Piccadilly and Northern Lines. Yerkes also built his own electrical generating station in Lots Road, Chelsea, to power the whole network. The dark red, glazed tiling of the tube stations, many with art nouveau decoration like Knightsbridge, are also part of Yerkes's legacy. Another of his brainwaves was to extend the Northern Line out to Hampstead and Golders Green, thus linking the inner-city subway system directly with suburbia. Yerkes died in 1905, before all this was realised, but he more than any other individual shaped the future of London's Underground. His ownership of several lines showed how coordination between them could be improved, and thus pointed the way to the London Passenger Transport Board, founded in 1933 as, in effect, the first nationalised industry in British history, to oversee the entire system. The new era became a reality in the 1920s with the birth of the Metroland concept, the line to suburban Harrow, Uxbridge and beyond into rural Buckinghamshire. This was created by the Metropolitan Railway, which set up its own property development company to build houses along the line. The other lines followed, extending deep into Essex and Hertfordshire. South London had already been covered by overland lines, so Kent and Surrey never joined the tube system in the same way. Much of this extension work was carried out in the 1930s, was publicly financed, and formed the first overall large-scale planning of the entire system. After a pause during the war, further extensions followed in the 1940s and 50s, but by then the Green Belt had been designated, and the march of suburbia had been halted. The Underground was not originally conceived to ease road traffic problems, but, as road congestion in the central zone became chronic in the 1930s, it became impossible to imagine London without its tube trains.

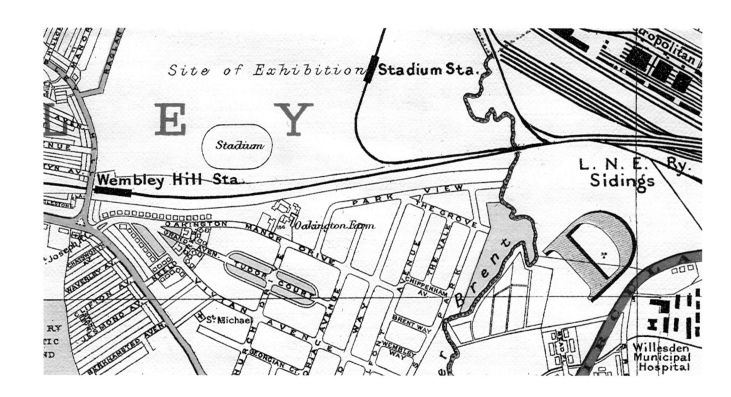

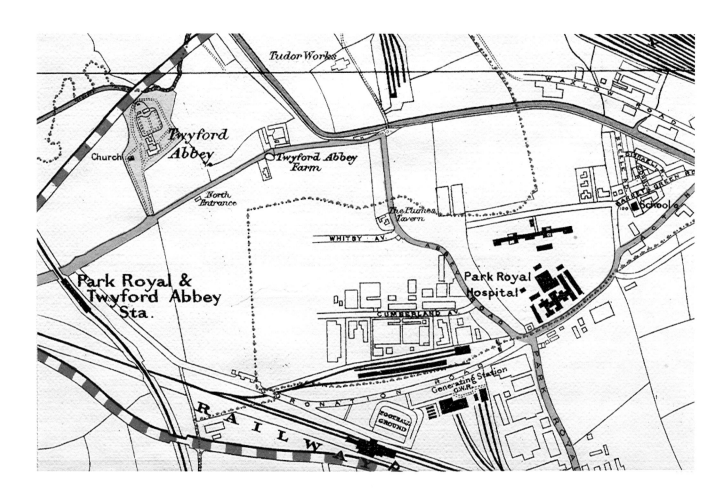

Wembley and Park Royal

Although Wembley was an Anglo-Saxon settlement (Wemba Leigh, recorded in the eighth century) its character is entirely that of a twentieth-century suburb, while the neighbouring district of Park Royal was the archetype of the modern industrial estate. The fanciful name Park Royal arose from the selection of this site, in 1902, as the permanent showground for the Royal Agricultural Society – trees planted there during the opening ceremony by King Edward still stand among the factories. This venture proved short-lived, but the site was pressed into service for munitions factories during the Great War, and after the war the buildings were colonised by private industries. These were not the traditional heavy industries of the East End, but new light industries to produce the consumer goods which would drive the twentieth-century economy: cars, electrical and household goods, processed food and drinks, and pharmaceuticals. From the mid 1920s onwards, the Park Royal site spread along what would become the Western Avenue, while the same industrial pattern was repeated along the Great West Road and through the northern suburbs to Hendon and Edmonton, linked by the North Circular Road, built in the 1930s. This growth was not planned or directed, but was entirely market-led, the work of shrewd individual developers.

The growth of Wembley was equally accidental and it, too, followed from plans for large-scale public entertainments. Already, in the 1890s, a large site had been acquired by the Metropolitan Railway, who, as part of their strategy to attract people to live in the north-western suburbs, proposed to build a vast pleasure-garden there, with a gigantic replica of the Eiffel Tower. This plan failed, but the same site was chosen to be the home to the British Empire Exhibition of 1924, an event which had been talked about since before the war, as a counter-attack against the growing economic might of America and Germany. Wembley Stadium – an innovative structure in reinforced concrete – was the first feature to be completed, and was christened in the 1923 Cup Final, when thousands of spectators spilled onto the pitch, an event captured in several famous photographs. The stadium was only one part of the show, which featured replicas of the Taj Mahal and Victoria Falls, and palaces of industry and art, based on the traditional nineteenth-century model. From the public's point of view, however, the centre of excitement was undoubtedly the American-style funfair, with its electric rides, dodgems and roller-coasters – the first time such things had been seen in Britain. The exhibition was a huge success, running for two years and attracting twenty million visitors. Roads and railways were built to service the site, and, as with Park Royal, the empty buildings were later bought for industrial use, but also this time for entertainment – cinemas, dance halls and restaurants. The stadium remained the national sports arena for seventy years and hosted the 1948 Olympic Games.

The Wembley-Park Royal district might easily have become just another standard residential suburb, but instead the strange legacy of parks and exhibitions turned it into London's first modern industrial estate. The whole area was a great generator of London's wealth during the 1920s and 30s. Hundreds of thousands of people worked there to produce the new consumer goods which marked the modern lifestyle. The new type of electrically powered factory on the American model contrasted sharply with the older-style, heavy, dirty foundries and refineries of the East End. This was a completely different England from the depressed industrial districts of the north, for it brought with it the typical south-eastern cityscape of factories, cinemas, parades of shops, swimming pools and suburban semis – a foretaste of what was to come throughout England after the Second World War.

Opposite: Wembley, (*top*), and Park Royal, (*bottom*), in the 1920s: a few suburban streets, railway lines and large empty spaces waiting to be filled.
B.L. Maps 3480(357).

Right and far right: the result – London's first industrial estate, and the Exhibition and Stadium.
Simmons Aerofilms.

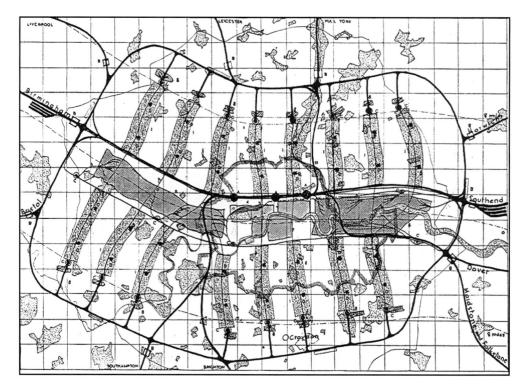

Right: the radical MARS plan of the late 1930s, which involved recreating London's entire transport network from a drawing-board plan. B.L. 7822 d.6.

Below: the Abercrombie master-plan: concentric ring roads, radial motorways, six airports and a dozen new towns. B.L. 7822 d.6.

Opposite: 1920s traffic jams. Private collection.

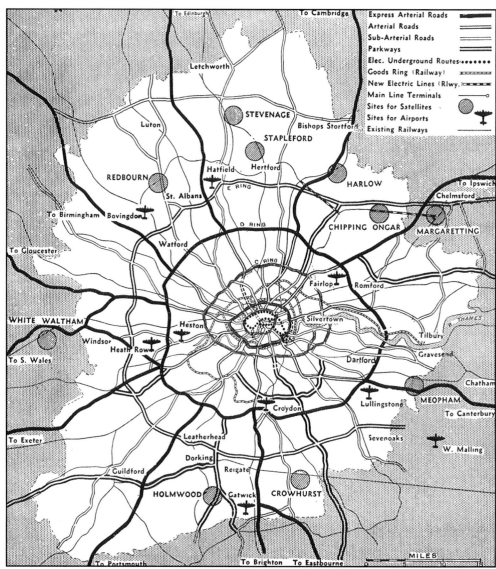

Road-planning: Early Visions

When the motor car first appeared on the streets of Edwardian London, it seemed to promise a solution to traffic congestion in the city. The car was smaller, faster, cleaner, and more manoeuvrable than the horse-drawn carriage – that was the logical view. What was not foreseen, of course, was the democratisation of car ownership, and the thousands of vehicles that would soon be crowding the roads of the capital. This was an unplanned transport revolution which crept up on London, as it did on western society as a whole. By the mid-1930s, central London was gridlocked for much of the day, and it was evident that plans must be made to meet this new challenge. The government had included a Minister of Transport since 1919, but it was some years before the regulation of traffic was seen to be essential, with driving tests, a highway code, traffic lights and so on, and before full-scale studies and reports on the problem were commissioned.

The most far-reaching of these early documents was the one written by Sir Charles Bressey, and published in 1938. The thrust of his report was the recognition that London was being choked by a tide of motor traffic for which its streets had never been intended. Bressey put forward radical plans which would effectively redraw the map of London's main roads. The new pattern which he proposed was simple and logical: it resembled a spider's web of ring roads, intersected by radial routes leading in and out of the centre. Three ring roads were proposed, with big roundabouts at the intersections. The main rail termini, which generated so much traffic congestion, would be pushed out to the mid-

dle of the rings. Bressey conceded that some of the new roads could be tunnelled, under Hyde Park for example, but others would have to be carried on overhead viaducts, the most conspicuous being an elevated road slicing across London from Barnet to Croydon. These high-level roads always looked exciting on plans, like visions of a Wellsian future brought to London. The cost of the Bressey scheme was, for its time, astronomical, at £120 million, while the demolition required would be ruthless. It was these two issues which sank the Bressey plan, although it would in any case have been overtaken by the war. Immediately before the outbreak of the war, an even more radical plan was published by the Modern Architectural Research Group (and later known as the MARS Plan) which envisaged huge raised arteries more than 200 feet broad crossing London at rooftop level, carrying trains and buses, while the streets below were to be handed over to private cars. This scheme involved virtually the total redesigning of London for a new age of transport.

The destruction left by the Blitz gave a great opportunity for post-war road planning, while it also removed some of the objections to the Bressey plan. Two further plans had been produced during the war years, both of which generally accepted the road model proposed by Bressey. The doyen of British planners, Sir Patrick Abercrombie, was the architect of two monumental plans, one for the County of London and another for the London Region. Abercrombie shared the spider's web vision of London's main road system, aiming now for no fewer than six ring roads and ten radial roads. This massive road-building programme was justified on the grounds that fast through traffic must be separated from local traffic – indeed, it was one of Abercrombie's central arguments that London was composed of cellular communities which should be carefully nurtured. These should be sealed, as far as possible, from the main roads around them. The design of the giant new roads, bridges and intersections were openly copied from American models, in the belief that they would solve urban traffic problems.

At the same time a second plan, restricted to the central area only, emerged from the Royal Academy of Arts, under the guidance of the architects Sir Edwin Lutyens and Sir Giles Gilbert Scott. Not unnaturally this was more concerned with the fabric and aesthetic quality of London, and a large part of the plan was to open architectural vistas throughout the city, by demolition and by laying out new roads. One of its unique features was a great traffic roundabout at St George's Circus, massive enough to contain a whole park, from which

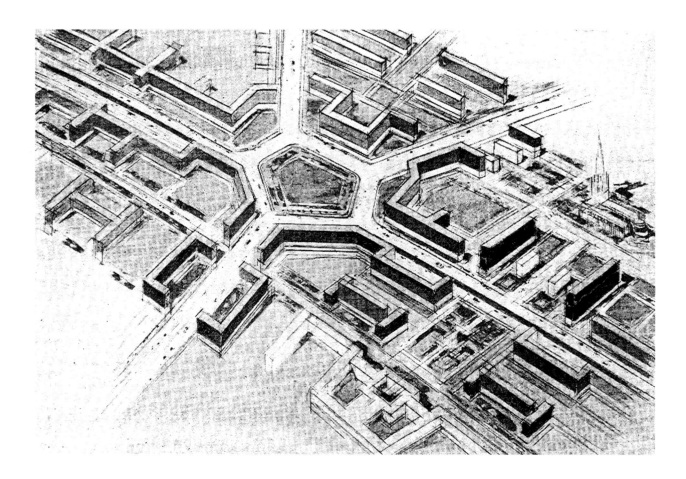

Above: Abercrombie's plan for motorways to cut through London. Private collection.

Opposite: one of the dozens of Abercrombie intersections, where the radial roads crossed the ring roads.
B.L. Cup. 1253.bb.2.

Right: the Royal Academy plan produced during the war envisaged London's aesthetic transformation.
B.L. 7822.d.6.

new roads would radiate to all the Thames bridges. A magnificent new vista of St Paul's from the river would be created by opening a new avenue from the cathedral down to the waterside. The key to the Royal Academy plan was to be a new purpose-built inner ring road, sunken in some places and elevated in others, which would speed traffic rapidly throughout London.

What happened to all these plans? None of them was implemented. Instead, in typical London fashion, hundreds of piecemeal improvements to the roads were made year by year. Roads were widened, new intersections were created, one-way systems, underpasses and flyovers were all tried, to smooth the flow of traffic. The inner ring road was never built, although the North Circular did evolve in stages, while the South Circular always remained more of an idea than a reality.

Should we regret the withering of these grandiose plans as great lost opportunities, which could have averted later traffic chaos? Almost certainly not, because the fallacy that underlay all of them was the failure to foresee that traffic volumes would rise remorselessly as long as they were allowed to. All the new roads desired by Bressey and Abercrombie would have rapidly been filled, the tunnels and high-speed intersections would have become clogged, and the sealed precincts would

probably now be car parks. The high-level viaducts carving through the capital would have spread intolerable noise and exhaust fumes. The outermost ring proposed by Bressey and Abercrombie finally materialised in the 1980s as the M25, and was instantly filled to capacity and beyond.

The early planners saw traffic problems as static and finite, soluble by specific measures, usually the building of a new road. Instead, these problems are dynamic, changing as society changes. These same planners were also convinced of the need to reduce London's population, moving people out to new towns and overspill estates. Bizarre as it now seems, they had no conception of reducing traffic volumes in the city: traffic flow was a good thing, a sign of economic vitality, and its path must be smoothed at all costs. A subsidiary doctrine, always associated with the name of Colin Buchanan, was the separation of pedestrians from road traffic by means of split-level walkways. Initially attractive as a theory, this idea would produce the lifeless, threatening concrete passageways of the 1960s city centres, and the roads devoted to traffic where it is all but impossible to walk. In urban planning, as in all things, fashions change, and the real solution of keeping traffic out of the capital was a solution that had not yet dawned on anyone.

A PROSPECT OF THE **CITY** OF **LONDON** FROM THE SOVTH EAST
IN THE YEAR 1945 SHEWING ITS ARCHITECTVRE. THE DESTRVCTION CAVSED
BY THE KING'S ENEMIES DVRING THE PREVIOVS FIVE YEARS AND SOME OF
THE MEANS WHEREBY THE SAFETY OF THE CITIZENS WAS MAINTAINED.

1939

This Drawing is dedicated by the Artist.
without permission, to the CITIZENS OF LONDON *who during five years*
withstood bombardment in various forms. "You worked. From your needed efforts you
would not be deterred. You carried on and from your midst arose no cry for mercy
no wail of defeat. Your faith and endurance have finally been rewarded."

General Eisenhower at the Guildhall June 12th 1945   *Cecil Brown Delineavit*

The City Blitzed

On the night of 29 December 1940, the German air force carried out a ferocious air-raid on the City, which was slumbering in its post-Christmas repose. The Blitz on London and other English cities had, by then, been under way since September, and had already claimed many thousands of lives. Defences and means of counter-attack had been devised, but nothing could really protect the capital from the onslaught of the bombers. Winston Churchill's prophetic fears had been realised. 'London,' he said, 'was the greatest target in the world, a kind of tremendous fat, valuable cow, tied up to attract the beasts of prey.' By the morning of 30 December, the heart of London from Farringdon Road to Aldgate had been laid waste. Churches, offices, banks, the livery company halls, and the Guildhall itself had been crushed or consumed by fire. It was the greatest destruction seen in the City since the Great Fire of 1666. It yielded, however, one extraordinary symbol of defiance: St Paul's Cathedral had suffered only minor damage, and the structure was miraculously untouched. Photographs of Wren's dome rising above the smoke and devastation were to become one of the best-known images from London's long history.

Two years after that momentous night, the architect and artist, Cecil Brown, began work on his magnificent panorama of the war-torn city. He called it 'A Tribute to London', for as well as recording a scene of appalling destruction, it does indeed celebrate how much of the city had survived under the protective wings of the great defending angel. Some of the quirky details are reminiscent of a Brueghel painting: a running track has been laid out near St Paul's on which athletes are racing; on a vegetable allotment off Gresham Street, people are following the government slogan 'Dig for Victory'; there is a rifle range in Aldermanbury. These little vignettes show life continuing in the shattered city. Business as usual it certainly was not, but Cecil Brown's message is clearly that London had passed through its worst ordeal for three centuries, and would arise again when the war was over.

Rather strangely, we have no clear idea how Brown created this masterly work of art in 1942. It has been suggested that he must have worked from a balloon tethered to a vehicle, which was parked in various locations, but there is no firm evidence that this actually happened. No one seems to have seen an artist working in such a balloon, and he himself never explained what he did. Brown was a devoted student of London and its history, who died in 1983. He left behind him a magnificent work in the tradition of Wyngaerde and Hollar, and like them he left an element of mystery concerning its genesis.

Above: Cecil Brown's unique 1945 panorama of the blitzed City, with St Paul's defended by guardian angels.
Guildhall Library, City of London.

Opposite: the miraculous preservation of the cathedral revealed in this photograph, 1940.
Simmons Aerofilms.

Right: Docklands burning, a German view.
US National Archives.

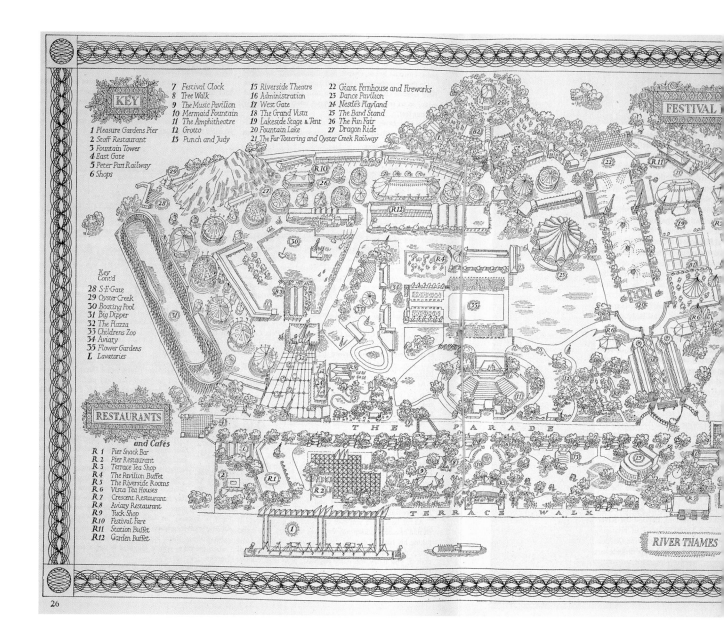

KEY

1 Pleasure Gardens Pier
2 Staff Restaurant
3 Fountain Tower
4 East Gate
5 Peter Pan Railway
6 Shops
7 Festival Clock
8 Tree Walk
9 The Music Pavilion
10 Mermaid Fountain
11 The Amphitheatre
12 Grotto
13 Punch and Judy
15 Riverside Theatre
16 Administration
17 West Gate
18 The Grand Vista
19 Lakeside Stage & Tent
20 Fountain Lake
21 The Far Tottering and Oyster Creek Railway
22 Giant Fernhouse and Fireworks
23 Dance Pavilion
24 Nestlé's Playland
25 The Band Stand
26 The Fun Fair
27 Dragon Ride

Key Cont'd

28 S.E.Gate
29 Oyster Creek
30 Boating Pool
31 Big Dipper
32 The Piazza
33 Childrens Zoo
34 Aviary
35 Flower Gardens
L Lavatories

RESTAURANTS and Cafés

R 1 Pier Snack Bar
R 2 Pier Restaurant
R 3 Terrace Tea Shop
R 4 The Pavilion Buffet
R 5 The Riverside Rooms
R 6 Vista Tea Houses
R 7 Crescent Restaurant
R 8 Aviary Restaurant
R 9 Tuck Shop
R 10 Festival Fare
R 11 Station Buffet
R 12 Garden Buffet

FESTIVAL

THE PARADE

TERRACE WALK

RIVER THAMES

The Festival of Britain

In the austere Britain of the late 1940s, the mid-point of the century loomed up as a moment of hope that invited celebration. It was also recalled that 1951 would be the centenary of the Great Exhibition, that great display of Victorian self-confidence. In February 1949, therefore, Atlee's Labour government announced that a Festival of Britain would be staged in the summer of 1951. Events would be organised throughout the country, but the focus of attention would naturally be on the capital. The chosen London site was the semi-derelict land on the South Bank between Waterloo Bridge and County Hall. The ideal inspiring the festival was '... to demonstrate the contribution to civilisation made by British advances in science, technology and industrial design', but this formal aim was to be brightened by more relaxed celebrations. It was, in fact, an extended public party hosted by the government.

Under the overall control of Herbert Morrison, London's leading politician, the South Bank site was filled with more than two dozen exhibition halls, above all by the 'Dome of Discovery', housing jet engines, radar equipment, penicillin, a model of a nuclear power station and other objects of national pride. Much was made of the 'Skylon', a slender, rocket-like obelisk that towered 150 feet over the entire site. The design of the halls and of much of their contents was fervently modern, with Scandinavian polished wood, plastic, glass and aluminium. The word 'contemporary' now acquired its special meaning, as a style badge firmly rooted in 1950s fashions.

All these exhibits were temporary, but the permanent legacy of the Festival came in the form of the Royal Festival Hall, the first major public building in London in the ultra-modern style, and the cornerstone of the South Bank's identity as a centre of the arts. Two miles west, in Battersea Park, there appeared the more informal face of the Festival: a huge funfair designed by John Piper and Osbert Lancaster, which survived until the mid-1970s. The other exhibition halls were removed in the autumn of 1951, but might have lasted longer had not victory in the general election gone to the Conservatives, who made no secret of their distaste for the whole event. The huge Shell office block now overshadows the site, although the Jubilee Gardens is where the Dome of Discovery once stood. There was a third London focus for the Festival in Poplar, in the new Lansbury Estate, promoted as an 'Exhibition of Living Architecture'. Here the low-rise council housing, the wide-open Chrisp Street market, the clock-tower and the two ultra-modern pubs all seemed inspired at the time.

It is easy now to smile at the festival: it showed a naïve faith in symbols of progress and planned regeneration. The Lansbury Estate and the architecture of the South Bank now look tawdry and dated, the latter made even worse by the Queen Elizabeth Hall and the Hayward Gallery, dating from the early 1960s, which resembled war-time bunkers. But, at the time, the festival was a great event, capturing perfectly the optimistic belief that a better future could be engineered out of concrete, glass and aluminium.

Above: Battersea Park – the party which lasted for twenty years. B.L. 010349.m.34.

Right: all the newspapers published their South Bank Festival special guides. B.L. Cup. 1253.c.27.

Opposite: the Royal Festival Hall and the Dome of Discovery. Simmons Aerofilms.

Above: an early picture of Dagenham, largest of the LCC estates, planted in the Essex marshes. Simmons Aerofilms.

Right: post-war East End - the new slums loom over the old.
Tower Hamlets Library.

Below: the Old Oak Estate, the LCC estate built in 1912 around the tube station. B.L. Maps 3480(357).

Opposite: Bellingham, an arabesque of streets designed on somebody's drawing board. B.L. Maps 3480(357).

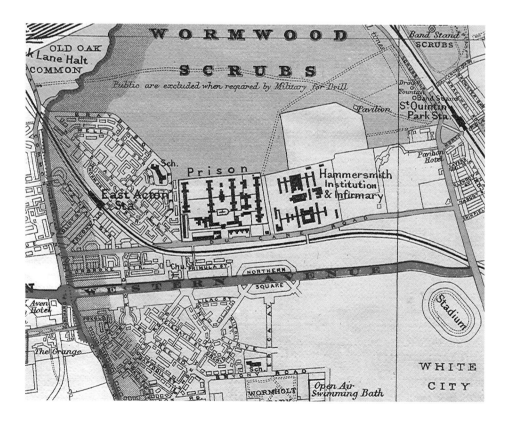

Planning the Capital

Within a decade of its birth in 1889, the London County Council had embarked on the process of rehousing the hundreds of thousands of the capital's inhabitants who were still living in Victorian slums, a process which eventually made the LCC the greatest landlord in England. The first LCC housing estates, conceived and built between 1898 and 1902, were at Millbank, behind the Tate Gallery, and in Shoreditch, where the notorious slum known as the Nichol was demolished and replaced. On both sites the new buildings were five-storey blocks of flats, well designed in the Arts and Crafts style in brick and terracotta, with greens or open squares as part of the layout. Within the next few years, however, current Garden City ideas influenced the LCC architects, and settlements such as those in Acton and Tooting were typical of the cottage-style estates that would become standard throughout the inter-war years. Old Oak in Acton was conceived as a dispersal community, and was built around the new Central Line station. The Great War halted these plans for some years, but they resumed in the 1920s with the Bellingham Estate in south London, remarkable for its highly designed arabesque pattern of streets. Above all there was the Becontree-Dagenham estate built between 1928 and 1932, housing 100,000 people and probably the largest planned settlement anywhere in the world. This estate

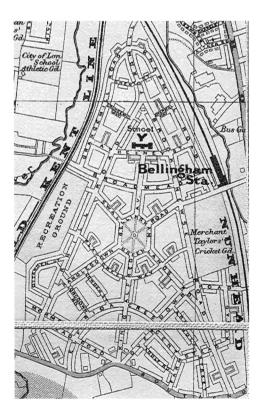

was the first fruit of the official doctrine that London's many problems could only be solved by moving large masses of people out of the city, in this case virtually into the middle of nowhere, until the arrival of the Ford factory in 1931 transformed Dagenham's prospects. St Helier in Surrey and Burnt Oak in Middlesex were similar but smaller 'overspill' estates, and by 1939 some 250,000 people lived in eight or nine of these LCC-designed communities. By the standards of the day, the new houses were comfortable and attractive, and they suffered none of the problems that would wreck the planned estates of a later generation. They represented the first phase of modern social engineering in London.

The aftermath of World War Two presented London's planners with a wholly new challenge, especially in the devastated City and East End. Moreover, architectural ideas had moved on dramatically, and modern influences from the continent now reigned. These two factors combined to produce a thirty-year period that proved traumatic and destructive for the fabric of London and the lives of its people. Garden City ideas were now entirely eclipsed, in favour of repetitive ranks of blocks and towers, which grew ever bigger – and ever more inhuman. The archetype of these estates, Roehampton, seemed daring and visionary, but it was entirely untypical, redeemed by the green spaces which surrounded it. When these blocks were replicated in Bethnal Green, Brixton or Peckham, only the term brutalism was adequate. It was not height alone that was the problem, but the lack of privacy and individuality in these structures which created alienation in those compelled to live there. They were designed by young theorists for tenants who were neither young nor theoretically minded. They sprang from an ideological confidence in demolition and reconstruction as the way out of social problems.

Nor were these developments restricted to public housing: economic pressure and architectural fashion produced exactly the same results in the City and the West End. The tower-block of the hapless working classes and the tower-blocks of the rich companies became almost indistinguishable. In the twenty years between 1955 and 1975, London's skyline was transformed by endless palisades of tower-clones. One of the first sites, which should have acted as a warning of things to come, was William Holford's 1961 rebuilding of Paternoster Square, which fenced St Paul's Cathedral within concrete blocks of terrifying ugliness, so offensive that their demolition was being planned just thirty years later. Yet, incredibly, this scheme was highly

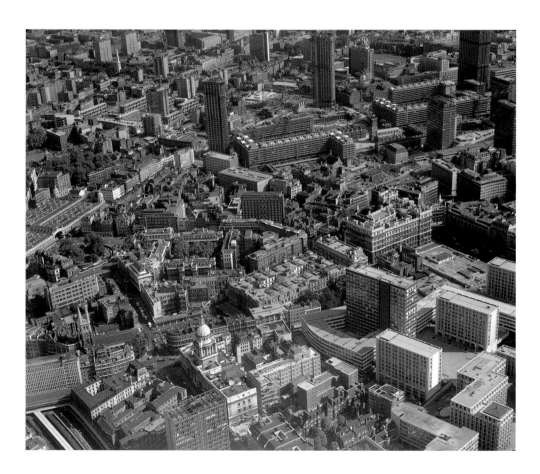

praised by no less a critic than Lewis Mumford, the great historian of the city; such was the temper of the times that even he was carried away by the rage for 'urban renewal'. Piccadilly Circus narrowly escaped the same fate at Holford's hands, and further developments of this kind would include the notorious Barbican, with its desolate walkways and 400-foot towers. The Barbican looked like a symbol of social division: within, luxurious apartments and breathtaking views over the city; without, brutal ugliness. Added to these architectural follies was the planners' determination to carve up the city in order to make room for traffic, and their continuing obsession with moving people out to overspill estates and new towns. These policies lay at the root of the years of urban decline that followed.

The challenge to planning orthodoxy began in the mid-1970s, coinciding with the world oil crisis and the rise of environmental awareness. Even before this, however, there had been several *causes célèbres* which focused public attention on the destruction lurking behind the words 'planning' and 'redevelopment', such as the demolition of Euston Station and of the Coal Exchange on Lower Thames Street, both superb Victorian structures sacrificed to greed and philistinism. But these controversies were trivial compared to the major planning battles of the late 70s: Covent Garden, the Motorway Box, and the Third London Airport. When the market left Covent Garden in 1972, the planners and developers were poised to move in and Manhattanise the whole area, but a strong alliance of local interests managed to prevent them. The urban motorway ring was part of the Greater London Development Plan of 1969, but it merely revived the Bressey –Abercrombie schemes. It was to cost £2 billion, or perhaps £3 billion, or was it £4 billion, destroy 40,000 or perhaps 50,000 houses in its path, and take twenty years to complete. A huge campaign against it gathered momentum from a cross-section of Londoners, including the Royal Institute of British Architects, who unearthed a prophetic plea that had been published in 1869: 'Any means which could be devised to diminish vehicular traffic in the city would be more successful than endeavours to accommodate it.' After six years of controversy, the plan was abandoned, leaving just a few fragments as reminders, such as the approach road to Blackwall tunnel. It was officially admitted that 'new primary routes are no longer acceptable to the GLC'. The Third London Airport presented the planning crisis in the clearest possible terms, for the commission examining the problem admitted that no single factor could determine the answer. All the possible sites had strong reasons for being chosen, and equally strong reasons for being ruled out, so no new airport was built, and instead the existing ones were steadily enlarged. What was already there could be accepted and endured, but nothing so major could now be created anew.

Battles of this kind effectively put an end to strategic planning because it became politically impossible to reach major decisions. Consultation was interminable and consensus became impossible; lead-times were too long, and both public needs and public attitudes were changing even while issues were being examined. At the same time architecture was in crisis as the fundamental faults of modernism were being revealed. Both style and materials were dating with terrifying speed, and the harsh realities of trying to live in the new environment were becoming apparent. Confidence in the ability of professionals to renew the urban fabric ebbed away, and conservation became the new orthodoxy.

The evolution of planning ideas over these thirty years highlights the central paradox of conservation: that which we wish to preserve may well be a haphazard collection of survivals, or things that were never planned at all in our sense. No one was consulted before Inigo Jones or Wren went to work, or before the aristocratic estates were built up into the West End, or before Nash and the Prince Regent cooked up their plans for London, yet we treasure what they created. Private money and totally undemocratic patronage built up London, then somehow the secret, the flair and the confidence were lost, and we, with all our sophistication and skills, cannot emulate the achievements of the past.

Opposite: towers for living and towers for working, but they are indistinguishable, whether in Hackney, (*top*), or in the City, (*bottom*), where Paternoster Square and the Barbican are captured in one image. Simmons Aerofilms.

Top and above: thirty years of social change, decline, and dramatic but partial rebirth in the West India Docks and the Royal Docks. Simmons Aerofilms.

Opposite: the Docklands' transformation spurred the City into renewed building, with massive projects such as the Broadgate Centre. Private collection.

The Transformation of Docklands

With hindsight, the most blatant failure of London's planners was not to recognise what was happening in the city's docks. After the end of the war, the docks enjoyed fifteen boom years before going into sudden and catastrophic decline, the twin causes of which were technical changes in cargo handling, coupled with chronic labour problems. The first dock closure, that of the East India Dock, came in 1967 but it went largely unnoticed. Open conflict between dockers and the government in the early 1970s brought the issue into public notice, but by 1980 the Royal Docks closed, and all heavy river traffic now halted at Tilbury, while the docks and the river itself lay almost deserted. It was the end of a long era of history, for the City and the docks had grown together, but the modern City no longer needed its archaic and truculent neighbour. Some 5,000 acres in the heart of East London suddenly became available for new users with new ideas, probably the biggest rebuilding opportunity ever presented to any world city. If this had been foreseen and understood, even by 1965, the entire slum clearance and rebuilding operation in the East End might have taken a different course.

From the late 1960s, the eventual fate of the whole dock system had been obvious, but no plan for the region's future emerged for many years. The size of the challenge seemed to paralyse anyone who looked at it. There were discussions, committees, reports and consultations, but nothing was decided; everyone was involved and no one was in charge. The logjam was not broken until 1981, when Docklands was designated an enterprise zone, governed by a development corporation empowered to override normal planning procedures. The heart of the strategy was to bring in private finance to regenerate the region in a way that officialdom could not. Local community groups were appalled, but unlike Covent Garden they could not demand conservation because the basis of their way of life had vanished: there was nothing to conserve. Financial corporations and newspaper publishers were lured to new sites in Docklands. Former wharfs and warehouses were converted into flats, offices and studios, yacht marinas and a small airport were opened, and the social character of much of the east riverside was transformed. It was, however, the first major redevelopment to take conservation seriously, and a variety of old buildings which would surely have been swept away a few years earlier were restored and converted. This came too late for many Dockland communities which had been seen as slums, and had been cleared and rebuilt in the lifeless style of the 1960s - places like Poplar, Deptford and Woolwich.

The centrepiece of this transformation was Canary Wharf in the old West India Dock. Completed in 1992, it was a massively ambitious building resembling a slice of Chicago or Hong Kong - planned as virtually a second City of London, a world financial centre. From being a triumphalist vision of the future, however, it became a national joke when it fell victim to the economic slump of the early 1990s, but it was eventually completed and leased. It is forbidding and unlovable, but it is there and it showed how the planning paralysis of the 1970s could be broken. As it took shape, however, it frightened the City into a new phase of building of its own, in a rush to create more office space and preserve its own hegemony. Architectural lessons had been learned, and this new phase made claims to inaugurate a post-modern era in which the square block was banished and replaced by structures which were no less massive, but which at least employed arches, terraces, pillars, curves and

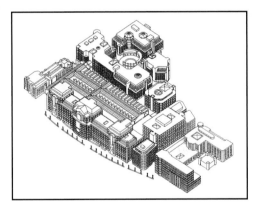

asymmetries. One of the first was the gigantic Broadgate complex on Bishopsgate, completed in 1992 and containing 3.5 million square feet of office space, with a titanic façade worthy of Speer's plans for Nazi Berlin. The post-modern style spread throughout London, and some of its products such as the new Charing Cross or Vauxhall Cross seem to be taking London away from Manhattanisation to Hollywoodisation, with structures which resemble vast film sets. The global corporations which inhabit them seem to relish these theatrical statements of their power, much as the banks and imperial offices had once been addicted to the glories of Edwardian baroque.

Top and above: the primitive life of Hoxton captured by the pen of James Boswell. B.L. Maps X8009/6127.

Right: the streets of Hoxton in the 1920s, many of them now obliterated by modern estates. The Bridport Arms in Bridport Place, centre, was the eternal haunt of Williams's drunken father.
B.L. Maps 3480(357).

A Hoxton Childhood

Hoxton is one of those districts of London that people find hard to place on the map, even though it is just one mile from St Paul's and even less from the Bank of England. Unlike Shoreditch, it was never celebrated in nursery rhymes, and unlike Whitechapel, it had no Ripper to make it infamous. People know that it used to be shady and disreputable, and its very name made it sound as though the whole place was in hock. Hoxton, in fact, lies just north of Shoreditch, between the City Road and Kingsland Road. It is not exactly the East End – its postal district is N1 – but it is very definitely Cockney: it was singled out by Shaw in *Pygmalion* as furnishing the very worst Cockney accent. In the Second World War it was badly blitzed, and today it is a mixture of shoddy post-war housing and trendy artists' studios in converted warehouses. Ninety-five years ago, on the eve of the Great War, it was a post-Victorian warren of mean terraces, pubs, street markets, pawn shops and music halls. It was peopled by a near-Dickensian underclass, scratching their hand-to-mouth existence, sometimes employed in the furniture workshops and shoe-makers which filled the district, and other times supporting themselves through petty crime. We know all this because in 1969 a man named Jan Williams published (under a pseudonym) a vivid personal memoir entitled *A Hoxton Childhood*. When it appeared this book provoked two kinds of response: young or middle-class readers were filled with amazement and disbelief at the squalor of the life which he described; older readers, who had lived through those years, were moved to see a vanished way of life which they had almost forgotten miraculously recalled on the page.

The overwhelming impression that we get from Williams's book is that Hoxton was a totally enclosed world. Their whole life was concentrated in this cluster of mean streets, tied there by a kind of territorial instinct. No one ventured outside it, there were no trips to the river, or the West End or the countryside. To these people, royal London, historic London, fashionable London, or cultural London meant nothing. London was merely the name of the great machine of which they happened to be part. This intense isolation was both geographical and psychological. No one ever thought of moving out, seeking a new career, breaking away from their family, or anything of that kind. There was simply no sense of the wider world outside. The Great War was just a noise offstage, a nuisance that took youngsters away from home and interfered with the supply of coal or food. Their only pleasures were the pub or the eel-and-pie shop. Even the music hall and Hoxton's famous Britannia Theatre were beyond them. Any money that came their way was spent instantly on beer and getting clothes out of pawn, and then it was back to penury. A family of six would be squeezed into two or three rooms, and when grown-up children married, their husbands or wives moved in too. Older brothers on the verge of trouble at the age of fifteen were packed off to the merchant navy, and if they returned a year or two later they were like strangers, because they had broken out of this claustrophobic world.

The dynamic force in this memoir is the incessant conflict between the shiftless, drunken father and the warm, unselfish mother around whom family life revolved. Each day was a struggle to scrape together the few shillings necessary to pay the rent, and to prevent the father from wasting it on drink. There was no clear distinction between the honest man and the criminal: anyone would steal if they could, it was an approved tactic in life's battle.

Williams's memoir is a reminder of the minimal life that will always exist in a great city – a life without imagination, without ideas, and where every day is the same. This life had perhaps only two virtues. The first was a stoical self-reliance: no one would help you, so you had to help yourself. Nobody turned to authority for support: police, welfare, schools, local government, the Church – all these organisations existed on entirely another level, and to cooperate with them was to betray your roots. The second was a basic, crude honesty: if they had no culture, at least it was their own culture that they didn't have, for their lives were not yet awash with phoney images and values absorbed from films and television and the consumer world. *A Hoxton Childhood* now looks like a series of snapshots from a dark age before people had woken up to life's possibilities, but apparently this was real life in the back streets of England's capital.

A View from a Bridge

London is now too vast to be captured in any single image, but this evocative night shot looking west from Waterloo Bridge encapsulates all the major themes of London's history - political, commercial and cultural. Significantly, it doesn't show London at all, not the historic heartland of the City itself, but Westminster, London's western neighbour, which became the seat of the court and the national government. The highway between the two centres - the Strand - became a neutral zone, first of aristocratic residencies, then of commerce and entertainment, as it remains today.

Across the centre stretches Hungerford Bridge, the Victorian wrought-iron railway bridge which incorporated a pedestrian crossing that was long known as as a dark, squalid path to the south bank, until it was modernised to create the cones of light seen here. On the right is Shell-Mex House, built in 1931, the first modern office block in Lon-

don on the American model, but still a miniature in comparison with the office blocks of Manhattan. Later, post-war office towers, leaner and glassier, can be seen in the Millbank Tower and the south-bank Shell Centre. To the right of the bridge stands the new over-building on Charing Cross Station, one of the first of London's structures to proclaim itself, in 1990, post-modern; still colossal but replacing the stark brutality of the 60s and 70s with far more imaginative forms and materials. Behind the lights of the bridge, and veiled in symbolic shadow, loom the vague forms of the government offices in Whitehall. By contrast, Parliament itself is floodlit, but Barry's magnificent Victorian Gothic is completely overshadowed by the towers of modernism. Still more diminished is Westminster Abbey, one of London two great surviving links with the Middle Ages, its towers just visible in the darkness. On the left we have the

A panoramic view of the Thames, showing, from *left* to *right*: the Royal Festival Hall, the Shell Centre, Old County Hall, the London Eye, Millbank Tower, the Houses of Parliament, Westminster Abbey, the Ministry of Defence, Charing Cross Station, the Adelphi, the Shell-Mex Building.

vulgarity of the London Eye - confirmation of the fairground mentality that surrounded the millennium hype of the year 2000. Beside the wheel stands the relic of a hundred years of London's self-government, the former County Hall, now converted into an international hotel. The Royal Festival Hall is the only permanent legacy of the 1951 Festival of Britain. Together with the National Theatre, added twenty years later, it symbolises the south bank as a cultural centre. The hideous concrete outside and vibrant music and theatre inside seem to typify the London of that era.

In the foreground of this panorama flows the River Thames, without which London would never have been founded or have grown to greatness. It is now empty, gone back to nature, just a sheet of water to mirror the structures of the city that tower over it. Now people, things, and ideas arrive in the city by road, by air, or as electronic data. The river belongs to an earlier era, when being a capital city meant ships and cargoes.

If we could rewind time's tape two hundred years or so, this entire skyline would vanish, to be replaced by a muddle of houses, a few private palaces and a few churches. The diversity of social life which has created buildings of commerce, administration and entertainment simply did not exist before that.

This one picture shows the inexorable forces of change at work on the face of London, change which no human power can predict or halt, yet which springs always from the dynamic of human life. Physically it is the modern structures which dominate this picture, but the spell of the past lies invisibly behind it, for the only reason those modern structures are there and not somewhere else, is that this is London.

Select Bibliography

Abercrombie, P.: *Greater London Plan*, 1944.

Barker, F. & Hyde, R.: *London as it Might Have Been*, 1982.

Barker, F. & Jackson, P.: *The History of London in Maps*, 1990.

Brett-James, N.G.: *The Growth of Stuart London*, 1935.

Carr, R.J.M. ed.: *Dockland*, 1986.

Clout, H.: *The Times London History Atlas*, 1991.

Clunn, H.: *The Face of London*, 1932.

Dyos, H.J. & Wolff, M.: *The Victorian City*, 2 vols. 1973.

Esher, L.: *A Broken Wave: the Rebuilding of Britain 1940-1980*, 1983.

Forshaw, J.H. & Abercrombie, P.: *County of London Plan*, 1943.

Harwood, E. & Saint, A.: *Exploring London's Heritage*, 1991.

Howgego, J.: *Printed Maps of London c.1553-1850*, 1979.

Inwood, S.: *A History of London*, 1998.

Jasper, A.S.: *A Hoxton Childhood*, 1969.

Jenkins, S.: *Landlords to London: the Story of a Capital and its Growth*, 1975.

Jenner, M.: *London Heritage: the Changing Style of a City*, 1988.

Jones, E. & Woodward, C.: *A Guide to the Architecture of London*, 2000.

Olsen, D.: *The Growth of Victorian London*, 1983.

Porter, R.: *London: a Social History*, 1994.

Powell, K.: *London: World City*, 1990.

Saint, A. & Darley, G.: *The Chronicles of London*, 1994.

Schofield, J.: *The Building of London from the Conquest to the Great Fire*, 1984.

Schofield, J.: *The London Surveys of Ralph Treswell*, 1987.

Sheppard, F.: *London 1808-1870, the Infernal Wen*, 1971.

Sheppard, F.: *London: a History*, 1998.

Summerson, J.: *Georgian London*, 1962.

Summerson, J.: *Architecture in Britain, 1530-1830*, 1993.

Weinreb, B. & Hibbert, C.: *The London Encyclopedia*, 1983.

Weightman, G. & Humphries, S.: *The Making of Modern London, 1815-1914*, 1983.

Weightman, G. & Humphries, S.: *The Making of Modern London, 1914-1939*, 1984.

Index